MCSE NT Workstation 4.0 Ace It!

MCSE NT
Workstation
4.0 Ace It!

Mark B. Cooper

IDG Books Worldwide, Inc.
An International Data Group Company
Foster City, CA • Chicago, IL • Indianapolis, IN • New York, NY

MCSE NT Workstation 4.0 Ace It!

Published by
IDG Books Worldwide, Inc.
An International Data Group Company
919 E. Hillsdale Blvd., Suite 400
Foster City, CA 94404
www.idgbooks.com (IDG Books Worldwide Web site)

Library of Congress Catalog Card Number: 98-073345

ISBN: 0-7645-3264-2

Printed in the United States of America

10 9 8 7 6 5 4 3 2 1

1P/QZ/RQ/ZY/FC

Distributed in the United States by IDG Books Worldwide, Inc.

Distributed by Macmillan Canada for Canada; by Transworld Publishers Limited in the United Kingdom; by IDG Norge Books for Norway; by IDG Sweden Books for Sweden; by Woodslane Pty. Ltd. for Australia; by Woodslane (NZ) Ltd. for New Zealand; by Addison Wesley Longman Singapore Pte Ltd. for Singapore, Malaysia, Thailand, Indonesia, and Korea; by Norma Comunicaciones S.A. for Colombia; by Intersoft for South Africa; by International Thomson Publishing for Germany, Austria, and Switzerland; by Toppan Company Ltd. for Japan; by Distribuidora Cuspide for Argentina; by Livraria Cultura for Brazil; by Ediciencia S.A. for Ecuador; by Ediciones ZETA S.C.R. Ltda. for Peru; by WS Computer Publishing Corporation, Inc., for the Philippines; by Unalis Corporation for Taiwan; by Contemporanea de Ediciones for Venezuela; by Computer Book & Magazine Store for Puerto Rico; by Express Computer Distributors for the Caribbean and West Indies. Authorized Sales Agent: Anthony Rudkin Associates for the Middle East and North Africa.

For general information on IDG Books Worldwide's books in the U.S., please call our Consumer Customer Service department at 800-762-2974. For reseller information, including discounts and premium sales, please call our Reseller Customer Service department at 800-434-3422.

For International Order Queries & Customer Service: Tel: 1-317-596-5530 Fax: 1-317-596-5692

For information on foreign language translations, please contact our Foreign & Subsidiary Rights department at 650-655-3021 or fax 650-655-3281.

For sales inquiries and special prices for bulk quantities, please contact our Sales department at 650-655-3200 or write to the address above.

For information on using IDG Books Worldwide's books in the classroom or for ordering examination copies, please contact our Educational Sales department at 800-434-2086 or fax 317-596-5499.

For press review copies, author interviews, or other publicity information, please contact our Public Relations department at 650-655-3000 or fax 650-655-3299.

For authorization to photocopy items for corporate, personal, or educational use, please contact Copyright Clearance Center, 222 Rosewood Drive, Danvers, MA 01923, or fax 978-750-4470.

is a trademark under exclusive license to IDG Books Worldwide, Inc., from International Data Group, Inc.

ABOUT IDG BOOKS WORLDWIDE

Welcome to the world of IDG Books Worldwide.

IDG Books Worldwide, Inc., is a subsidiary of International Data Group, the world's largest publisher of computer-related information and the leading global provider of information services on information technology. IDG was founded more than 25 years ago and now employs more than 8,500 people worldwide. IDG publishes more than 275 computer publications in over 75 countries (see listing below). More than 90 million people read one or more IDG publications each month.

Launched in 1990, IDG Books Worldwide is today the #1 publisher of best-selling computer books in the United States. We are proud to have received eight awards from the Computer Press Association in recognition of editorial excellence and three from *Computer Currents'* First Annual Readers' Choice Awards. Our best-selling *...For Dummies*® series has more than 50 million copies in print with translations in 38 languages. IDG Books Worldwide, through a joint venture with IDG's Hi-Tech Beijing, became the first U.S. publisher to publish a computer book in the People's Republic of China. In record time, IDG Books Worldwide has become the first choice for millions of readers around the world who want to learn how to better manage their businesses.

Our mission is simple: Every one of our books is designed to bring extra value and skill-building instructions to the reader. Our books are written by experts who understand and care about our readers. The knowledge base of our editorial staff comes from years of experience in publishing, education, and journalism — experience we use to produce books for the '90s. In short, we care about books, so we attract the best people. We devote special attention to details such as audience, interior design, use of icons, and illustrations. And because we use an efficient process of authoring, editing, and desktop publishing our books electronically, we can spend more time ensuring superior content and spend less time on the technicalities of making books.

You can count on our commitment to deliver high-quality books at competitive prices on topics you want to read about. At IDG Books Worldwide, we continue in the IDG tradition of delivering quality for more than 25 years. You'll find no better book on a subject than one from IDG Books Worldwide.

John Kilcullen
CEO
IDG Books Worldwide, Inc.

Steven Berkowitz
President and Publisher
IDG Books Worldwide, Inc.

WINNER

*Eighth Annual
Computer Press
Awards ≥1992*

WINNER

*Ninth Annual
Computer Press
Awards ≥1993*

WINNER

WINNER

*Tenth Annual
Computer Press
Awards ≥1994*

WINNER

*Eleventh Annual
Computer Press
Awards ≥1995*

IDG Books Worldwide, Inc., is a subsidiary of International Data Group, the world's largest publisher of computer-related information and the leading global provider of information services on information technology. International Data Group publishes over 275 computer publications in over 75 countries. More than 90 million people read one or more International Data Group publications each month. International Data Group's publications include: **ARGENTINA:** Buyer's Guide, Computerworld Argentina, PC World Argentina; **AUSTRALIA:** Australian Macworld, Australian PC World, Australian Reseller News, Computerworld, IT Casebook, Network World, Publish, Webmaster; **AUSTRIA:** Computerwelt Österreich, Networks Austria, PC Tip Austria; **BANGLADESH:** PC World Bangladesh; **BELARUS:** PC World Belarus; **BELGIUM:** Data News; **BRAZIL:** Annuário de Informática, Computerworld, Connections, Macworld, PC Player, PC World, Publish, Reseller News, Supergamepower; **BULGARIA:** Computerworld Bulgaria, Network World Bulgaria, PC & MacWorld Bulgaria; **CANADA:** CIO Canada, Client/Server World, ComputerWorld Canada, InfoWorld Canada, NetworkWorld Canada, WebWorld; **CHILE:** Computerworld Chile, PC World Chile; **COLOMBIA:** Computerworld Colombia, PC World Colombia; **COSTA RICA:** PC World Centro America; **THE CZECH AND SLOVAK REPUBLICS:** Computerworld Czechoslovakia, Macworld Czech Republic, PC World Czechoslovakia; **DENMARK:** Communications World Danmark, Computerworld Danmark, Macworld Danmark, PC World Danmark, Techworld Denmark; **DOMINICAN REPUBLIC:** PC World Republica Dominicana; **ECUADOR:** PC World Ecuador; **EGYPT:** Computerworld Middle East, PC World Middle East; **EL SALVADOR:** PC World Centro America; **FINLAND:** MikroPC, Tietoverkko, Tietoviikko; **FRANCE:** Distributique, Hebdo, Info PC, Le Monde Informatique, Macworld, Reseaux & Telecoms, WebMaster France; **GERMANY:** Computer Partner, Computerwoche, Computerwoche Extra, Computerwoche FOCUS, Global Online, Macwelt, PC Welt; **GREECE:** Amiga Computing, GamePro Greece, Multimedia World; **GUATEMALA:** PC World Centro America; **HONDURAS:** PC World Centro America; **HONG KONG:** Computerworld Hong Kong, PC World Hong Kong, Publish in Asia; **HUNGARY:** ABCD CD-ROM, Computerworld Szamitastechnika, Internetto online Magazine, PC World Hungary, PC-X Magazin Hungary; **ICELAND:** Tolvuheimur PC World Island; **INDIA:** Information Communications World, Information Systems Computerworld, PC World India, Publish in Asia; **INDONESIA:** InfoKomputer PC World, Komputek Computerworld, Publish in Asia; **IRELAND:** ComputerScope, PC Live!; **ISRAEL:** Macworld Israel, People & Computers/Computerworld; **ITALY:** Computerworld Italia, Macworld Italia, Networking Italia, PC World Italia; **JAPAN:** DTP World, Macworld Japan, Nikkei Personal Computing, OS/2 World Japan, SunWorld Japan, Windows NT World, Windows World Japan; **KENYA:** PC World East African; **KOREA:** Hi-Tech Information, Macworld Korea, PC World Korea; **MACEDONIA:** PC World Macedonia; **MALAYSIA:** Computerworld Malaysia, PC World Malaysia, Publish in Asia; **MALTA:** PC World Malta; **MEXICO:** Computerworld Mexico, PC World Mexico; **MYANMAR:** PC World Myanmar; **NETHERLANDS:** Computer! Totaal, LAN Internetworking Magazine, LAN World Buyers Guide, Macworld Netherlands, Net, WebWereld; **NEW ZEALAND:** Absolute Beginners Guide and Plain & Simple Series, Computer Buyer, Computer Industry Directory, Computerworld New Zealand, MTB, Network World, PC World New Zealand; **NICARAGUA:** PC World Centro America; **NORWAY:** Computerworld Norge, CW Rapport, Datamagasinet, Financial Rapport, Kursguide Norge, Macworld Norge, Multimediaworld Norge, PC World Ekspress Norge, PC World Nettverk, PC World Norge, PC World ProduktGuide Norge; **PAKISTAN:** Computerworld Pakistan; **PANAMA:** PC World Panama; **PEOPLE'S REPUBLIC OF CHINA:** China Computer Users, China Computerworld, China InfoWorld, China Telecom World Weekly, Computer & Communication, Electronic Design China, Electronics Today, Electronics Weekly, Game Software, PC World China, Popular Computer Week, Software Weekly, Software World, Telecom World; **PERU:** Computerworld Peru, PC World Profesional Peru, PC World SoHo Peru; **PHILIPPINES:** Click!, Computerworld Philippines, PC World Philippines, Publish in Asia; **POLAND:** Computerworld Poland, Computerworld Special Report Poland, Cyber, Macworld Poland, Networld Poland, PC World Komputer; **PORTUGAL:** Cerebro/PC World, Computerworld/Correio Informático, Dealer World Portugal, Mac*In/PC*In Portugal, Multimedia World; **PUERTO RICO:** PC World Puerto Rico; **ROMANIA:** Computerworld Romania, PC World Romania, Telecom Romania; **RUSSIA:** Computerworld Russia, Mir PK, Publish, Seti; **SINGAPORE:** Computerworld Singapore, PC World Singapore, Publish in Asia; **SLOVENIA:** Monitor; **SOUTH AFRICA:** Computing SA, Network World SA, Software World SA; **SPAIN:** Communicaciones World España, Computerworld España, Dealer World España, Macworld España, PC World España; **SRI LANKA:** Infolink PC World; **SWEDEN:** CAP&Design, Computer Sweden, Corporate Computing Sweden, Internetworld Sweden, it.branschen, Macworld Sweden, MaxiData Sweden, MikroDatorn, Nätverk & Kommunikation, PC World Sweden, PCaktiv, Windows World Sweden; **SWITZERLAND:** Computerworld Schweiz, Macworld Schweiz, PCtip; **TAIWAN:** Computerworld Taiwan, Macworld Taiwan, NEW ViSiON/Publish, PC World Taiwan, Windows World Taiwan; **THAILAND:** Publish in Asia, Thai Computerworld; **TURKEY:** Computerworld Turkiye, Macworld Turkiye, Network World Turkiye, PC World Turkiye; **UKRAINE:** Computerworld Kiev, Multimedia World Ukraine, PC World Ukraine; **UNITED KINGDOM:** Acorn User UK, Amiga Action UK, Amiga Computing UK, Apple Talk UK, Computing, Macworld, Parents and Computers UK, PC Advisor, PC Home, PSX Pro, The WEB, UNITED STATES: Cable in the Classroom, CIO Magazine, Computerworld, DOS World, Federal Computer Week, GamePro Magazine, InfoWorld, I-Way, Macworld, Network World, PC Games, PC World, Publish, Video Event, THE WEB Magazine, and WebMaster; online webzines: JavaWorld, NetscapeWorld, and SunWorld Online; **URUGUAY:** InfoWorld Uruguay; **VENEZUELA:** Computerworld Venezuela, PC World Venezuela; and **VIETNAM:** PC World Vietnam.   5/7/98

Welcome to *Ace It!*

Looking to get certified? The *Ace It!* series is what you're looking for! The *Ace It!* series has been designed to meet your need for a quick, easy-to-use study tool that helps you save time, prioritize your study, and cram for the exam. *Ace It!* books serve as a supplement to other certification resources, such as our award-winning *Study Guides* and *MCSE...For Dummies* series. With these two series' and *Ace It!*, IDG Books offers a full suite of study tools to meet your certification needs, from complete tutorial and reference materials to quick exam prep tools.

Ace It's exam-expert authors give you the ace in the hole: our unique insider's perspective on the exam itself — how it works, what topics are really important, and *how you really need to think* to ace the exam. Our features train your brain to understand not only the essential topics covered on the exam, but also how to decipher the exam itself. By demystifying the exam, we give you that extra confidence to know you're really prepared!

Ace It! books help you study with a wealth of truly valuable features in each chapter:

- **Official Word** lists the official certification exam objectives covered in the chapter.

- **Inside Scoop** immediately follows the Official Word and gives you the author's insight and expertise about the exam content covered in the chapter.

- **Are You Prepared?** is a chapter pretest that lets you check your knowledge beforehand: if you score well on the pretest, you may not need to review the chapter! This helps you focus your study. The questions are immediately followed by answers with cross-references to the information in the chapter, helping you further target your review.

- **Have You Mastered?** is a chapter post-test that includes five to ten multiple-choice questions with answers, analysis, and cross-references to the chapter discussion. The questions help you check your progress and pinpoint what you've learned and what you still need to study.
- **Practice Your Skills** consists of three to five exercises related to specific exam objectives. They provide an opportunity to relate exam concepts to real-world situations by presenting a hypothetical problem or guiding you through a task at the computer. These exercises enable you to take what you've learned for the exam and put it to work.

Within each chapter, icons call your attention to the following features:

 give hints and strategies for passing the exam to help strengthen your test-taking skills.

 warn you of pitfalls and loopholes you're likely to see in actual exam questions.

 Pop Quizzes offer instant testing of hot exam topics.

 Know This provides a quick summary of essential elements of topics you *will* see on the exam.

In the front and back of the book, you'll find even more features to give you that extra confidence and prepare you to get certified:

- **Ace Card:** Tear out this quick-review card for a distilled breakdown of essential exam-related terms and concepts to take with you and review before the exam.

- **Insider's Guide:** This helpful certification profile describes the certification process in general, and discusses the specific exam this book covers. It explains the exam development process, provides tips for preparing for and taking the exams, describes the testing process (how to register for an exam, what to expect at the testing center, how to obtain and evaluate test scores, and how to retake the exam if necessary), and tells you where to go for more information about the certification you're after.

- **Practice Exam:** A full-length multiple-choice practice exam. Questions and answer selections mimic the certification exam in style, number of questions, and content to give you the closest experience to the real thing.

- **Exam Key** and **Exam Analysis:** These features tell you not only what the right answers are on the Practice Exam, but why they're right, and where to look in the book for the material you need to review.

- **Exam Revealed:** Here's your ace in the hole — the real deal on how the exam works. Our exam-expert authors deconstruct the questions on the Practice Exam, examining their structure, style, and wording to reveal subtleties, loopholes, and pitfalls that can entrap or mislead you when you take the real test. For each question, the author highlights part of the question or answer choices and then, in a sentence or two, identifies the possible problem and explains how to avoid it.

- **Glossary:** Not familiar with a word or concept? Just look it up! The Glossary covers all the essential terminology you need to know.

With this wealth of features and the exclusive insider's perspective provided by our authors, you can be sure that *Ace It!* completes your set of certification study tools. No matter what you've got, you still need an *Ace It!*

Credits

Acquisitions Editor
Tracy Thomsic

Development Editors
Jennifer Rowe
Steve Anderson

Copy Editors
Nicole Fountain
Brian MacDonald

Project Coordinator
Ritchie Durdin

Cover Coordinator
Cyndra Robbins

Book Designer
Dan Ziegler

*Graphics and Production
Specialists*
Stephanie Hollier
Jude Levinson

Quality Control Specialists
Mick Arellano
Mark Schumann

Illustrator
Hector Mendoza

Proofreader
Arielle Carole Mennelle

Indexer
Liz Cunningham

About the Author

Mark B. Cooper has been working with enterprise networking technologies for the last ten years. The last six years he has been working as a consulting engineer for the Fortune 500, providing consulting and solution designs for large complex networking environments. He is also the director of publishing for the Enterprise Networking Association's *Enterprise Networking* magazine. Mark is an MCSE, MCT, CBE, Compaq ASE, Sun CSSA, and CNP.

To my loving wife Heather, who completes me, and to our daughter Briar Elise, who completes my world.

Insider's Guide to MCP Certification

The Microsoft Certified Professional Exams are *not* easy, and require a great deal of preparation. The exam questions measure real-world skills. Your ability to answer these questions correctly will be greatly enhanced by as much hands-on experience with the product as you can get.

About the Exams

An important aspect of passing the MCP Certification Exams is understanding the big picture. This includes understanding how the exams are developed and scored.

Every job function requires different levels of cognitive skills, from memorization of facts and definitions to the comprehensive ability to analyze scenarios, design solutions, and evaluate options. To make the exams relevant in the real world, Microsoft Certified Professional exams test the specific cognitive skills needed for the job functions being tested. These exams go beyond testing rote knowledge — you need to *apply* your knowledge, analyze technical solutions, solve problems, and make decisions — just like you would on the job.

Exam Items and Scoring

Microsoft certification exams consist of four types of items: multiple-choice, multiple-rating, enhanced, and simulation. The way you indicate your answer and the number of points you receive differ depending on the type of item.

Multiple-choice item

A traditional multiple-choice item presents a problem and asks you to select either the best answer (single response) or the best set of answers (multiple response) to the given item from a list of possible answers.

For a multiple-choice item, your response is scored as either correct or incorrect. A correct answer receives a score of 1 point and an incorrect answer receives a score of 0 points.

In the case of a multiple-choice, multiple-response item (for which the correct response consists of more than one answer), the item is scored as being correct only if all the correct answers are selected. No partial credit is given for a response that does not include all the correct answers for the item.

For consistency purposes, the question in a multiple-choice, multiple-response item is always presented in singular form, regardless of how many answers are correct. Always follow the instructions displayed at the bottom of the window.

Multiple-rating item

A multiple-rating item presents a task similar to those presented in multiple-choice items. In a multiple-choice item, you are asked to select the best answer or answers from a selection of several potential answers. In contrast, a multiple-rating item presents a task, along with proposed solution. Each time the task is presented, a different solution is proposed. In each multiple-rating item, you are asked to choose the answer that best describes the results produced by one proposed solution.

Enhanced item

An enhanced item is similar to a multiple-choice item because it asks you to select your response from a number of possible responses. However, unlike the traditional multiple-choice item that presents you with a list of possible answers from which to choose, an enhanced item may ask you to indicate your answer in one of the following three ways:

- Type the correct response, such as a command name.

- Review an exhibit (such as a screen shot, a network configuration drawing, or a code sample), and then use the mouse to select the area of the exhibit that represents the correct response.
- Review an exhibit, and then select the correct response from the list of possible responses.

As with a multiple-choice item, your response to an enhanced item is scored as either correct or incorrect. A correct answer receives full credit of 1 point, and an incorrect answer receives a score of 0 points.

Simulation item

A simulation imitates the functionality of product components or environments, complete with error messages and dialog boxes. You are given a scenario and one or more tasks to complete by using that simulation. A simulation item's goal is to determine if you know how to complete a given task. Just as with the other item types, the simulation is scored when you complete the exam. A simulation item may ask you to indicate your answer in one of the following ways:

- Review an exhibit (such as a screen shot, a network configuration drawing, or a code sample), and then use the GUI simulation to resolve, configure or otherwise complete the assigned task.
- Based on information in the exam scenario, resolve, configure, or otherwise complete the assigned task.

As with the other item types, you receive credit for a correct answer only if all of the requested criteria are met by your actions in the scenario. There is no partial credit for a incomplete simulation item.

Exam Formats

Microsoft uses two different exam formats to determine how many questions are going to be presented on the exam. The majority of Microsoft exams have historically used fixed length exams, with between 50 and 100 questions per exam. Each time you take the exams, you are presented with a different set of questions, but still comprising an equal amount of questions. Recently, Microsoft has attempted to increase the reliability of its testing procedures, and has implemented new strategies to that end. The newest format is called *computer adaptive testing*. A *computer adaptive test* (CAT) is tailored to the individual exam taker. You start with an easy-to-moderate question; if you answer the question correctly, you get a more difficult follow-up question. If that question is answered correctly, the difficulty of subsequent questions likewise increases. Conversely, if the second question is answered incorrectly, the following questions will be easier. This process continues only until the CAT determines the your ability. As a result, you may have an exam that is only 15 questions, but contains extremely difficult questions. Likewise, you may have an exam that contains 50 moderately difficult questions.

Preparing for a Microsoft Certified Professional Exam

The best way to prepare for an exam is to study, learn, and master the job function on which you'll be tested. For any certification exam, you should follow these important preparation steps:

1. Identify the objectives on which you'll be tested.
2. Assess your current mastery of those objectives.
3. Practice tasks and study the areas you haven't mastered.

This section describes tools and techniques that may be helpful as you perform these steps to prepare for the exam.

Exam Preparation Guides

For each certification exam, an Exam Preparation Guide provides important, specific information about what you'll be tested on and how best to prepare. These guides are essential tools for preparing to take certification exams. You'll find the following types of valuable information in the exam preparation guides:

- **Tasks you should master:** Outlines the overall job function tasks you should master
- **Exam objectives:** Lists the specific skills and abilities on which you should expect to be measured
- **Product resources:** Tells you the products and technologies with which you should be experienced
- **Suggested reading:** Points you to specific reference materials and other publications that discuss one or more of the exam objectives
- **Suggested curriculum:** Provides a specific list of instructor-led and self-paced courses relating to the job function tasks and topics in the exam

You'll also find pointers to additional information that may help you prepare for the exams, such as *Microsoft TechNet, Microsoft Developer Network* (MSDN), online forums, and other sources.

By paying attention to the verbs used in the "Exam Objectives" section of the Exam Preparation Guide, you will get an idea of the level at which you'll be tested on that objective.

To view the most recent version of the Exam Preparation Guides, which include the exam's objectives, check out Microsoft's Training and Certification Web site at `www.microsoft.com/train_cert/`.

Assessment Exams

When preparing for the exams, take lots of assessment exams. Assessment exams are self-paced exams that you take at your own computer. When you complete an assessment exam, you receive instant score feedback so you can determine areas in which additional study may be helpful before you take the certification exam. Although your score on an assessment exam doesn't necessarily indicate what your score will be on the certification exam, assessment exams give you the opportunity to answer items that are similar to those on the certification exams. The assessment exams also use the same computer-based testing tool as the certification exams, so you don't have to learn the tool on exam day.

An assessment exam exists for almost every certification exam.

Taking a Microsoft Certified Professional Exam

This section contains information about registering for and taking a Microsoft Certified Professional exam, including what to expect when you arrive at the testing center to take the exam.

How to Register for an Exam

Candidates may take exams at any of more than 700 Sylvan Prometric testing centers around the world. For the location of a Sylvan Prometric testing center near you, call (800) 755-EXAM (755-3926). Outside the United States and Canada, contact your local Sylvan Prometric Registration Center.

You can also take exams at any of the over 160 different Virtual University Enterprises testing centers around the world. To register for an exam at VUE at a testing center in your area, call (888) 837-8616. Outside the United States and Canada, contact your local Virtual University Enterprises Registration Center.

Sylvan Prometric offers online registration for Microsoft exams at its Microsoft registration Web site https://www.slspro.com/msreg/microsof.asp. You can also register for an exam at a VUE testing center by visiting http://www.vue.com/ms.

To register for a Microsoft Certified Professional exam:

1. Determine which exam you want to take and note the exam number.
2. Call the Sylvan Prometric Registration Center or VUE nearest to you. If you haven't registered with them before, you will be asked to provide information to the Registration Center.

3. You can then schedule your exam at your choice of locations. Once the exam is scheduled, you will be asked to provide payment for the exam. Both of the testing centers take major credit cards and offer pre-payment options for purchasing exam certificates for future or corporate use.

When you schedule the exam, you'll be provided instructions regarding the appointment, cancellation procedures, and ID requirements, as well as information about the testing center location.

Exams must be taken within one year of payment. You can schedule exams up to six weeks in advance, or as late as one working day prior to the date of the exam. You can cancel or reschedule your exam if you contact the testing center at least one working day prior to the exam.

Although subject to space availability, same-day registration is available in some locations. Where same-day registration is available, you must register a minimum of two hours before test time.

What to Expect at the Testing Center

As you prepare for your certification exam, it may be helpful to know what to expect when you arrive at the testing center on the day of your exam. The following information gives you a preview of the general procedure you'll go through at the testing center:

- You will be asked to sign the log book upon arrival and departure.
- You will be required to show two forms of identification, including one photo ID (such as a driver's license or company security ID), before you may take the exam.
- The test administrator will give you a Testing Center Regulations form that explains the rules you will be expected to comply with during the test. You will be asked to sign the form, indicating that you understand the regulations and will comply.
- The test administrator will show you to your test computer and will handle any preparations necessary to

start the testing tool and display the exam on the computer.

- You will be provided a set amount of scratch paper for use during the exam. All scratch paper will be collected from you at the end of the exam.
- The exams are all closed-book. You may not use a laptop computer or have any notes or printed material with you during the exam session.
- Some exams may include additional materials, or exhibits. If any exhibits are required for your exam, the test administrator will provide you with them before you begin the exam and collect them from you at the end of the exam.
- Before you begin the exam, the test administrator will tell you what to do when you complete the exam. If the test administrator doesn't explain this to you, or if you are unclear about what you should do, ask the administrator before beginning the exam.
- The number of items on each exam varies, as does the amount of time allotted for each exam. Generally, certification exams consist of about 50 to 100 items and have durations of 60 to 90 minutes. You can verify the number of items and time allotted for your exam when you register.

Because you'll be given a specific amount of time to complete the exam once you begin, if you have any questions or concerns, don't hesitate to ask the test administrator before the exam begins.

As an exam candidate, you are entitled to the best support and environment possible for your exam. In particular, you are entitled to following:

- A quiet, uncluttered test environment
- Scratch paper
- The tutorial for using the online testing tool, and time to take the tutorial
- A knowledgeable and professional test administrator

- The opportunity to submit comments about the testing center and staff, or the test itself

The Certification Development Team will investigate any problems or issues you raise and make every effort to resolve them quickly.

Your Exam Results

Once you have completed an exam, you will be given immediate, online notification of your pass or fail status. You will also receive a printed Examination Score Report indicating your pass or fail status and your exam results by section. (The test administrator will give you the printed score report.) Test scores are automatically forwarded to Microsoft within five working days after you take the test. You do not need to send your score to Microsoft.

If you pass the exam, you will receive confirmation from Microsoft, typically within two to four weeks.

If You Don't Receive a Passing Score

If you do not pass a certification exam, you may call the testing center to schedule a time to retake the exam. Before retaking the exam, you should review the appropriate Exam Preparation Guide and focus additional study on the topic areas where your exam results could be improved. Please note that you must pay again for each exam retake.

One way to determine areas where additional study may be helpful is to review your individual section scores carefully. The section titles in your score report generally correlate to specific groups of exam objectives listed in the Exam Preparation Guide.

Here are some specific ways you can prepare to retake an exam:

- Go over the section-by-section scores on your exam results, noting objective areas where your score could be improved.
- Review the Exam Preparation Guide for the exam, with a special focus on the tasks and objective areas that

correspond to the exam sections where your score could be improved.

- Increase your real-world, hands-on experience and practice performing the listed job tasks with the relevant products and technologies.
- Consider taking or retaking one or more of the suggested courses listed in the Exam Preparation Guide.
- Review the suggested readings listed in the Exam Preparation Guide.
- After you review the materials, retake the corresponding Assessment Exam.

For More Information

To find out more about Microsoft Education and Certification materials and programs, to register with a testing center, or to get other useful information, check the following resources. Outside the United States or Canada, contact your local Microsoft office or testing center.

- **Microsoft Certified Professional Program:** (800) 636-7544. Call for information about the Microsoft Certified Professional program and exams, and to order the *Microsoft Certified Professional Program Exam Study Guide* or the Microsoft Train_Cert Offline CD-ROM.
- **Sylvan Prometric Testing Centers:** (800) 755-EXAM. Call to register to take a Microsoft Certified Professional exam at any of more than 700 Sylvan Prometric testing centers around the world, or to order the *Microsoft Certified Professional Program Exam Study Guide.*
- **Virtual University Enterprises Testing Centers:** (888) 837-8616. Call to register to take a Microsoft Certified Professional exam at any of the over 160 different Virtual University Enterprises testing centers around the world.
- **Microsoft Sales Fax Service:** (800) 727-3351. Call for Microsoft Certified Professional Exam Preparation

Guides, Microsoft Official Curriculum course descriptions and schedules, or the *Microsoft Certified Professional Program Exam Study Guide.*

- **Education Program and Course Information: (800) SOLPROV.** Call for information about Microsoft Official Curriculum courses, Microsoft education products, and the Microsoft Solution Provider Authorized Technical Education Center (ATEC) program, where you can attend a Microsoft Official Curriculum course, or to order the *Microsoft Certified Professional Program Exam Study Guide.*

- **Microsoft Certification Development Team: Fax #: (425) 936-1311.** Use this fax number to volunteer for participation in one or more exam development phases or to report a problem with an exam. Address written correspondence to: Certification Development Team, Microsoft Education and Certification, One Microsoft Way, Redmond, WA 98052.

- **Microsoft TechNet Technical Information Network: (800) 344-2121.** Call for support professionals and system administrators. Outside the United States and Canada, call your local Microsoft subsidiary for information.

- **Microsoft Developer Network (MSDN): (800) 759-5474.** MSDN is the official source for software development kits, device driver kits, operating systems, and information about developing applications for Microsoft Windows and Windows NT.

- **Online Services: (800) 936-3500.** Call for information about Microsoft Connection on CompuServe, Microsoft Knowledge Base, Microsoft Software Library, Microsoft Download Service, and Internet.

- **Microsoft Online Institute (MOLI): (800) 449-9333.** Call for information about Microsoft's new online training program.

Preface

Welcome to the MCSE Ace It Series! This book is designed to help you hone your existing knowledge of Windows NT Workstation 4.0 and gain a greater understanding so you'll have the ability to pass Microsoft Certified Professional Exam No. 70-073: Implementing and Supporting Microsoft Windows NT Workstation 4.0.

This book is designed to be the only book you'll need to prepare for and pass the Workstation exam. However, the goal of this book is *not* to make you into an NT guru. I cover Windows NT Workstation 4.0 to the depth of the exam objectives, but not beyond that point. If, during the course of your study, you find yourself wanting more depth, detail, and advanced technical tidbits, I heartily recommend *Windows NT® Workstation 4.0 MCSE Study Guide* (IDG Books Worldwide, 1998).

How This Book Is Organized

Chapters begin with an introductory paragraph, followed by "Official Word" and "Inside Scoop" — bulleted summaries of official exam objectives *and* exclusive inside exam information covered in the chapter. The first list, "Official Word," includes the Microsoft objectives; the second, "Inside Scoop," includes the author's synthesis of topic priorities within the objectives (the functional objectives) and other important insights on exam coverage. Following these lists is the "Are You Prepared?" section — a short self-assessment test of three multiple-choice questions with answers and cross-references to the chapter content. Chapter content includes a concise conceptual discussion of essential exam material. Chapters end with "Have You Mastered?" — five to ten multiple-choice questions with answers, analyses, and cross-references to chapter discussions — followed by a "Practice Your Skills" section, consisting of three to five hands-on or critical-thinking review activities.

The supplemental materials at the back of the book contain a wealth of information. This part features a full-length Practice Exam highlighting the most likely question types you will see on the actual MCP exam. The exam is followed by the Exam Analysis section that details why the correct answer is true, and offers a look at why the distracters might have been chosen. This part also includes the MCSE Ace It! exclusive, "Exam Revealed." This section offers an insider's look at the makeup of MCP exam questions, and what to look for when you are taking your exam. You gain insight into reducing the complexity of typical questions, and gain skills to help you determine the correct answer quickly.

How to Use This Book

This book can be used either by individuals working independently or by groups in a formal classroom setting.

For best results (and the only acceptable result is a passing score on the exam), I recommend the following plan of attack as you use this book. First, read the chapter, the Test Tips and Traps highlights, and the "Inside Scoop." Then use the "Have You Mastered" and "Practice Your Skills" sections to see if you've really got the key concepts under your belt. If you don't, go back and reread the section(s) you're not clear on. When you are preparing for the exam, review the "Are You Prepared" sections at the beginning of each chapter, and review the material you need to refresh. Just before taking the exam, tear out the Ace Card and use it to study the key points of the book, even up to the time you walk into the testing center — if possible. Remember, the important thing is to master the tasks that are tested on the exam.

The chapters of this book are designed to be studied sequentially. In other words, it would be best if you complete Chapter 1 before you proceed to Chapter 2. A few chapters could probably stand alone, but all in all, I recommend a sequential approach.

After you've completed your study of the chapters, reviewed the "Have You Mastered" questions, and done the "Practice Your Skills" exercises, take the Practice Exam included in the back of the book. The Practice Exam will help you assess how much you've learned from your study, and will familiarize you with the types of questions you'll face when you take the real exam. Once you identify a weak area, you can restudy the corresponding chapters (including the "Have You Mastered" questions) to improve your knowledge and skills in that area.

Prerequisites

Although this book is a comprehensive study and exam preparation guide, it does not start at ground zero. I assume you have the following knowledge and skills at the outset:

- Basic terminology and basic skills to use a Microsoft Windows product. (This could be Windows 95, Windows for Workgroups, or a Windows NT product.)
- Basic mouse skills: being able to left-click, right-click, use the pointer, and so on.
- Networking knowledge or experience equal to the scope required to pass the Microsoft Certified Professional Networking Essentials Exam (Exam No. 70-58).
- Some hands-on experience with Windows NT Workstation, or the aptitude to jump into this material with a running start.

If you meet these prerequisites, you're ready to begin this book.

If you don't have the basic Windows experience or mouse skills, I recommend you either take a one-day Windows application course or work through a self-study book, such as *Windows 95 For Dummies* (IDG Books Worldwide, 1995), to acquire these skills *before* you begin this book.

If you don't have the networking knowledge or experience, I recommend you use a tool such as the *Networking Essentials MCSE Study Guide* by Jason Nash (IDG Books Worldwide, 1998), to obtain this knowledge, and pass the Networking Essentials exam *before* you begin this book.

Icons Used in This Book

Several different icons are used throughout this book to draw your attention to matters that deserve a closer look:

 This icon identifies quick notes that warn readers of pitfalls and loopholes in Microsoft exam questions.

This icon points out advice that strengthens readers' test-taking skills with helpful hints and strategies for passing the exam.

 This icon highlights quick summaries of essential elements of exam topics.

 This icon includes three to five true/false questions that offer instant testing of hot exam topics.

This concludes the owner's manual on how to operate this book. It's time to get started, and get you on your way to passing the Windows NT Workstation 4.0 exam. Now, let's get certified!

Acknowledgments

There have been few other times in my life as precious as these last few months while I have been preparing this book. With this book project and the birth of my first daughter, it is unlikely I will ever forget this time. To that end I owe a great deal of gratitude to a number of people who have made it their lives to support me and get this book to you.

First I would like to thank Alan Carter for his supreme wisdom in getting me to talk with IDG Books. Without his intervention I would not be here today.

My appreciation goes out to the entire team at IDG Books who worked on this book tirelessly for several months. Special thanks to Jennifer Rowe, lead development editor; Tracy Thomsic, acquisitions editor; Steve Anderson, development editor, Nicole Fountain, lead copy editor, and Brian MacDonald, copy editor. Also, thanks to the graphics and production staff. I wish to send thanks to Tony Houston for his efforts in technically reviewing this book, and my sincerest appreciation to the Director of Publishing for the Computer Publishing Group at IDG Books, Steve Sayre.

Of course, I also want to thank all of my family and friends who supported me during this tremendous effort. To my wife and darling daughter, your support and understanding made this project a success and a pleasure to work on.

Contents
at a Glance

Contents

Installing Windows NT Workstation

G ET READY TO DIVE RIGHT INTO the thick of the
Workstation exam. Do you have experience installing
Windows NT Workstation, including the hardware
requirements? Do you know the difference between
using Winnt.exe or Winnt32.exe? This chapter looks
at the entire installation process, phase-by-phase, and
discusses how to uninstall Windows NT Workstation. It also prepares
you for questions about installing in a dual boot configuration and troubleshooting common NT installation problems.

Exam Material in This Chapter

Based on Microsoft Objectives

Installing and Configuring

- Install Windows NT Workstation on an Intel platform in a given situation.
- Set up a dual-boot system in a given situation.
- Remove Windows NT Workstation in a given situation.
- Upgrade to Windows NT Workstation 4.0 in a given situation.

Troubleshooting

- Choose the appropriate course of action to take when the installation process fails.

Based on Author's Experience

- You need to know the hardware requirements for installing Windows NT.
- Expect a few questions on configuring a computer to boot to either Windows NT or another OS.
- The exam may present questions to test your knowledge on what partition types you can use on the C drive of a dual boot Windows NT Workstation.
- You should be familiar with how to automate the installation of Windows NT setup program using command-line switches.
- You should understand how to convert from NTFS to FAT on a partition.

Are You Prepared?

Do you have what it takes? Try out these self-assessment questions to see if you have prepared for the material in this chapter or if you should review problem areas.

1. **Which command-line option for** Winnt.exe **enables you to start your installation without creating the setup boot disk set?**

   ☐ A. Winnt.exe /S
   ☐ B. Winnt.exe /F
   ☐ C. Winnt.exe /B
   ☐ D. Winnt.exe /X
   ☐ E. Winnt.exe /C

2. **What utility helps you determine if Windows NT can detect the hardware in your computer before starting the installation process?**

   ☐ A. NTHQ
   ☐ B. Winnt32.exe /F
   ☐ C. MSInfo

3. **What is the minimum free disk space required to install Windows NT Workstation?**

   ☐ A. 210MB
   ☐ B. 430MB
   ☐ C. 50MB
   ☐ D. 117MB
   ☐ E. 12MB

Answers:

1. C   *The /B command-line switch configures Windows NT to install without creating startup disks. See the section entitled "The Installation Process."*

2. A   *NTHQ helps you determine if Windows NT can detect your hardware, and it identifies the hardware settings used for each adapter. See the section entitled "Installation Requirements."*

3. D   *Windows NT Workstation requires a minimum of 117MB of free disk space to install. See the "Installation Requirements" section.*

The Microsoft Windows NT Workstation Operating System

Windows NT Workstation 4.0 is a 32-bit operating system that is optimized to run as a desktop operating system. It can also be used on personal computers that are networked in a peer-to-peer workgroup configuration, or on a workstation computer that is part of a Windows NT Server domain configuration.

The minimum hardware required to successfully run Windows NT Workstation 4.0 consists of an Intel-based computer with a 486/33 processor, 12MB of RAM (16MB recommended), 117MB of free hard disk space, and a VGA graphics card. Windows NT Workstation provides only minimal support for Plug and Play.

Windows NT Workstation supports most MS-DOS-based applications, most 16-bit and 32-bit Windows-based applications, POSIX 1.*x* applications, and most OS/2 1.*x* applications. It does not support applications that require direct hardware access because this could compromise Windows NT Workstation's security. It also does not support software applications that require a *terminate-and-stay-resident* (TSR) program or a virtual device driver.

User logon and authentication are required to use the Windows NT Workstation operating system and in order to access local or network resources.

Workgroups and Domains

Computers and their users may be grouped based on common usage requirements or on departmental or geographical traits. Workgroups and domains are two prevalent methods of grouping networked computers for common purposes. For example, all members of an accounting department or all computers on the third floor of a building may be grouped together.

Workgroups

A *workgroup* is a logical grouping of networked computers in which one or more of the computers has one or more shared resources, such as a shared folder or a shared printer.

 The terms *folder* and *directory* are synonymous in the world of Windows NT. The NT user interface does not use these terms consistently. Sometimes the interface refers to a *folder*, and sometimes it calls the same (or similar) item a *directory*. Expect to find these terms on the test.

In a workgroup environment, the security and user accounts are all maintained individually at each separate computer. Resources and administration are distributed throughout the computers that make up the workgroup. In a workgroup configuration there is no centrally maintained user accounts database, or any centralized security. Figure 1-1 illustrates how security is distributed throughout a workgroup environment. Notice that security is maintained individually at each separate computer in the workgroup.

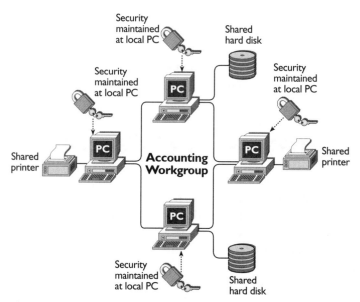

Figure 1-1 *Security in a workgroup environment*

Typically, all of the computers in a workgroup run desktop operating systems, such as Windows NT Workstation or Windows 95.

Domains

A *domain* is a logical grouping of networked computers in which all of the computers share a common, central domain directory database that contains user account and security information. One distinct advantage of using a domain (or *domain model*, as it is sometimes called), particularly on a large network, is that administration and security for the entire network can be managed from a centralized location. Figure 1-2 illustrates how security is centralized in a domain environment. Note that all user account security is maintained at the domain controller.

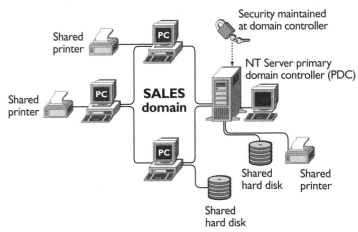

Figure 1-2 *Security in a domain environment*

In a Windows NT domain, at least one of the networked computers is a server computer that runs Windows NT Server. The server computer is configured as a *primary domain controller* (PDC), which maintains the domain directory database. A domain may contain only one PDC. Typically, there is at least one additional server computer that also runs Windows NT Server. This additional computer is usually configured as a *backup domain controller* (BDC). There is no limit to the number of BDCs in an NT Domain.

Workgroups Versus Domains

Choosing the appropriate model of grouping computers and managing shared network resources depends upon the size and security needs of the network. Small- to medium-sized networks (two to 20 computers) can be managed fairly easily by using the workgroup model, with the user of each computer controlling the security to the specific resources shared by that user's computer. In a larger network environment, administration and security become harder to manage; thus, the domain model, which provides centralized account administration and greater security, is usually the preferred choice.

POP QUIZ True or False?

1. A Windows NT Workgroup has a PDC.

2. In large corporate networks, Windows NT Workstations should participate in workgroups rather than domains because workgroups have a common directory service.

3. A Windows NT Domain may have only one PDC and more than one BDC.

4. Windows NT Workstations support applications that require direct hardware access.

5. You can run most OS/2 1.x applications on Windows NT Workstation.

Answers: *1. False 2. False 3. True 4. False 5. True*

Installation Requirements

Before you can install NT, you should make sure you have the appropriate hardware. To avoid problems, only use hardware that appears on the Windows NT *Hardware Compatibility List* (HCL). The HCL, which is updated periodically, ships with the NT products.

Table 1.1 shows the minimum hardware required for installing Windows NT Workstation. The requirements listed apply only to Intel-based platforms.

TABLE 1.1 Minimum Hardware Required for Installation of Windows NT Workstation 4.0

Hardware Component	Minimum Requirement
Processor	486/33
Memory	12MB of RAM
Hard disk space	117MB
Display	VGA or better
Floppy disk drive	3.5-inch high-density
CD-ROM drive	Required (If your computer does not have a CD-ROM drive, you can still install NT Workstation by using an over-the-network installation.)
Network adapter	Optional (Required for over-the-network installation)
Mouse	Optional

Make sure you know the minimum hardware requirements to install Windows NT Workstation. You will likely see a few questions on the exam that ask you to determine which configurations you can install Windows NT on.

You can use the *NT Hardware Qualifier* (NTHQ) utility that comes with Windows NT to examine and identify your hardware configuration. NTHQ helps you determine if Windows NT can detect your hardware, and it identifies the hardware settings used for each adapter. To use NTHQ, you must create an NTHQ diskette, which you then use to boot your computer.

Configuring Dual Boot

When you install Windows NT 4.0 in a different directory than the original operating system, Windows NT automatically configures itself to *dual boot* between Windows NT 4.0 and the previously installed operating system. Windows NT 4.0 can also dual boot between Windows NT 4.0 and Windows 3.*x* when you install Windows NT 4.0 in the same directory as Windows 3.*x*.

When Windows NT Workstation installs on a MS-DOS computer, the boot sector program that loads MS-DOS is moved to a file called `bootsect.dos`. Windows NT then replaces the boot sector information to load the Windows NT loader. When the installation is completed and the computer is rebooted, the boot process will load the Windows NT loader, which displays a boot menu to the user. The menu will enable the user to load Windows NT Workstation or load MS-DOS. If the user chooses to boot into MS-DOS, the Windows NT loader uses the information in the `bootsect.dos` file to load MS-DOS.

If the user does not choose which operating system to load, or if the computer is booted while unattended, the Windows NT loader, by default, waits 30 seconds and then loads Windows NT.

Because a dual boot computer has multiple operating systems on one or more disks, some OS features may cause interruption or loss of data if not properly configured. Windows NT includes NTFS (Windows NT File System), which provides increased management capabilities and improved disk utilization. As a result, other operating systems such as MS-DOS and Windows are incapable of using any partition that has been formatted as NTFS. To dual boot between Windows NT Workstation and other operating systems, the boot drive must be formatted as a *FAT* (File Allocation Table) partition.

Dual Boot Partition Requirements

A dual boot computer must have the C drive formatted as FAT. MS-DOS and Windows are incapable of seeing or using any partitions formatted as NTFS. If Windows NT is already installed with the disk formatted as NTFS, and you want to install MS-DOS or Windows, you must remove Windows NT, repartition the drive, and format the partition as FAT.

Types of partitions

Within the Windows NT operating system there are two important types of partitions: a *system partition* and a *boot partition*. These two terms are Windows NT jargon for primary and extended partitions that contain specific files and perform specific functions in Windows NT.

- **System Partition:** The system partition is located on the active primary partition of the first hard disk in the computer (usually the C: drive). It contains several files that are required to boot Windows NT, including: `ntldr`, `Ntdetect.com`, `Boot.ini`, and sometimes `Bootsect.dos`, and `Ntbootdd.sys`, depending on the installation type and hardware configuration.

- **Boot Partition:** The boot partition can be located on either a primary or extended partition. It contains the Windows NT installation directory (usually the `Winnt` directory) and all of the Windows NT operating system files.

The names of these two partitions often confuse people. Because of the types of files the partitions contain, many people think the boot partition should be called the system partition, and vice versa. You might find it helpful to make a mental note that these two partitions are named the opposite of what you intuitively think they should be!

The Installation Process

Now that you know the minimum hardware required to install Windows NT Workstation and have all the information required to perform the installation, you're ready to move on to the actual installation process.

There are three ways to start the installation process: from a CD-ROM drive, by using `Winnt.exe`, and by using `Winnt32.exe`. Installation can be done locally, from a CD-ROM drive; or over the network.

Setup from a CD-ROM Drive

To start the installation from a CD-ROM drive, your computer must be configured with a local CD-ROM drive that is on the HCL. Place the

Windows NT Workstation compact disc in the CD-ROM drive. Next, boot the computer from the Windows NT Setup Boot Disk.

Setup Using Winnt.exe

You can use `Winnt.exe` to start the installation from an unsupported CD-ROM drive (a CD-ROM drive that is not listed on the HCL), or to start an over-the-network installation. First boot the computer to MS-DOS, load either the CD-ROM drivers or network drivers (depending on the type of installation), and then use `Winnt.exe` to start the install.

`Winnt.exe` has several command-line switches that enable customization of the setup process. Table 1.2 lists these switches and describes their functions.

 KNOW THIS **Command-Line Switches**

Command-line switches are not case-sensitive. You may type them in either uppercase or lowercase.

TABLE 1.2 Winnt.exe Command-Line Switches

Switch	What the Switch Does
`/S[:]sourcepath`	Specifies the source location of NT files. You must specify a full path, in the form `x:\[path]` or `\\server\share[\path]`. Default sourcepath is the current directory.
`/T[:]tempdrive`	Specifies the drive that contains NT's temporary setup files during installation. If not specified, Setup uses the first drive it finds (that it thinks has enough free space) for the temp-drive.
`/I[:]inffile`	Specifies the filename (no path) of the file containing setup information. Default inffile is `DOSNET.INF`.
`/OX`	Instructs Setup to create the Setup Boot Disk set.

Switch	What the Switch Does
/X	Instructs Setup *not* to create the Setup Boot Disk set.
/F	Instructs Setup not to verify files as they are copied to the Setup Boot Disk set (during the creation of the Setup Boot Disk set).
/C	Instructs Setup to skip the disk free-space check during the creation of the Setup Boot Disk set.
/B	Enables you to install NT without using the Setup Boot Disk set. Requires you to specify the source path by using the /S switch.
/U	Enables you to perform an unattended NT installation and use an optional script file. Requires you to specify the sourcepath by using the /S switch.
/R	Specifies an optional directory to be installed during installation.
/RX	Specifies an optional directory to be copied to the local hard drive during installation.
/E	Specifies a command to be executed at the end of the installation/setup process.
/UDF	Specifies that a Uniqueness Database File is used during an unattended NT installation.

The most common command-line questions are about the /U, /B, /X, and /I. Make sure you understand their purpose and how to use them in various scenarios.

The syntax for the Winnt.exe command is:

```
WINNT [/S[:]sourcepath] [/T[:]tempdrive] [/I[:]inffile
[/OX] [/X | [/F] [/C]] [/B] [/U[:scriptfile]]
[/RX]:directory] [/E:command]
```

To illustrate how the switches are used, suppose that you want to install Windows NT from a network drive (named drive K:) without using the Setup Boot Disk set. (This is often referred to as a disk-less installation). To accomplish this, use the following command:

```
K:\I386\Winnt /B /S:K:\I386
```

Notice the /B switch is used to permit you to perform a disk-less installation, and the /S switch is used to specify that the sourcepath (the location of the NT files that will be installed on your computer) is a network drive named K:.

Setup Using Winnt32.exe

Winnt32.exe functions in the same way as Winnt.exe except that Winnt.exe is designed to run on a MS-DOS-based or Windows-based computers, and Winnt32.exe is designed to be used on Windows NT computers. All Winnt32.exe command-line options are the same as Winnt.exe, with the exception of /F and /C, which are not supported by Winnt32.exe. Additionally, Winnt32.exe performs the functions quicker because it can launch multiple threads in Windows NT. As a result, your installation process will proceed more quickly if you use Winnt32.exe.

POP QUIZ   True or False?

1. The /U command-line switch enables you to specify a script file to use during the installation.

2. Winnt.exe performs an installation faster than Winnt32.exe.

3. Winnt.exe works only on Windows NT computers.

4. The /B command-line switch enables you to perform a disk-less installation.

5. A dual boot Windows NT and MS-DOS computer can have the boot drive formatted as NTFS.

Answers: *1. True 2. False 3. False 4. True 5. False*

Setup Flow

The installation of Windows NT Workstation takes place in four or five phases, depending on whether you install from a CD-ROM or use Winnt.exe. These phases are: the pre-copy phase, phase 0, and phases 1-3. During each phase, you perform specific tasks and enter requested information. The Windows NT installation program (Setup) causes the computer to reboot after the pre-copy phase, and again after phase 0.

Pre-copy phase

The pre-copy phase is the initial phase of the installation process. This phase applies only when the Winnt.exe or Winnt32.exe installation option is used. Setup creates a set of three floppy disks to use during the installation process. These diskettes are similar to the diskettes used to perform an installation from a CD-ROM drive (except they point to the directory that has a copy of the installation files instead of to a CD-ROM drive). The floppy disks are not created if the /B or /U switches are used. Setup then creates a Win_NT.~ls folder on the first local drive with enough free space, and then copies the installation files from the source directory to this folder. (The installation program deletes this folder after the installation is complete.)

Phase 0

Phase 0 begins when you boot the computer with the Setup boot disk, or when you reboot the computer after starting Winnt.exe using either the /B or /U switch. During this phase you will be prompted to Confirm all SCSI and CD-ROM adapters, and add drivers for adapters by using driver disks supplied by the manufacturer. You are also permitted to choose the installation directory and whether to upgrade previously installed versions of Windows 3.x or Windows NT, or to install Windows NT in a different directory to create a dual boot system, which can boot to more than one operating system.

Setup will then examine your computer's hard disk for corruption, and then cause the computer to reboot. After the computer reboots, Setup prompts you to remove the floppy disk from drive A: if one is there.

FAT and NTFS File Systems

The *file allocation table* (FAT) file system is supported by Windows NT and many other operating systems. If you want your computer to dual boot between Windows NT and another operating system, choose the FAT file system. The FAT file system supports neither extended attributes nor file-level security.

The *Windows NT file system* (NTFS) is supported only by Windows NT. Choose NTFS if you do not want your computer to dual boot between Windows NT and another operating system and you want the added advantages provided by NTFS, including extended attributes and file-level security.

You can select FAT as the file system to be used during installation of Windows NT, and then later choose to convert the file system to NTFS; however, if you choose NTFS as the file system to be used during installation of Windows NT and then later want to convert to FAT, the process isn't so easy. To convert from NTFS to FAT, you need to back up all files, repartition and format the drive, reinstall Windows NT, and restore all the files from backup.

Windows NT 4.0 does not support the *high performance file system* (HPFS) used by OS/2. If you want to install Windows NT 4.0 on a computer that uses HPFS, you must back up all data, repartition and format the computer's drive with FAT or NTFS, and then restore all the files from backup before you can install Windows NT 4.0.

Phase 1

In phase 1, the NT Setup Wizard starts. Setup gathers more information from you about your computer and specific installation details. You are prompted to enter information such as your name, CD key number, computer name and an administrator account password. At this point, you can choose which optional Windows NT components you want to install.

Phase 2

In phase 2, Setup installs and configures networking components. To accomplish this, you provide more information about how (or if) the computer connects to the network. You are then permitted to configure your network adapters, protocols, and network groups to determine which workgroup or domain the computer should join.

Phase 3

In phase 3, Setup completes the installation (which is very short). You are prompted to configure the date, time, time zone information, and test the computer's video adapter settings. You can also create an Emergency Repair Disk at this time.

The Windows NT installation is complete.

Removing Windows NT Workstation

If you have incorrectly installed Windows NT, or want to remove it from your computer for any other reason, this section outlines the necessary steps.

If your computer is configured to dual boot between Windows NT and MS-DOS, it is fairly easy to remove Windows NT. You must first boot your computer to MS-DOS from a floppy disk that has the Sys.com utility on it. At the command prompt, type **Sys c:**. This will replace the Windows NT boot sector with the boot sector for your other operating system. Reboot the computer, and MS-DOS should start automatically.

If you want to remove Windows NT from an NTFS partition, you must delete that partition, repartition the drive, and reformat the disk because no other operating system supports NTFS. Depending on your situation, to accomplish this you need to either delete an NTFS primary partition, or delete NTFS from an extended partition.

Be certain you understand that only Windows NT can see and use NTFS partitions in a computer. MS-DOS and Windows-based computers cannot use a NTFS partition. The partition must be repartitioned and formatted before they can be used by an operating system other than Windows NT.

Troubleshooting Common Installation Problems

Most of the common problems that cause your installation of Windows NT Workstation to fail occur because of hardware incompatibilities. Your first troubleshooting step is to ensure that all of your hardware is on the HCL or is supported by the manufacturer. The following table lists some common Windows NT installation problems and their possible causes and solutions.

TABLE 1.3 Troubleshooting Common Installation Problems

Problem:	Possible Cause/Solution:
You have the recommended amount of free disk space, but still run out of disk space during installation.	The recommended amount of disk space is based on the expectation that you are using 16K sectors on your hard disk. If you have a very large partition, you could be using 32K or 64K sectors.
A blue screen or STOP message is displayed during installation or after a reboot.	This can be caused by several things. Some of the most common causes are a *corrupt boot sector* or a *boot sector virus*, which you can usually repair by using `Fdisk /mbr` from MS-DOS (many virus scanners can also repair this error); and *hardware conflicts*, which you can check for by using NTHQ to examine all of your hardware settings.

Problem:	Possible Cause/Solution:
You can't install from your CD-ROM drive.	This could be caused by an unsupported CD-ROM drive or by an unsupported SCSI adapter. Some SCSI adapters, such as PC card SCSI adapters, are not supported during installation but you can install the drivers for them after the installation is complete.
You can't join a domain during installation.	Make sure that all network settings, both hardware and software, are correct. Confirm that you have correctly typed in the domain name and the administrator's user account name and password. (All passwords in Windows NT are case-sensitive.) Check the network cable and connections and verify that the PDC is up and accessible on the network.
Network services don't start correctly.	Verify that all network adapter and network protocol settings are correct, including interrupt, I/O port, and transceiver type. Confirm that the newly assigned computer name is unique — that it does not match any other computer, domain, or workgroup name used on the network.

POP QUIZ True or False?

1. You should always use NTFS on the C drive of a dual boot computer.

2. To convert a NTFS partition to FAT you must repartition and format the disk.

3. FAT partitions support neither extended attributes nor file-level security.

Answers: *1. False 2. True 3. True*

Have You Mastered?

Now it's time to apply what you've learned in this chapter by testing your mastery of the material. These questions provide you with a means to determine if you are ready to move on to the next chapter or if you need to review the material again.

1. **You are upgrading a Windows NT Workstation 3.51 computer to Windows NT Workstation 4.0. What can you do to increase the speed of the upgrade?**

    ☐ A. Run NTHQ before starting the upgrade.
    ☐ B. Start the upgrade with `Winnt32.exe`.
    ☐ C. Start the upgrade with `Winnt.exe`.
    ☐ D. Remove all of the network components in NT 3.51 before starting the upgrade.

    The correct answer is **B**. `Winnt32.exe` performs installations and upgrades faster because it can start multiple threads of the installation simultaneously, rather than sequentially as `Winnt.exe` does. `Winnt32.exe` can only be run on computers that are already running Windows NT, so it can only increase the performance during upgrades and installations to different directories on a Windows NT computer. For more information, see the section entitled "The Installation Process."

2. **You are planning a new network that will have 50 Windows NT Workstation computers and 5 Windows NT Server computers. You want to centrally manage user accounts and security**

privileges for all of the computers. What type of network should you implement?

- ☐ A. Create a workgroup and place all of the computers in the workgroup.
- ☐ B. Create a workgroup, place all of the computers in the workgroup, and configure one of the Windows NT Server computers as a PDC.
- ☐ C. Create a domain, place all of the computers in the domain, and configure all of the Windows NT Server computers as a PDC.
- ☐ D. Create a domain, place all of the computers in the domain, and configure one of the Windows NT Server computers as a PDC.

The correct answer is **D**. To centrally manage user accounts and security privileges, you must have an NT domain. Additionally, a domain can only have one PDC at a time. The other servers can be configured as BDCs. A Workgroup does not support central user accounts because there is no common directory for the computers. For more information, see the section entitled "Workgroups and Domains" earlier in this chapter.

3. **You are installing a new application on your Windows NT 4.0 computer. The application requirements state that it must have direct access to your computer's hardware. What can you do to get this application to run on your computer?**

- ☐ A. Do nothing, Windows NT Workstation 4.0 directly supports these types of applications.
- ☐ B. Place the computer in a Workgroup rather than an NT Domain.
- ☐ C. Install MS-DOS on the computer and run the application from MS-DOS.
- ☐ D. Configure the application run in the POSIX environment.

The correct answer is **C**. Windows NT does not support any application that requires direct access to the computer hardware. Direct access may compromise the security features of Windows NT. Of the presented solutions, only the MS-DOS scenario would resolve the problem and permit the application to run on the computer. For more information, see the "Microsoft Windows NT Workstation Operating System" section of this chapter.

4. **You want to configure your computer to dual boot between Windows NT Workstation and Windows 95. Your computer is currently running Windows NT Workstation and has its only hard disk formatted as an NTFS partition. What should you do to install Windows 95?**

    ☐ A. Boot to the Windows NT desktop and run the Windows 95 setup program.

    ☐ B. Boot the computer with an MS-DOS disk and start the Windows 95 setup program.

    ☐ C. Convert the NTFS partition to FAT and start the Windows 95 setup program.

    ☐ D. Repartition and format the drive as FAT, start the Windows 95 setup program, and then install Windows NT Workstation.

The correct answer is **D**. The most important aspect of this scenario is that the only drive in the computer is formatted as NTFS. No other operating system can use a NTFS partition other than NT Workstation. Also, there is no way to convert from a NTFS partition to a FAT partition. For more information, refer back to the "Configuring Dual Boot" section.

5. **What is the minimum processor, amount of RAM, and hard disk space required to install Windows NT Workstation on an Intel-based computer?**

    ☐ A. Processor: 386/33
           RAM: 8MB
           Hard disk: 500MB

☐ B. Processor: 486/33
RAM: 12MB
Hard disk: 117MB

☐ C. Processor: 486/66
RAM: 16MB
Hard disk: 220MB

☐ D. Processor: Pentium/100
RAM: 16MB
Hard disk: 330MB

The correct answer is **B**. Microsoft Windows NT Workstation does not support the Intel 386 processor and the minimum amount of free space is 117MB, depending on the options installed. For diskless installs add an additional 100MB-200MB during the install process. For more information, see the "Installation Requirements" section of this chapter.

6. What file system types does Microsoft Windows NT Workstation 4.0 support?

☐ A. FAT
☐ B. FAT32
☐ C. HPFS
☐ D. NTFS
☐ E. POSIX

The correct answer is **A** and **D**. Windows NT Workstation 4.0 supports older FAT partitions, as well as newer NTFS partitions. NT Workstation 4.0 does not support the newer FAT32 file system that ships with Windows 98, nor can it use HPFS drives. POSIX is a computing subsystem, not a file system.

Practice Your Skills

Here is a chance to apply your practical, hands-on experience and material from this chapter. These exercises are designed for you to apply not only the material in the book, but to gain greater experience and exposure to the product. These exercises are a critical part of understanding the product and gaining valuable experience using the product and passing the certification exam. For each of the following problems, consider the given facts and determine what you think are the possible causes of the problem and what course of action you might take to resolve the problem.

1. Planning NT Workstation Groups

EXERCISE   You are installing 50 new Windows NT Workstation computers on your network. You create a workgroup called **NT Computers** and place all of the Workstation computers in the workgroup. When users try to access network shares on other computers they get access denied errors. What is the problem and what can you do to resolve it?

ANALYSIS   Workgroups do not provide a central directory service or security management. When the computers were added to the workgroup, there was no sharing of user accounts between the computers. To resolve the issue, the computers should be added to a Windows NT domain and managed by a Windows NT Domain Controller that provides a central account directory.

2. Troubleshooting Windows NT installation problems

EXERCISE You are installing Windows NT Workstation 4.0 to your new computer. During the installation, the process stops and you see a blue screen containing error information on your display. What should you do to resolve the problem and determine the solution?

ANALYSIS The most likely cause of the problem is that of hardware compatibility. Try removing all add-on devices that are not required for the installation, and then attempt the installation again. If the error reoccurs, try installing from a new CD-ROM or other location. If the problem still occurs, check the HCL to ensure there is Windows NT support your computer hardware.

3. Joining a domain during installation

EXERCISE You are installing Windows NT Workstation 4.0 on your new computer. During the installation you try to join a domain and an error message is displayed. It states that the domain controller for this domain cannot be located. What should you do to join the domain?

ANALYSIS Click the *Back* button in the installation dialog boxes until you are returned to the Network configuration dialog. Verify all of your network configuration information and alternatively, select an additional supported protocol. Proceed with the installation to determine if the domain controller is now accessible. If not, make a quick scan of the physical network components, status LEDs and cable, and then make sure the domain controller is online.

Server-Based Deployment

BEING ABLE TO INSTALL WINDOWS NT on a single computer is not enough to pass the exam. You must understand how to perform server-based installation and deployments for multiple computers. Do you understand how to create unattended installation script files using the Windows NT Setup Manager? How about creating bootable installation disks using the Network Client Administrator? In this chapter we focus on these topics and include a look at how to automate the installation of applications during an automated installation of Windows NT.

Exam Material in This Chapter

Based on Microsoft Objectives

Planning

- Create unattended installation files
- Set up a dual-boot system in a given situation
- Remove Windows NT Workstation
- Upgrade to Windows NT Workstation 4.0 in a given situation

Troubleshooting

- Choose the appropriate course of action to take when the installation process fails

Based on Author's Experience

- You should know how to use the Network Client Administrator to create a Network Installation Startup Disk.
- You should understand the difference between a Network Installation Startup Disk and an Installation Disk Set.
- There will be questions on how to install Microsoft client operating systems over the network.
- Be sure to review the process of how to use an unattended.txt file to preselect the install process of Windows NT Workstation.
- You should understand what a UDF file contains and how it is used during an automated installation.

Are You Prepared?

Do you have what it takes? Try out these self-assessment questions to see if you have prepared for the material in this chapter or if you should review problem areas.

1. **Which of the following processes enable you to install applications automatically at the end of the Windows NT Workstation installation? (Choose two.)**

   - ☐ A. OEM
   - ☐ B. Unattended.txt
   - ☐ C. Sysdiff.exe
   - ☐ D. UDF
   - ☐ E. Setup Manager

2. **What can you use to automate the installation of applications that don't support scripted installation and that would otherwise require user interaction during the installation process?**

   - ☐ A. Sysdiff.exe
   - ☐ B. OEM
   - ☐ C. Setup Manager
   - ☐ D. Network Client Administrator

3. **What is the purpose of an Installation Disk Set?**

   - ☐ A. Install an operating system (OS), such as Windows NT over the network.
   - ☐ B. Install the network drivers to connect to an NT Server and download the installation disks.

☐ C. Contains the files required to install client software, such as TCP/IP for Windows for Workgroups.

☐ D. Installs client operating systems on an NT Server to
enable clients to install from the server.

Answers:

1. A+C *The OEM directory structure and* Sysdiff.exe
*enable you to install Applications at the end of the
Windows NT Workstation installation routine. See the
section titled, "Automating Application Installation
During Setup."*

2. A *The* Sysdiff.exe *utility creates a before and after
picture of your computer when you install the
application. See the section titled "Automating
Application Installation During Setup."*

3. C *An Installation Disk Set contains installation files for
client software for most DOS environments and can
contain services, such as TCP/IP for Windows for
Workgroup computers. See the section titled "Network
Client Administrator."*

Server-Based Deployment

Server-based deployment is a process that involves automating the installation and setup of Windows NT, other OSs, and applications on multiple computers on a network.

This process is primarily designed for rolling out large networks quickly and efficiently.

Because you may not use server-based deployment in your environment (unless you manage a large network), you should study this chapter carefully, and revisit it just before you take the Workstation exam. Don't study just one or two sections; the truth is that the whole chapter is fair game on the exam.

In server-based deployment, source files are placed on a centrally located Windows NT Server computer. Then floppy disks are created and, when run on the computers that need to be set up, they cause these computers to connect to the server automatically and to run a partially or fully automated installation and setup routine.

Server-based deployment is commonly used in two types of environments. First, *original equipment manufacturers* (OEMs) use this process to install and configure large numbers of computers at the factory prior to shipping them to customers and retail outlets. Second, organizations that install a new network or add several new computers to an existing network use this process to install operating systems and applications on their new computers in an efficient manner.

Deployment Preparations

To begin the preparation, copy the `Clients` folder, including all files and subfolders, from your Windows NT Server compact disc to one of the drives on the Windows NT Server computer. This drive must have enough free space to hold the entire contents of the `Clients` folder and the source files for any additional operating systems and applications you want to install using server-based deployment.

Next, share the `Clients` folder on the Windows NT Server computer as `CLIENTS.` If the only OS you want to deploy is Windows 95, you are finished preparing your Windows NT Server computer. To deploy

Windows NT, create a subfolder in the Clients folder named Winnt and create a subfolder in the Clients\Winnt folder named Netsetup. Copy the Windows NT installation files and subfolders from the I386 folder on your Windows NT CD-ROM to the Netsetup folder.

Network Client Administrator

Network Client Administrator is a Windows NT Server tool that is used to create an installation disk set to install network clients or services on client computers. For example, to install TCP/IP on several Windows for Workgroups computers you can use Network Client Administrator to create a TCP/IP installation disk set, and then use this disk set on each computer on which you want to install TCP/IP.

The network clients and services for which you can create an installation disk set are: Network Client *v*3.0 for MS-DOS and Windows, Remote Access *v*1.1a for MS-DOS, TCP/IP 32 for Windows for Workgroups 3.11, LAN Manager *v*2.2c for MS-DOS, and LAN Manager *v*2.2c for OS/2.

KNOW THIS — Installation Disks

An installation disk set can only be used to install the network client software and services for DOS and OS/2 computers. These disks can be used to configure an existing DOS computer to use real-mode client software. They can then be used to connect to an NT Server to install Windows NT Workstation.

A network installation startup disk is used to boot a computer, load the MS-DOS network client software, and start an installation automatically. These disks are generally used for computers that do not have an existing OS or are not bootable.

You can also use Network Client Administrator to create a *network installation startup disk*. This runs on the computer that needs to be set up (the *target computer*) and causes it to connect to the server automatically and start an interactive installation/setup routine. For example, to install Windows NT Workstation on several new client computers on your network, you can use Network Client Administrator to create a single disk for use on each of the new client computers. This automatically begins an interactive, over-the-network installation of Windows NT Workstation.

You can create a network installation startup disk for use in installing any of the following operating systems: Windows for Workgroups, Windows 95, Windows NT Workstation, or Windows NT Server. (A separate disk is required for each different operating system.)

Network Client Administrator is only included with Windows NT Server — it is not available on a Windows NT Workstation computer.

True or False?

1. The `Clients` folder is automatically installed on NT Server computers when they are first installed.

2. A network installation disk set is used to copy network client software to a computer.

3. Network Client Administrator is only included with Windows NT Server.

4. An installation disk set can be used to install RAS on MS-DOS client computers.

5. Network installation startup disk works only on computers that have identical network adapters installed in them.

Answers: *1. False 2. False 3. True 4. True 5. True*

Automating Setup of Windows NT

To automate the Windows NT installation and setup process fully, you must create an answer file to be used by the Windows NT setup program. You must also edit the Autoexec.bat file on the network installation startup disk so it uses this answer file during the installation. You also need to know how to create and use Uniqueness Database Files (UDFs) to automate the Windows NT installation and setup process fully.

Answer Files (Unattend.txt)

Answer files are text files that contain stylized responses to the queries posed by the Windows NT Setup program during installation. You can use an answer file in conjunction with a network installation startup disk to automate the installation of Windows NT on a single computer (that is, perform an unattended installation). The default name for an answer file is Unattend.txt, but you can use any filename you want for your answer files. Listing 2-1 presents a sample answer file.

Listing 2-1 *Sample* Unattend.txt *file*

```
[Unattended]
OemPreinstall = yes
NoWaitAfterTextMode = 1
NoWaitAfterGUIMode = 1
FileSystem = ConvertNTFS
ExtendOEMPartition = 0
ConfirmHardware = no
NtUpgrade = no
TargetPath = *
OverwriteOemFilesOnUpgrade = no

[UserData]
FullName = "MCSE Candidate"
OrgName = "MCSE Candidates Company"
```

```
ComputerName = NTW2
ProductId = "975-4769754"


[GuiUnattended]
TimeZone = "(GMT-08:00) Pacific Time (US & Canada);
Tijuana"


 [Network]
DetectAdapters = ""
InstallProtocols = ProtocolsSection
InstallServices = ServicesSection
InstallInternetServer = InternetParamSection
JoinDomain = LAB
CreateComputerAccount = administrator, password


 [TCParamSection]
DHCP = no
IPAddress = 192.168.59.7
Subnet = 255.255.255.0
Gateway = 192.168.59.1
```

There are two ways you can create an answer file. You can use any text editor, such as Notepad, to type in all of the appropriate responses in the correct format. Or, you can use Windows NT Setup Manager (`Setupmgr.exe`) to create an answer file, which is the easiest and preferred method.

TEST TIP Windows NT Setup Manager is used to create answer files for unattended installation.

To use an answer file, run the Windows NT Setup program (`Winnt.exe` or `Winnt32.exe`) with the /U switch.

For example, to use an answer file from the command line, you can type the following line: **z:\Winnt\Netsetup\Winnt.exe /U:z: \Winnt\Netsetup\Unattend.txt /S:z:\Winnt\Netsetup**

In this example, `Winnt.exe` starts the installation process with the unattended switch (/U) to specify that `Winnt.exe` will use a specific answer file (z:\Winnt\Netstup\Unattend.txt). `Winnt.exe` uses the

/S switch to specify that the source folder for all Windows NT Workstation files is Z:\Winnt\Netsetup.

Setup Manager

Windows NT Setup Manager (Setupmgr.exe) is a graphical tool that provides an easy way to create an answer file (Unattend.txt) that you can use to install Windows NT in unattended mode. Setup Manager is located on both the Windows NT Server and Windows NT Workstation compact discs. You can find it in the \Support\Deptools\I386 folder (for Intel-based computers).

When you start Setup Manager, the Windows NT Setup Manager main dialog box appears, as shown in Figure 2-1.

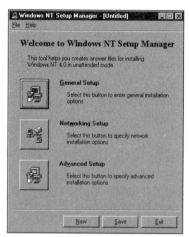

Figure 2-1 *Windows NT Setup Manager main dialog box*

Notice that you can choose from three options: General Setup, Networking Setup, and Advanced Setup.

- The General Setup options in Windows NT Setup Manager are used to configure the user information, computer role, installation directory, display settings, time zone, and license mode entries in an answer file.

- The Networking Setup options in Windows NT Setup Manager are used to configure the adapters, protocols, services, Internet, and modem entries in an answer file.

- The Advanced Setup options in Windows NT Setup Manager are used to configure the file system, mass storage, display driver, keyboard, pointing device, and boot files entries in an answer file.

Uniqueness Database Files

Uniqueness Database Files (UDFs) are text files that make it possible for one answer file to be used for the installation of many computers with different identifying characteristics. For example, each computer has a different computer name and user name. A UDF, used in conjunction with a network installation startup disk and an answer file, makes it possible to fully automate the installation of Windows NT on multiple computers on a network.

The UDF is structured like an answer file, and uses the same types of entries that are used by an answer file. The UDF has an additional section, named [UniqueIds]. When the appropriate command-line switch is used, selected entries in the UDF replace entries with the same name in the answer file.

The only types of entries you can't use in a UDF are entries that are used during the text-mode portion (phase 1) of the installation routine. In other words, entries from the following section headings *must* be specified in the answer file — they can't be used in a UDF:

- [Unattended]
- [OEMBootFiles]
- [MassStorageDrivers]
- [KeyboardDrivers]
- [PointingDeviceDrivers]

KNOW THIS

Answer files for multiple hardware configurations

If you have computers with different hard disk controllers, keyboards, or mice, you must use a different answer file for each hardware configuration.

Listing 2-2 presents a sample UDF named `Authors.txt`.

Listing 2-2 *Sample UDF,* `Authors.txt`

```
[UniqueIds]
Wshakespeare = Wshakespeare:UserData
Sclemens = Sclemens:UserData

[Wshakespeare:UserData]
FullName = "William Shakespeare"
OrgName = "Playwrights, Inc."
ComputerName = Willie
ProductId = "975-4769755"

[Sclemens:UserData]
FullName = "Samuel Clemens"
OrgName = "The Mark Twain Book Company"
ComputerName = Huck
ProductId = "975-4769756"
```

Notice in the `Authors.txt` UDF that the names listed in the `[UniqueIds]` section map to the other section headings in the UDF.

Automated Installation Files

An `unattended.txt` file is used to automate the installation process by preselecting which components to install, and how to configure the computer. The file will install every workstation exactly the same.

A UDF file is used to preselect the per-user configuration settings and customization. The UDF file is referenced during the installation based on the user name that is entered by the installer. The installation then uses the configuration information in the `unattended.txt` file for that user. However, this file does not specify which NT components to install or how to configure the network.

The command-line switches for most NT applications are usually off limits for MCSE exams, but you may want to bone up on the switches used for the NT exams.

Using the `Authors.txt` UDF file as an example, assume that you want to use a UDF, an answer file, and a network installation startup disk to install Windows NT Workstation on Samuel Clemens's computer. To configure the network installation startup disk, you must edit the last line of the `Autoexec.bat` file on this disk so it reads as does the following line:

```
Z:\Winnt\Netsetup\Winnt.exe /U:Z:\Winnt\Netsetup\
Unattend.txt /S:Z:\Winnt\Netsetup /UDF:Sclemens,
Authors.txt
```

This command instructs `Winnt.exe` to use the entries in the `[Sclemens:UserData]` section of the `Authors.txt` UDF to replace the entries with the same name in the answer file during the installation. In this case, the user name, organization name, computer name, and product ID specified in the `[Sclemens:UserData]` section of the `Authors.txt` UDF is used during the installation of Windows NT Workstation; and the user name, organization name, computer name, and product ID specified in the answer file is disregarded.

True or False?

1. You can use the `Winnt.exe /D` command-line switch to specify the source directory to install NT Workstation.

2. A UDF file enables you to specify a Windows NT product number for each person.

3. You can stipulate specific keyboard and pointing device drivers for each person.

4. You can use an UDF file to configure which NT components will be installed.

5. You can only use an UDF file when you are also using an `unattend.txt` file.

Answers: *1. False 2. True 3. True 4. False 5. False*

Automating Application Installation During Setup

In addition to automating the installation of Windows NT, you may also want to automate the installation of various applications at the same time. In this section, you learn how the OEM subfolder and Sysdiff.exe can be used to install applications at the end of the automated installation/setup process automatically.

The OEM Subfolder

The OEM subfolder is used to store the source files that are used to install applications, components, or files that do not ship with Windows NT. You must create the OEM subfolder — it does not exist as part of Windows NT distribution files.

To create a OEM subfolder to use in conjunction with an automated installation/setup of Windows NT Workstation, create the OEM subfolder in the Clients\Winnt\Netsetup folder. You can use the OEM subfolder to store source files of applications that support scripted installation. Scripted installation permits complete installation of an application from a single command line. Most Microsoft applications support scripted installation.

For example, to prepare for automated installation of a scripted application (in conjunction with a Windows NT Workstation automated installation) on your computer's C: drive, first create a OEM subfolder in the Clients\Winnt\ Netsetup folder. Next, create a subfolder named C in the OEM folder, and a subfolder named *name_of_appli-cation* in the OEM\C folder. Then copy the application's source files, including all subfolders, to the Clients\Winnt\Netsetup\OEM\C*name_of_application* folder and create a Cmdlines.txt file in the OEM subfolder that uses the following syntax:

```
[Commands]
"complete command line to install the application"
```

Cmdlines.txt Syntax Requirements

The use of quotation marks around the command line is required in the `Cmdlines.txt` file.

Finally, add an `OemPreinstall = yes` entry to the answer file to instruct `Winnt.exe` to execute the commands in the `Cmdlines.txt` file. (If the answer file is *not* edited, `Winnt.exe` will ignore the `$OEM$` subfolder and all of its contents during automated installation.)

As an alternative to placing files in a subfolder of the `$OEM$` folder, particularly when you have only one application to install, you can place files directly into the `$OEM$` folder.

While it is important to understand the `$OEM$` feature, don't expect a lot of questions about it on the Workstation exam.

Sysdiff.exe

`Sysdiff.exe` is used to automate the installation of applications that don't support scripted installation and that would otherwise require user interaction during the installation process. `Sysdiff.exe` is designed for use when the same application must be installed on many different computers, and you want to install the application automatically during an unattended installation of Windows NT.

Using `Sysdiff.exe` to install an application automatically requires a fair amount of work in advance of the actual unattended installation. First, you must install Windows NT Workstation on a computer, and then use `Sysdiff.exe` to take a snapshot of the computer's current configuration. Next, you must manually install the application (the one for which you want to automate the installation), and finally, use `Sysdiff.exe` to create a difference file. This difference file will then be used to automate the installation of this application on future unattended installations of Windows NT.

`Sysdiff.exe` is located on both the Windows NT Server and Windows NT Workstation compact discs. You can find it in the `\Support\Deptools\I386` folder (for Intel-based computers).

Sysdiff.exe is typically used with the following switches:

- **/snap:** When this switch is used after Windows NT is installed but before any applications are installed, Sysdiff.exe takes a snapshot of a the computer's current configuration.

- **/diff:** When this switch is used after the desired application is installed, Sysdiff.exe creates a difference file that contains all of the files that were added and Registry changes that were made as a result of installing the application.

- **/apply:** When this switch is used, Sysdiff.exe will apply the difference file to a Windows NT installation.

Have You Mastered?

Now it's time to apply what you've learned in this chapter by testing your mastery of the material. These questions provide you with a means to determine if you are ready to move on to the next chapter or if you need to review the material again.

1. **You are preparing to deploy Windows NT Workstation to 40 new computers on your network. What can you do to enable the computers to boot up, access a shared folder on an NT Server, and install Windows NT Workstation?**

    ☐ A. Use the Windows NT Setup Manager to create a boot disk.

    ☐ B. Use the Network Client Administrator on a Windows NT Server computer to create a boot disk.

    ☐ C. Use the Network Client Administrator on a Windows NT Workstation computer to create a boot disk.

    ☐ D. Use the contents of the `clients` folder to create a boot disk.

    The correct answer is **B**. The Network Client Administrator (NCA) can create a bootable disk to start up a computer and begin the installation of Windows NT Workstation without installing drivers or software on the PC first. The NCA is available only on a Windows NT Server computer. The NT Setup Manager is used to create an unattended installation file. For more information, see the "Network Client Administrator" section.

2. You want to install Microsoft client software for MS-DOS, Windows 3.1, and Windows for Workgroups computers. Which folder must be copied from the Windows NT Server compact disc to the Windows NT Server computer to be able to use the Network Client Administrator to create setup disks?

    ☐ A. `Drivers`
    ☐ B. `Clients`
    ☐ C. `I386`
    ☐ D. `Winnt`

The correct answer is **B**. The `Client` folder contains the required files to create installation disk sets and network installation startup disks. The `I386` folder contains the source files for installation on Intel platforms, the `Drivers` directory contains files for additional driver support. For more information, see the "Server-Based Deployment" section.

3. You want to install TCP/IP 32 for Windows for Workgroups 3.11 on 20 computers on your network. What can you create, using Network Client Administrator, to help you accomplish this task efficiently?

    ☐ A. Network installation startup disk
    ☐ B. A shared folder containing the required installation files
    ☐ C. Installation disk set
    ☐ D. An unattended installation file

The correct answer is **C**. The installation disk set can be created to contain the TCP/IP installation files for the computers. The NCA cannot be used to create a shared folder or an unattended installation file. For more information, see the "Network Client Administrator" section.

4. You are installing Windows NT Workstation on 400 new computers on your network. The computers are connected to the network and do not have a CD-ROM drive installed. You want to install as many computers as possible quickly. What can

you do to install Windows NT Workstation faster than by using a floppy disk?

☐ A. Create a shared folder with the contents of the NT Workstation CD-ROM I386 folder, use the network installation setup disk, and use the shared folder as the installation source.

☐ B. Use the Network Configuration Administrator to create an installation disk set for Windows NT.

☐ C. Create a shared folder with the contents of the NT Workstation CD-ROM, boot the new computer with the first setup disk and specify the source directory as the shared folder.

☐ D. Use the Windows NT Setup Manager to create an installation disk set for Windows NT.

The correct answer is **A**. By creating a shared folder, you make the contents of the CD accessible on the network. You can then specify the network share as the installation source directory, rather than a drive letter for a CD-ROM. Windows NT Setup Manager cannot be used to create an installation disk set. For more information, see the "Network Client Administrator" section.

5. **You are preparing for the unattended installation of Windows NT Workstation onto 200 new computers. Some of the computers are used by people with disabilities. As a result, some of the computers have specialized keyboards and pointing devices. What can you do to install the specialized drivers for these devices on the computers during the automated installation?**

☐ A. Create an `unattended.txt` file that selects the Accessibilities options to install.

☐ B. Create a `UDF` file that has a profile for each person and which devices should be installed.

☐ C. Create a network installation setup disk for each person with a unique `unattended.txt` file.

☐ D. Place a `custom.txt` file on the root of the computer that has a `drivers` section for each custom device.

The correct answer is **B**. The UDF file can be constructed to have the customized drivers preselected for installation based on the user name entered for the profile. An unattended installation file can be used to install the Accessibility options, but it cannot be used to install the special keyboard and pointing devices. For more information, see the "Automating Setup of Windows NT" section.

6. **You are using an** `unattended.txt` **file to install Windows NT Workstation on 250 new computers. You also want to install Microsoft Office at the same time you install NT Workstation. You already have a scripted installation to install Office. What process should you use to install Office in your roll-out?**

☐ A. Add a `commands` section to the `unattended.txt` file and enter the Office installation script program name in the section.

☐ B. Add a `commands` section to a UDF file and enter the Office installation script program name in the section.

☐ C. Create a OEM subdirectory in your shared folder for Windows NT Workstation, place the installation script and required files in the folder, and create the required `cmdlines.txt` file.

☐ D. Use the `sysdiff.exe` utility to add the installation script to your shared folder installation directory.

The correct answer is **C**. The OEM directory and `cmdlines.txt` are used to install applications that have there own scripted install. The `commands` section does nothing to include the Office installation with your roll out. For more information, see the "Automating Setup of Windows NT" section.

7. You have created a sysdiff image for your network deployment
   of Windows NT Workstation 4.0. After copying the files to the
   OEM subfolder, you use a network installation setup disk to
   start the installation process. When Windows NT Workstation is
   installed and the computer is rebooted, the sysdiff image is not
   applied. What can you do to have the sysdiff image applied at
   the end of the installation process?

   ☐ A. Add the command Start OEM\cmd.bat in to
        the autoexec.bat file on the network installation
        startup disk.
   ☐ B. Create a cmdlines.txt file, which includes with
        the sysdiff /apply command on the network
        installation startup disk.
   ☐ C. Create a cmdlines.txt file, which includes with
        the sysdiff /apply command and place it in the
        OEM subfolder.
   ☐ D. Add the command cmdlines.txt to the UDF file
        used for each workstation.

The correct answer is C. The cmdlines.txt file, when placed in the
OEM directory, automatically runs if the OEMPREINSTALL command is entered in the unattended.txt file. If the cmdlines.txt
will only be used if it is placed in the OEM directory, it will not be
used if placed anywhere else. For more information, see the
"Automating Application Installation during Setup" section.

Practice Your Skills

Here is a chance to apply your practical, hands-on experience and material from this chapter. These exercises are designed for you to apply not only the material in the book, but to gain greater experience and exposure to the product. These exercises are a critical part of understanding the product and gaining valuable experience using the product and passing the certification exam. For each of the following problems, consider the given facts, determine possible causes of the problem, and what course of action you might take to resolve the problem.

1. Network Installation Startup Disks

EXERCISE Your organization has been using a network installation startup disk to install Windows NT Workstation. You recently purchased some new computers and you are attempting to install Windows NT Workstation using the network installation startup disks. When you boot the new computers with the disk, you are unable to access the network. What is the most likely problem?

ANALYSIS Network Installation Startup Disks are specific to a particular network adapter. The new computers most likely have different network adapter cards or are configured differently than the previous computer types. You may need to create a new disk set or update the settings on the current set to reflect the configuration changes.

2. Automating Unattended Installations

EXERCISE You have prepared an `unattended.txt` file to automate the installation of Windows NT Workstation. When you boot with your network installation start-up disk, you must start the installation process manually. What can you do to start the installation automatically after the computer has booted with the startup disk?

ANALYSIS You can add the `Winnt.exe` command along with the `unattended.txt` file specified with a `/U` switch and the source directory for the installation files with the `/S` command-line switch to the `autoexec.bat` file on the startup disk.

3. Application Installs

EXERCISE You want to deploy Microsoft Office along with your Windows NT Workstation deployment. You want to use the existing scripted install you have already created for use prior to deploying NT Workstation. What is the best way to deploy Microsoft Office at the same time as Windows NT Workstation?

ANALYSIS Because you already have a scripted install, you should leverage that investment. By placing the Office install files and script in the `$OEM$` directory and configuring the `cmdlines.txt` file you do not need to recreate your install process. If you were to use the sysdiff process, you would not only need to create the image by installing Office and configuring it as you wanted, but you could use that image to install Office on other platforms or computers. An existing or standalone install, such as a scripted Office installation, could be used not only during the Windows NT Workstation deployment, but on non-NT computers as well.

4. Applying Images

EXERCISE   You have a need to roll out several in-house applications to your new Windows NT Workstation computers. You already installed NT Workstation, and you have a "test" computer that is configured exactly the same as the user workstations. You also need to install a few standalone support files and create some directories on each computer. What is the best way to update all of the existing NT Workstations to this new configuration?

ANALYSIS   You could reinstall NT Workstation on every computer, but that would not be practical or economical. You can, however, use sysdiff to create an "update" image that contains only the changes to the existing desktop. When you run sysdiff the first time, using the /snap command-line switch, the process creates a before image. After configuring the computer as you need it, the sysdiff /diff process determines what has changed since the image. So if you install the custom application, create the directories, and install your support files in between the SNAP and DIFF processes, those changes will become the sysdiff image. So sysdiff can be used not only during deployments, but also during the maintenance period of the computer.

Configuring Disks

O ne of the most challenging sections of the Workstation exam involves configuring and supporting hard disks. You will be tested on the strengths, limitations, and special features of the two file systems that Windows NT supports: FAT and NTFS. Are you prepared? Do you know how to convert from FAT to NTFS and vice versa? Do you know how to establish volume and stripe sets? This chapter looks at those topics and examines the types of configuration where stripe and volume sets cannot be used and how to use an Emergency Repair Disk.

Exam Material in This Chapter

Based on Microsoft Objectives

Planning

- Choose the appropriate file system to use in a given situation. File Systems and situations include:
  - NTFS
  - FAT
  - HPFS
  - Security
  - Dual-boot systems

Based on Author's Experience

- You should know which types of partitions are supported by Windows NT, Microsoft Windows 3.x, Windows 9.x, and MS-DOS.

- You should know how to convert an HPFS partition to NTFS.

- You should know how FAT and NTFS handle partitions of various sizes.

- Watch for questions about NTFS file-level security.

- The exam will present scenarios to test your understanding of how to convert a FAT partition to NTFS, and how to convert NTFS to a FAT partition.

- Expect questions on what software fault-tolerant methods can be used on boot and system partitions.

- You should be aware of the function of the Emergency Repair Disk and how to create one.

Are You Prepared?

Do you have what it takes? Try out these self-assessment questions to see if you have prepared for the material in this chapter or if you should review problem areas.

1. You are updating your Emergency Repair Disk. What command-line option should you use to back up the local SAM database at the same time?

        ☐ A. /S
        ☐ B. /BU
        ☐ C. /SAM
        ☐ D. /REG

2. You are configuring your computer to dual boot between Windows NT Workstation and Windows 95. What file format must you use on the C drive to enable you to dual boot between the two operating systems?

        ☐ A. FAT
        ☐ B. NTFS
        ☐ C. HPFS
        ☐ D. FAT32

3. You are running low on disk space on your Windows NT Workstation computer. You want to reduce the size of some files that are not used often. Which file formats can Windows NT Workstation provide folder and file compression for?

        ☐ A. FAT32
        ☐ B. FAT

☐ C. NTFS
☐ D. HPFS

Answers:

1. A   *When updating or creating an Emergency Repair Disk, you can use the /S switch to back up the local SAM database. For more information, refer to the section entitled "Emergency Repair Disk" of this chapter.*

2. A   *When dual booting between Windows NT and MS-DOS or Windows 95, you must use FAT on the C drive as it is the only file format supported between all of the operating systems. For more information, refer to the "File Systems" section of this chapter.*

3. C   *Windows NT can provide compression on a per-folder or per-file basis on NTFS volumes, thus reducing the amount of space consumed on the volume. This is covered in the "File Systems" section.*

File Systems

Windows NT Workstation 4.0 supports three file systems: the *file allocation table* (FAT) *file system*, the *Windows NT file system* (NTFS), and the *Compact Disc Filing System* (CDFS). Windows NT 4.0 does *not* support the *high performance file system* (HPFS), although earlier versions of NT did. (If you are upgrading from an earlier version of Windows NT that used HPFS, you must convert to NTFS before performing the upgrade.) Table 3.1 shows which file systems are supported by various operating systems.

TABLE 3.1 File System Support by Operating System

Operating System	File Systems Supported
Windows NT 4.0	FAT, NTFS, and CDFS
Windows NT 3.51 (and earlier versions)	FAT, NTFS, CDFS, and HPFS
Windows 95	FAT and CDFS
Windows 3.x and 3.1x	FAT, and CDFS
OS/2	FAT, CDFS, and HPFS
MS-DOS	FAT and CDFS

Don't expect to see any questions regarding Compact Disc Filing System (CDFS) on the exam.

FAT

The *file allocation table* (FAT) *file system* used on Windows NT is a modified version of the FAT file system used by MS-DOS. FAT is the only hard disk file system supported by Windows 3.x, Windows 3.1x, Windows 95, Windows 98, and MS-DOS. To configure a Windows NT computer to dual boot between Windows NT and Windows 3.1x, Windows 95, Windows 98, or MS-DOS, your computer's first partition must use the FAT file system.

Don't confuse the FAT file system with the FAT32 file system. Windows NT does not support the FAT32 file system (an enhanced rendition of FAT) that is supported on the original equipment manufacturer (OEM) version of Windows 95 that includes Service Pack 2 and in Windows 98.

KNOW THIS Dual Boot Partition Requirements

The ability to dual boot between Windows NT and any other Microsoft OS requires that the C Drive be formatted as a FAT partition. Most of the file system-related questions will deal with the support of dual-boot computers and NTFS file system security. These are the areas that you should focus on!

Security

The FAT file system does *not* support file and folder security in Windows NT. Because file and folder security is not supported on a FAT partition, any user who is logged on locally to a computer has full control of all of the files and folders located in the FAT partition(s) on that computer. This applies only to local access.

You can use share permissions to control users' access to shared folders over the network, however. Share permissions affect only the access to files and folders over the network, not when someone is logged on locally. So, if you need local file and folder security, you should use an NTFS partition instead of a FAT partition.

Naming conventions

The FAT file system, as used by Windows NT, supports the use of long filenames. This file system permits the full path to a file (including the file name) to be up to 255 characters long. File names can contain any character *except* \ / : * ? " < > | and should begin with an alphanumeric character. File names can contain spaces and multiple periods, and the characters after the last period are considered the file name extension. The FAT file system preserves uppercase and lowercase in file names, but file names are not case-sensitive.

Speed of access to files

Access speed to files on a FAT partition is dependent on many factors, including file type, file size, partition size, number of files in a folder, and fragmentation. Windows NT accesses files on FAT partitions that are smaller than 500MB faster than it accesses files on other similar-sized file system partitions. Additionally, NT accesses certain types of files on FAT partitions more efficiently than on partitions formatted with other file systems.

On very large partitions, however, or when there is a large number of files in a folder, Windows NT accesses files on NTFS partitions much faster than it accesses files on a FAT partition of similar size. Windows NT usually accesses files on a highly fragmented FAT partition slower than it can access files on an NTFS partition of similar size.

Partition size

The maximum size of a FAT partition is 4GB. The maximum size of a file in a FAT partition is 4GB.

The FAT file system does *not* support file compression.

NTFS

The *Windows NT file system* (NTFS) is the most powerful file system supported by Windows NT. Only Windows NT supports NTFS — no other operating systems currently support this file system. When it comes to security, naming conventions, speed of access to files, and partition size, NTFS has its own unique characteristics. Additionally, NTFS has some features not supported by the FAT file system.

Security

NTFS provides file and folder security for both local and remote users on a network. NTFS is the only file system discussed here that permits the assigning of permissions to individual files and folders. NTFS security controls access to files on an NTFS partition by utilizing the user's *security identifier* (SID) to determine which files that user can access. (Each file and folder on an NTFS partition has an *access control list* (ACL) associated with it. The ACL is a list that contains user and group SIDs, with the associated privileges of each user and group.)

Naming conventions

Like the FAT file system, NTFS supports the use of long filenames. Names of files and folders (including extensions) can be up to 255 characters long.

You can use most characters in NTFS file and folder names; however, the characters ? " / \ < > * | : can't be used.

NTFS preserves uppercase and lowercase in file names. File names are not case-sensitive (except when used by a POSIX application). For example, a Win32 application does not distinguish between Money.DOC, MONEY.DOC, and money.doc — it treats all three names as though they were the same file.

The POSIX subsystem, however, is case-sensitive with respect to file names, because it does not translate a request for a file into all uppercase letters as do Win32 and other subsystems. A POSIX application treats the file names in the previous paragraph as though they were three separate files: Money.DOC, MONEY.DOC, and money.doc. You must use a POSIX application if you want to access these three different files — if you attempt to access Money.DOC with a Win32 application (no matter how you type the file name) you will typically always retrieve the MONEY.DOC file because the Win32 subsystem translates file requests into all uppercase letters.

Speed of access to files

NTFS usually provides faster access to files stored on a large partition containing many files than does the FAT file system. NTFS is capable of accessing files in this situation faster than the FAT file system because NTFS uses an enhanced binary tree to locate files. A binary tree search is a faster mechanism for searching through a large number of file names than is the sequential read mechanism used on FAT partitions.

Partition size

The maximum theoretical size of an NTFS partition is 16 exabytes (an *exabyte* is one billion billion bytes, or a giga-gigabyte). However, when you actually implement NTFS on current standard industry hardware, there is a functional limitation of 2 terabytes. (A terabyte is 1 trillion bytes.)

Additional features

NTFS has several other unique attributes and features that are not found in, or supported by, the FAT file system.

- NTFS supports a compression attribute for each file. You can choose which files to compress and which ones to leave uncompressed. The compression algorithm NTFS uses is similar to the one used by drive space in MS-DOS. Using compression provides an approximately 40 to 50 percent increase in hard disk space.

KNOW THIS **Compression Degradation**

Compression can cause some performance degradation on partitions with substantial write activity. Additionally, accessing uncompressed files is faster than accessing compressed files.

- NTFS is a highly reliable, recoverable file system. It is not necessary to periodically run `Chkdsk.exe` on an NTFS partition.

- Using NTFS greatly reduces fragmentation on partitions; however, a file can still become fragmented when its size is increased. Windows NT does not include an NTFS defragmentation utility, but there are several third-party utilities available.

- NTFS maintains a recycle bin for each user.

You can't use NTFS to format floppy disks, and NTFS does not permit you to change media in a removable media drive (such as a ZIP drive) without rebooting. (The FAT file system does support changing media without rebooting.)

True or False?

1. FAT partitions access files faster than NTFS partitions when they are under 500MB in size.
2. Only NTFS can use long filenames with up to 255 characters.
3. Windows NT supports drives formatted as FAT32.
4. FAT partitions may be as large as 16 exabytes.
5. Files on a FAT partition are case-sensitive.

Answers: *1. True 2. False 3. False 4. False 5. False*

Converting from FAT to NTFS

In Windows NT you can format a new partition with either FAT or NTFS; but, how do you change the file system on an existing partition?

You can change an existing FAT partition, and retain the data on it, into an NTFS partition by using Convert.exe. However, it is a one-way process—there is no way to convert an NTFS partition into a FAT partition without first backing up, reformatting the disk, and restoring the data.

Converting NTFS and FAT Partitions

There is no way to convert an NTFS partition into a FAT partition without first backing up, reformatting the disk, and restoring the data.

To convert a FAT partition into an NTFS partition, use the following syntax: CONVERT *drive:* /FS:NTFS [/V]

The following is an explanation of syntax:

- *Drive* specifies the letter of the drive to convert to NTFS.

- /FS:NTFS indicates that the file system should be converted to NTFS. This is an outdated switch because NTFS is the only file system that you can use Convert.exe to switch to in Windows NT 4.0; but its use, in terms of command syntax, is still required.

- /V specifies that `Convert.exe` will run in verbose mode.

For example, to convert drive D: from FAT to NTFS, use the following command line: `CONVERT D: /FS:NTFS`.

Partitions

Before you can format a hard disk with a file system, such as FAT or NTFS, you must mark the disk to identify which parts of it will contain a file system (or systems). This is called *partitioning*. A hard disk can be separated into a maximum of four partitions, or one partition can occupy all of the space on a disk.

You may recall, back in Chapter 1, that when you installed Windows NT Workstation 4.0 you were presented with the option to create a partition on your computer's hard disk. Once Windows NT is installed, the primary tool for creating, formatting, and managing various types of partitions is Disk Administrator.

Windows NT supports two partition types: primary and extended. Both types of partitions can coexist on the same hard disk. A disk can have more than one primary partition, but it can have only one extended partition.

Primary Partitions

A *primary partition* can occupy all of the space on a disk, or any portion of it. A hard disk can have up to four partitions, and all four can be primary partitions. A primary partition can be formatted as a single logical drive (but not as multiple logical drives).

Any primary partition on the first hard disk in the computer can be designated as the active partition. The active partition is significant because when the computer boots, it attempts to load the operating system from the active primary partition on the first hard disk in the computer.

The Windows NT 4.0 system partition must be located on the active primary partition on the first hard disk in a computer.

Extended Partitions

There can be only one *extended partition* on a disk. An extended partition can't be marked active, and it can't be used for the system partition of a computer. The Windows NT boot partition, however, can be located on an extended partition.

An extended partition can be formatted as one or more logical drives, where each partition is assigned a different drive letter. Logical drives can be formatted with either FAT or NTFS. You can have one logical drive formatted with FAT, and another logical drive in the same extended partition formatted with NTFS.

Extended partitions are convenient for breaking up a physical disk into more than four logical drives.

Disk Administrator

Windows NT includes a useful tool, called Disk Administrator, to manage disks after NT has been installed. Disk Administrator can help you create, format, and otherwise manage various types of partitions.

Figure 3-1 shows a screen shot of the main dialog box of Disk Administrator.

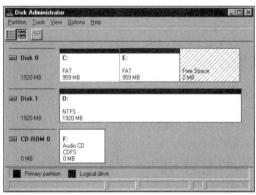

Figure 3-1 *Windows NT Disk Administrator*

Stripe Sets

In a *stripe set*, which is made up of 2 to 32 hard disks, data is stored, a block at a time, evenly and sequentially among all of the disks in the set.

Stripe sets are sometimes referred to as disk striping. *Disk striping* alludes to the process wherein a file is written, or striped, one block at a time; first to one disk, and then to the next disk, and so on, until all of the data has been evenly distributed among all of the disks.

 Neither the boot nor the system partition can be on a stripe set.

A stripe set is accessed by using a single drive letter, as if all of its disks were combined into a single drive. A stripe set is created from identical amounts of free space on each of the disks that belong to the set, as shown in Figure 3-2.

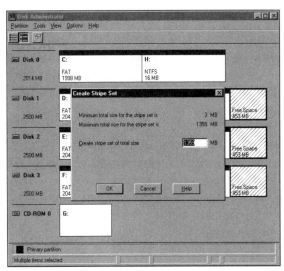

Figure 3-2 *Creating a stripe set*

Stripe sets provide faster disk access than volume sets or large individual hard disks because the stripe sets store a single file across multiple disks. The various pieces of the file can be read nearly simultaneously from the multiple disks, thus increasing performance. Access speed is the primary advantage and common reason for using a stripe set. The trade-off or downside to using a stripe set is that the potential disk failure rate is increased because there are more possible points of failure when a file is accessed across several disks.

Stripe sets do not provide any fault tolerance. If one partition or disk in a stripe set fails, all data on the stripe set is lost. A stripe set (or disk striping) is also known as *RAID level 0*.

Volume Sets

A *volume set* is a combination of free space areas over 2 to 32 hard disks that is treated as a single drive. (The free space areas do not need to be of identical size.)

 Neither the boot nor the system partition can be on a volume set.

The primary purpose and use of a volume set is to access disk space on more than one hard disk by using a single drive letter. A volume set is sometimes used when a drive becomes full and you want to enlarge its capacity.

A volume set is similar to a stripe set; however, a file in a volume set is usually fully contained on a single hard disk, instead of being striped over multiple hard disks.

 Volume sets, like stripe sets, do not perform any fault-tolerance function. If one disk in a volume set fails, all data on the volume may be lost. This occurs because Windows NT can't access data unless all of the disks that make up the volume set are functional.

Volume sets are said to be *created* when areas of free space only (not existing volumes) are combined into a volume set. Volume sets are said to be *extended* when an existing NTFS partition is enlarged. Extending a volume set is far more common than creating one — it's one way to approach a situation when a drive is filled to capacity and you still need additional space in that volume.

True or False?

1. The Windows NT system partition can be part of a stripe set.

2. You can perform a non-destructive conversion from FAT to NTFS, but not from NTFS to FAT.

3. An extended partition can be used for a bootable system drive.

4. A stripe set is created from an equal amount of free space on multiple partitions.

5. A volume set is usually striped over multiple physical disk drives.

Answers: *1. False 2. True 3. False 4. False 5. False*

Emergency Repair Disk

The *Emergency Repair Disk* is a floppy disk used to restore the Windows NT Registry to the configuration that existed when the Emergency Repair Disk was created (or updated).

If you have made any changes to your computer's system configuration since the Emergency Repair Disk was created or last updated, those changes will be lost during the emergency repair process. For this reason, you should update your Emergency Repair Disk *every time* you make a change to your computer's system configuration, including any changes to your disk configuration. Windows NT will prompt you to update your Emergency Repair Disk every time you make a change to your disk configuration in Disk Administrator.

The Emergency Repair Disk is initially created during the installation of Windows NT. To update it at any time after installation (or to create an Emergency Repair Disk after installation, if one was not created at that time), you must use the Rdisk.exe utility.

You won't find the Rdisk.exe utility in the Start menu. You need to run it from the command line, run it by selecting the Run option from the Start menu, or you can create a shortcut to it on your desktop.

When you run `Rdisk.exe`, a Repair Disk Utility dialog box is displayed. Figure 3-3 shows the first Repair Disk Utility dialog box.

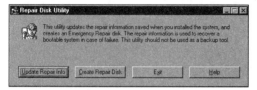

Figure 3-3 *The first Repair Disk Utility dialog box*

If you click the Update Repair Info command button in the Repair Disk Utility dialog box (and click Yes in the next dialog box displayed to confirm), `Rdisk.exe` will save all of your Registry (with the exception of the Security hive and the Security Accounts Manager [SAM] database) to the `<winntroot>\ repair` directory. `<winntroot>` is the directory that was specified for the installation of Windows NT, usually `C:\winnt`.

After `Rdisk.exe` saves your Registry configuration information, it will ask if you want to create an Emergency Repair Disk. Figure 3-4 displays this Repair Disk Utility dialog box.

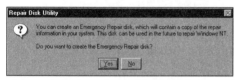

Figure 3-4 *Creating (updating) the Emergency Repair Disk*

Don't be thrown because `Rdisk.exe` asks if you want to *create* an Emergency Repair Disk when what you're really trying to do is to *update* it. `Rdisk.exe` uses the same process and terminology for both.

At this point, Repair Disk prompts you to insert a labeled 3.5-inch floppy disk into drive A:. If you have the Emergency Repair Disk you created during the installation of Windows NT, use this disk to create an updated Emergency Repair Disk. If you didn't create an Emergency Repair Disk during installation, insert any blank floppy disk to create an Emergency Repair Disk now.

A second way you can update your Emergency Repair Disk is to use the one command-line switch that can be used with `Rdisk.exe`, the /S switch. The S stands for security. Using the /S switch causes the entire Registry, including the Security hive and the SAM database, to be backed up. When you run `Rdisk.exe` with the /S switch, `Rdisk.exe` automatically begins saving your Registry information to the repair directory, and then prompts you to create the Emergency Repair Disk.

You can use the `Rdisk.exe` utility with the /S switch to back up the SAM database in addition to the one on your regularly scheduled tape backup.

To use the `Rdisk.exe` utility with the /S switch, select the Run option from the Start menu, and then type **rdisk /s** in the text box within the Run dialog box.

Have You Mastered?

Now it's time to apply what you've learned in this chapter by testing your mastery of the material. These questions provide you with a means to determine if you are ready to move on to the next chapter or if you need to review the material again.

1. **You are installing Windows NT Workstation onto a new computer. You plan on installing Windows 95 in the near future. What file system should you use on the C drive?**

   ☐ A. NTFS
   ☐ B. FAT32
   ☐ C. FAT
   ☐ D. HPFS

   The correct answer is **C**. The only file system that is accessible to both Windows NT and Windows 95 is FAT. If the C drive is formatted as NTFS, Windows 95 will not be capable of accessing the drive to install itself. Additionally, FAT32 is only available in Windows 95 OSR2 and is not supported by Windows NT. For more information, see the "File Systems" section.

2. **You are installing Windows NT Workstation on 10 new laptop computers. The users of these computers will be carrying sensitive company documents that need to be protected. What**

type of file system should be used on the drives containing the sensitive documents to ensure that only authorized users have access to them?

- [ ] A. NTFS
- [ ] B. FAT32
- [ ] C. FAT
- [ ] D. HPFS

The correct answer is **A**. NTFS is the only file system in which you can set access permissions on the local hard disks and files. These access rights are independent of any other security systems (including a Windows NT Domain) in that they are still in effect when away from the office. As mentioned before, FAT32 and FAT do not have any means of applying access rights at the file-system level. For more information, see the "File Systems" section.

3. **You are installing Windows NT Workstation onto your new computer. You have a 2GB disk installed in your computer and you would like to configure your disk for optimal performance. You want to separate your NT systems files from your user files. Which of the following steps should you take to configure your disk? (Choose three.)**

- [ ] A. Create a 500MB C drive and format it as FAT.
- [ ] B. Create a 500MB C drive and format it as NTFS.
- [ ] C. Place the NT System Files on the C Drive.
- [ ] D. Create a 1.5GB D drive and format it as FAT.
- [ ] E. Create a 1.5GB D drive and format it as NTFS.
- [ ] F. Place the NT System Files on the D Drive.

The correct answers are **A, C,** and **E**. Because FAT is faster than NTFS when working with volumes 500MB and under, you get the best performance by having a 500MB C drive with your NT system files for faster access. The D drive performs better as an NTFS partition because of the large size of the partition and additional features found in NTFS. For more information, see the "File Systems" section.

4. **You are upgrading your computer from Windows NT Workstation 3.51 to Windows NT Workstation 4.0. The computer is also configured to dual boot Windows NT and Windows 3.1. After upgrading NT Workstation and converting the only hard disk in the computer to NTFS, you are unable to boot to Windows 3.1. What should you do in order to use both Windows NT Workstation and Windows 3.1 on this computer?**

   ☐ A. Use the `convert` utility to convert the drive back from NTFS to FAT, and reinstall Windows NT Workstation and Windows 3.1.
   ☐ B. Use the Disk Administrator to convert the drive from NTFS to FAT.
   ☐ C. Backup your computer, repartition the drive, reformat the drive as FAT, install Windows 3.1 and Windows NT, and restore your backup.
   ☐ D. Uninstall Windows NT Workstation 4.0, and convert the drive back to FAT.

The correct answer is **C**. The `convert` utility can only convert a drive from NTFS to FAT, not vice versa. As a result, once a drive is formatted as NTFS, you must repartition and reformat the drive because the data on the drive will be lost. For more information, see the "File Systems" section.

5. **You are configuring the disks in your Windows NT Workstation. The computer has three 4GB drives and will be used for graphics-intensive applications that need quick access to files**

on the hard drives. You want to increase the performance of your disks. What should you do?

- ☐ A. Configure the three disks as a stripe set.
- ☐ B. Configure the three disks as a volume set.
- ☐ C. Configure each of the disks as a standalone NTFS volume.
- ☐ D. Configure each of the disks as a standalone FAT volume.

The correct answer is **A**. A stripe set spans across an equal space on multiple disks to create a high-performance drive. The resulting stripe set is accessed as a single drive, while the files are distributed throughout the disks. A volume set will not give you the best performance for this scenario. For more information, see the section entitled "Partitions."

6. You have three hard drives of different capacities in your Windows NT Workstation computer. You have two partitions on each of the drives. The C drive partition contains the Windows NT system files. You want to use the remaining space as a single drive letter, rather than having three more drive letters to use. What can you do without wasting any possible storage space?

- ☐ A. Create a stripe set that spans the remaining partitions.
- ☐ B. Create a stripe set that spans all of the drive partitions.
- ☐ C. Create a volume set that spans the remaining partitions.
- ☐ D. Create a volume set that spans all of the drive partitions.

The correct answer is **C**. A volume set can span multiple partitions, each of which can be different sizes. Whereas a stripe set must use partitions of equal size. Also, the system and boot files can be on a volume or stripe set. For more information, see the "Partitions" section.

7. **You are configuring a Windows NT Workstation 4.0 computer. The computer has a 3GB hard disk configured as a FAT partition and is nearing its capacity. You have a need to increase the amount of information stored on the hard disk. What can you do to increase the capacity of the computer?**

   ☐ A. Enable Windows NT compression for the hard disk.
   ☐ B. Convert the disk to NTFS and enable Windows NT compression for the hard disk.
   ☐ C. Repartition the drive into three FAT partitions and use a stripe set.
   ☐ D. Repartition the drive into three NTFS partitions and use a stripe set.

The correct answer is **B**. Windows NT only supports compression on NTFS volumes. The use of a stripe set would do nothing to increase the amount of usable disk space. For more information, see the "File Systems" section.

Practice Your Skills

Here is a chance to apply your practical, hands-on experience and material from this chapter. These exercises are designed for you to apply not only the material in the book, but to gain greater experience and exposure to the product. These exercises are a critical part of understanding the product and gaining valuable experience for using the product and passing the certification exam. For each of the following problems, consider the given facts and determine possible causes of the problem and what course of action you might take to resolve the problem.

1. Accessing NTFS partitions

EXERCISE You have installed Windows NT Workstation onto a new computer. When you boot with a MS-DOS disk to install Windows 95 you are unable to see the C drive. What is the most likely problem?

ANALYSIS The most likely scenario is that the hard disk was converted to NTFS during, or after, the installation of Windows NT Workstation. As a result, MS-DOS is incapable of accessing the NTFS volume. To resolve the problem, the disk must be reformatted as FAT and Windows NT Workstation and Windows 95 must be reinstalled.

2. File-level access permissions

EXERCISE You are using a Windows NT Workstation computer that is shared by a number of people. When you attempt to open some files a directory, called Company Documents, you are unable to successfully retrieve the document. When you attempt to open a file anywhere else you have no problem. What is most likely causing this to happen?

ANALYSIS Because you are using someone else's computer, the problem is mostly because the hard disk is formatted as NTFS and has permissions set on the Company Documents that are preventing you from accessing the files. To resolve the problem, you will need the primary user of the computer to grant you user ID permissions to these files.

3. Recovering from volume set failures

EXERCISE You have created a stripe set across three hard disks in your Windows NT Computer. What will happen to the files in the stripe set when one of the hard disks fails?

ANALYSIS Because a stripe set spans multiple disks and the data is spread evenly among them, all of the data in the set will be lost. If you create a volume set, only the data on the failed disk would be lost, the data on the other disks in the volume set will still be accessible.

Using Control Panel

U NDERSTANDING HOW TO configure Windows NT with the Control Panel is a critical component of passing the Workstation exam. Do you know how to install and configure hardware and device drivers using the Control Panel? Do you know how to use the Server icon in the Control Panel and how to configure virtual memory properly? This chapter also explores steps to troubleshoot common configuration problems.

Exam Material in This Chapter

Based on Microsoft Objectives

Installing and Configuring

- Install, configure, and remove hardware components for a given situation. Hardware components include:
  - Network adapter drivers
  - SCSI device drivers
  - Tape device drivers
  - UPS
  - Multimedia devices
  - Display drivers
  - Keyboard drivers
  - Mouse drivers
- Use Control Panel applications to configure a Windows NT Workstation computer in a given situation

Managing Resources

- Set up and modify user profiles

Based on Author's Experience

- You should be familiar with the different startup properties of Windows NT devices.
- You must know how to configure a Windows NT computer to belong to a workgroup or a domain.
- Know how to improve the performance of a Windows NT computer by optimizing the network bindings.
- You need to understand how to selectively disable devices and services on a per-adapter or per-protocol basis for security or optimization requirements.
- Understand how to configure multiple configurations for hardware devices on portable computers.
- Know how to create, modify, and remove user profiles.

Are You Prepared?

Do you have what it takes? Try out these self-assessment questions to see if you have prepared for the material in this chapter or if you should review problem areas.

1. If you want a system device to start only after another device has started, how should you configure the startup value for the device?

☐ A. System
☐ B. Automatic
☐ C. Boot
☐ D. Manual
☐ E. Disabled

2. What can you do to improve the performance of the workstation?

☐ A. Optimize the network bindings.
☐ B. Change the startup properties for the workstation service.
☐ C. Install more than one network protocol.

3. What protocol should only be used on nonrouted networks?

☐ A. NWLink IPX/SPX Compatible Transport
☐ B. PPP
☐ C. TCP/IP
☐ D. NetBEUI

Answers:

1. **D**   *Unless the device is specifically written to be dependent
on another device, or you use some of the Windows NT
Workstation resource kit utilities, there is no way to
configure when a device will be started, or in what
order. Because all devices configured as boot, system,
and automatic will automatically start when the system
is booted, none of these values will work in this
scenario. For more information, refer to the
"Peripherals and Devices" section of this chapter.*

2. **A**   *The network bindings order dictates in which order the
computer will attempt to access and locate resources
on the network. More than one protocol will actually
slow things down, because the workstation will attempt
to communicate with each device through each
protocol if it has difficulty locating the device. For more
information, refer to the "Networking" section of this
chapter.*

3. **D**   *NetBEUI is designed for small nonrouted networks. As
a result, NetBEUI is extremely fast for smaller networks,
but does not scale for larger environments. All of the
other protocols are designed for large, routed networks.
For more information, refer to the "Networking" section
of this chapter.*

Overview of Control Panel

Windows NT Control Panel is a collection of mini-applications, sometimes called applets. These applications are automatically installed with
Windows NT Workstation and Windows NT Server, and are used to
install and configure various options, hardware, protocols, and services.

Each Control Panel application is used for a different task. Some software packages and some installable services include their own Control
Panel icon, which is displayed in the Control Panel dialog box after the
new application or service is installed.

All of the common Control Panel applications are organized into sections in this chapter based on each application's functionality. The basic
application functions include: managing peripherals and devices, networking, managing services, managing the server, managing the system,
and miscellaneous other functions.

Peripherals and Devices

This section examines the Control Panel applications that are used to
install and/or configure options, hardware, and hardware drivers.

Devices

The *Devices* application is used to start and stop device drivers, to configure the startup behavior of device drivers, to view the status of a device
driver, and to enable or disable a device driver within a hardware profile.

The startup behaviors (or types) available in this application include
boot, system, automatic, manual, and *disabled.* If you choose boot, system,
or automatic, Windows NT starts the device driver automatically every
time the computer is booted. If you choose manual, a user (or another
device driver) must start the device driver. If you select disabled, the
device driver can't be started by a user.

One of the most common mistakes is not understanding
how the device startup properties work. Be sure to review
this section thoroughly before taking the test.

Display

The *Display* application is used to configure a computer's desktop background, screen saver options, desktop appearance, Microsoft Plus! options, and display adapter settings. You can also configure the display to use large fonts, large icons, and a high-contrast color scheme to accommodate a visually challenged person. The Display application can also be accessed by right-clicking the desktop and selecting Properties from the menu that appears.

Use the Settings tab to configure your computer's display adapter settings. Figure 4-1 shows the Settings tab of the Display Properties dialog box. Notice the various display options that you can configure, including: Color Palette, Font Size, Desktop Area, and Refresh Frequency.

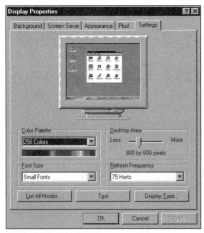

Figure 4-1 *The Settings tab*

If you make any changes on the Settings tab, you must test the changes before you can apply them or save them.

Keyboard

The *Keyboard* application is used to configure specific keyboard features, including speed of character repeat, cursor blink rate, input locale (including keyboard layout), and keyboard type.

The default input locale is English/United States. You can select other languages (localized for use in other countries) by clicking the Add command button on the Input Locales tab, and then scrolling through the drop-down list box.

A list of keyboard layout options is displayed when you click the Properties command button on the Input Locales tab, and then scroll through the drop-down list box.

Modems

The *Modems* application is used to install and configure modems and to configure dialing properties (see Figure 4-2). When you install a modem, you can instruct Windows NT to detect your modem automatically, or you can select your modem manually from a list. If you choose to select your modem manually and your modem does not appear on the list, you can choose from the list of standard modem types.

When you troubleshoot modem connection problems, consider configuring Windows NT to record a log file of your modem connection activity. This log file will contain a detailed record of all commands sent to and from your modem starting from the time that you enable this feature. Windows NT saves this log file in your Windows NT installation directory as `ModemLog_your modem name.txt`. You can use any text editor to view this file.

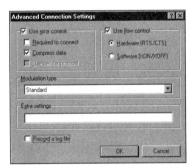

Figure 4-2 *Configuring the Modems application to record a log file*

Make sure you know how to configure and view a modem log file because you are likely to see a question about it on the exam.

You can use the Modems application to configure dialing properties, including the area code you are calling from, the country you are in, special instructions on how to access an outside line, whether to dial using a calling card, instructions on how to disable call waiting, and to specify tone or pulse dialing. To access the Dialing Properties dialog box, double-click Modems in Control Panel, and then click the Dialing Properties command button in the Modems Properties dialog box.

Mouse

The *Mouse* application is used to install and configure a mouse or other pointing device. You can choose the mouse button configuration, select a different pointer (this is the arrow on your screen that moves as you move your mouse), and configure pointer speed and double-click speed.

Multimedia

The *Multimedia* application is used to install and configure audio/visual devices. You can specify audio record and playback devices, MIDI output configuration, and how a video is shown on your computer's display. The types of devices you can install with this application include sound cards, MIDI devices and instruments, joysticks, video capture devices, and so on.

SCSI Adapters

The *SCSI Adapters* application is used to install, configure, and manage SCSI adapters. SCSI adapter drivers are usually installed and configured during the installation of Windows NT. The SCSI Adapters application, however, is a convenient tool to add additional SCSI adapters after installation, and to view the operational status, configuration, and resources used by your SCSI adapters.

Figure 4-3 shows the two SCSI adapters installed in my desktop computer (a dual-channel IDE controller and an Adaptec SCSI adapter), and the devices connected to each adapter. (Note: Windows NT treats dual-channel IDE controllers as SCSI adapters.) Clicking the Properties button in the SCSI Adapters dialog box displays the IDE CD-ROM dialog box, which shows the driver status and other information about the IDE controller.

Remember that any item that can be used to view configuration information is usually fair game for troubleshooting questions.

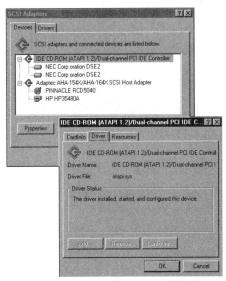

Figure 4-3 *SCSI adapters installed in a computer*

Tape Devices

The *Tape Devices* application is used to install drivers for tape backup devices and to view the status of tape backup devices connected to your computer. This application functions much like the PC Card (PCMCIA) and SCSI Adapters applications.

You must install a driver for your tape backup device before you can access it in the Windows NT Backup application.

UPS

The *UPS* application is used to install, configure, and manage an uninterruptible power supply. The Windows NT UPS application is adequate for managing an inexpensive UPS that does not include Windows NT-compatible UPS application software.

You can configure the UPS interface voltages, expected battery life, the name of an executable program to run thirty seconds before shutdown, and other settings using the Windows NT UPS application.

Most of the UPS devices on the market connect with a server through a serial communications port. As a result, many of the problems with premature UPS shutdowns or failure to shutdown have to do with a serial port problem.

True or False?

1. A device configured as a System device will only start when a user starts the device.

2. Windows NT Workstation does not have an automatic modem detection process.

3. You should always use the Windows NT UPS software, ignoring the manufacturer's software.

4. The SCSI Application allows you to view every device connected to a SCSI adapter in your computer.

5. If you are not sure what a Windows NT Workstation device is, you should configure it as disabled.

Answers: *1. False 2. False 3. False 4. True 5. False*

Networking

The *Network* application is used to control all aspects of networking services on the Windows NT computer, including changing the computer/domain/workgroup name, installing and configuring protocols and services, configuring bindings and network access order, and configuring network adapters. The Network application can also be accessed by right-clicking the Network Neighborhood icon and selecting Properties from the menu that appears.

Computer/Domain/Workgroup Names

Occasionally you may want to change the computer, domain, or workgroup name of a Windows NT Workstation computer. For example, you might change the computer name of a Windows NT Workstation computer that is assigned to a new employee to match the new user's name, instead of the name of the previous employee who used that computer.

The Network dialog box contains five tabs: Identification, Services, Protocols, Adapters, and Bindings. The Identification tab is on top initially. If you click the Change command button, the Identification Changes dialog box is displayed, as shown in Figure 4-4.

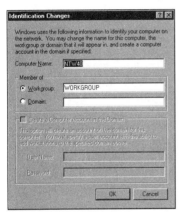

Figure 4-4 *Making identification changes on a*
Windows NT Workstation computer

Notice that in the Identification Changes dialog box you can change the computer name or change the domain or workgroup the computer belongs to. A Windows NT computer must belong to either a workgroup or a domain.

If you select the Workgroup option, button you can accept the workgroup name that is displayed or, if no name is displayed, you must type in a workgroup name. A Windows NT computer can be a member of any existing workgroup, or it can be the only computer in a new workgroup.

Joining a Domain

If you select the Domain option button, you must either accept the domain name that is displayed or type the name of any existing domain on the network. To be a member of a domain, a Windows NT computer must have a computer account in that domain. If a computer account does not exist in the domain for the computer you are configuring, you must check the Create a Computer Account in the Domain check box, and you must supply the administrator's user account name and password (or any other user account that has the right to add computer accounts to the domain). This entire process is called *joining a domain*.

Once a Windows NT computer has joined a domain, a user can log on to this computer interactively (locally) by using a user account in the domain directory database via a process known as *pass-through authentication*.

 Watch for exam questions regarding joining a domain. Remember that a Windows NT computer must have a computer account in the domain it is joining.

Protocols and Services

Windows NT supports a variety of protocols and services. The following list identifies each protocol that ships with Windows NT Workstation and briefly describes the functionality of each.

- **AppleTalk Protocol:** This protocol enables a Windows NT Workstation computer to connect to AppleTalk network print devices. (AppleTalk is usually associated with Macintosh computers and printers.)

- **DLC Protocol:** This protocol is a datalink protocol. In an NT environment, DLC is primarily used by Windows NT computers to communicate with Hewlett-Packard printers and IBM mainframe computers.

- **NetBEUI Protocol:** This protocol is designed for small, nonrouted networks. It doesn't require any configuration and has minimal overhead. NetBEUI is included with NT 4.0 primarily to provide backward compatibility with earlier networking software that uses NetBEUI as its only protocol.

- **NWLink IPX/SPX Compatible Transport:** This protocol is a routable protocol usually associated with NetWare networks. NWLink is fully supported for Windows NT networking.

- **Point-to-Point Tunneling Protocol:** This protocol is used to provide a secure network communications path between computers over the Internet.

- **Streams Environment:** Some applications require Streams for correct network functionality. I recommend you install Streams Environment only if it is required by an application or service you want to use.

- **TCP/IP Protocol:** This protocol provides the most robust capabilities for Windows NT networking. It is a fast, routable enterprise protocol. TCP/IP is the protocol used on the Internet. TCP/IP is supported by many other operating systems, including Windows 95, Macintosh, UNIX, MS-DOS, and IBM mainframes. Its only drawback is the extensive configuration required to implement it.

Not many questions relating to the abilities of each of these protocols will appear on the exam, but knowing that they exist and what they support is important.

Bindings and Network Access Order

Bindings and *network access order* specify which protocol or service Windows NT will use first when it attempts to connect to another computer.

Bindings and network access order don't have much effect on the speed of performance of the Server service on Windows NT. (The Server service is normally installed by default.) The Server service's performance is not affected because the Server service replies to the client computer that contacted it by using the same protocol the client computer used. For example, if a client computer uses NetBEUI to contact a server, the server will reply by using NetBEUI, even if TCP/IP is the server's first bound protocol.

Bindings and network access order *can* be very important to the performance of the Workstation service on Windows NT. The Workstation service's performance can be affected because the Workstation service will try each of the protocols installed, in the order they are bound, when attempting to connect to another computer.

Bindings affect network performance

If a Windows NT computer is primarily used as a client computer, you should configure the protocols and services that are used most often to appear at the top of the bindings and network access order lists.

Assume that most of the servers you want to connect to from this computer use NWLink NetBIOS. If this is the case, you should move NWLink NetBIOS to the top of the Workstation bindings list. The result of this configuration change is shown in Figure 4-5. Notice that NWLink NetBIOS is now the first protocol listed for the Workstation service. Making this configuration change will improve the performance of the Workstation service on this computer.

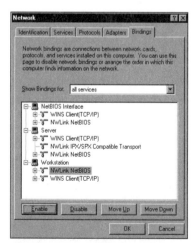

Figure 4-5 *Modified Workstation bindings order on a Windows NT computer*

Occasionally you may want to disable network services on one or more network adapters in your server. For example, if you have a server that has two network adapters, one of which is connected to your local network, and the other connected to the Internet, you might want to disable the Server service on the network adapter that is connected to the Internet so that users on the Internet can't connect network drives to your server. To disable a network binding, start the Network application in Control Panel, select the Bindings tab, highlight the protocol or service on which you want to disable the bindings, and click the Disable command button.

You may see an exam question in which a computer has two network adapters, one on the local network and the other connected to the Internet. You will most likely be asked to determine how to prevent users on the Internet from connecting to your computer.

When configuring bindings, the primary emphasis is on ordering protocols. When configuring network access order, the primary emphasis is on ordering network service providers, such as Microsoft Windows Network, or NetWare or Compatible Network. Figure 4-6 shows the network access order on a computer. Notice that Microsoft Windows Network is the first provider listed in the Network Providers list, and that NetWare or Compatible Network is listed second.

Figure 4-6 *Network access order on a Windows NT computer*

Assume that you use the computer that has the network access order shown in Figure 4-6 primarily to connect to NetWare servers. If this is the case, you should move NetWare or Compatible Network to the top of the Network Providers list. Making this configuration change will improve the performance of the Workstation service on this computer.

Network Adapters

Occasionally you may need to configure a network adapter. For example, assume you install an additional card (of any kind) in your computer. You might have to change the settings on your network adapter to resolve an interrupt or an I/O port address conflict between the existing network adapter and the newly installed card.

Configuring a network adapter in Windows NT is usually a two-step process. First, you must configure manually the hardware settings of the network adapter. This can include setting jumpers or switches, or using a manufacturer-supplied configuration program. Second, you must configure the network adapter driver settings used in Windows NT by using the Network application in the Control Panel.

Figure 4-7 shows a setup dialog box for a 3Com Etherlink III network adapter. Notice that you can modify the I/O port address, interrupt, and transceiver type.

Figure 4-7 *Configuring a network adapter*

True or False?

1. A Windows NT computer must belong to either a workgroup or a domain.

2. In order for a Windows NT computer to participate in a workgroup, it must have a computer account created for it.

3. You can improve the performance of the workstation by optimizing the network bindings.

4. You can selectively disable or enable services and protocols on a per adapter basis.

5. You can not improve the performance of the server service.

Answers: *1. True 2. False 3. True 4. True 5. False*

Server Application

The *Server* application is used to view user sessions (including the resources that users are accessing), disconnect users from the computer, view the status of shared resources, and configure administrative alerts. Most of the functions within the Server application are fairly intuitive and straightforward.

System Application

The *System* application is used to configure foreground application performance, virtual memory, system and user environment variables, startup and shutdown behavior, hardware profiles, and user profiles.

You can use the System application to set the performance boost for the foreground application and to configure your virtual memory paging file(s).

Application Performance

Foreground application performance involves giving a higher priority to the application running in the foreground than to other applications. The purpose of assigning a higher priority is to make the foreground application more responsive to the user.

To configure the foreground application priority, double-click the System icon in the Control Panel, and select the Performance tab. Adjust the slide bar for the amount of performance boost you want.

Virtual Memory

Virtual memory is implemented in Windows NT by the use of paging files. You should consider both performance and recoverability when configuring virtual memory paging files.

KNOW THIS   Configuring Page Files

If you want to configure your system for maximum paging file performance, you should put a small paging file on each physical disk, except for the disk that contains the Windows NT boot partition. This will provide the highest performance for virtual memory.

If you want to configure your system for optimum system recovery, you must put a paging file on the Windows NT boot partition that is at least as large as the amount of RAM in your computer. This paging file is used by Windows NT as a normal paging file, and also is required to enable Windows NT to write a memory.dmp file when the operating system crashes.

Hardware Profiles

You can use the System application to create and configure *hardware profiles.* Windows NT creates an initial hardware profile during installation.

The primary reason for creating hardware profiles is to manage the different hardware configurations of laptop computers. (A laptop computer that is used at the office in a docking station has a different hardware configuration than the same laptop computer when it is used at home or on the road without a docking station.) Hardware profiles make it possible to create custom configurations for the same laptop computer that is used both with and without a docking station.

Figure 4-8 shows the Hardware Profiles tab within the System application. Note that you can use the arrows on the right-hand side to move profiles up or down in the Available Hardware Profiles list box. Windows NT uses the first profile in this list when no other selection is made during the boot process.

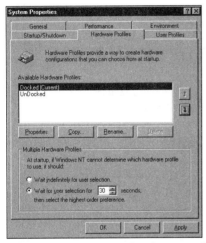

Figure 4-8 *Managing hardware profiles*

To configure a new or existing hardware profile, highlight the profile in the Available Hardware Profiles list box and click the Properties command button. Then select the docking status for this hardware profile, and specify whether this is a network-disabled profile. (A network-disabled profile prevents any network services from starting on a computer.)

You can also use the Services and Devices applications to enable and disable services and device drivers within each hardware profile.

Once you have created multiple profiles, Windows NT displays the Hardware Profile/Configuration Recovery menu after the boot loader menu when your computer boots to Windows NT. This menu permits you to select the hardware profile you want Windows NT to use. You can configure the length of time this menu is displayed in the Multiple Hardware Profiles section on the Hardware Profiles tab.

User Profiles

You can use the User Profiles tab within the System application to copy, delete, and change the type of user profiles. The System application is the only application in Windows NT that can copy user profiles. You can't copy user profiles by using Windows NT Explorer.

Troubleshooting Configuration Problems

Configuration problems are common and usually arise in two major areas: hardware and protocols. Troubleshooting configuration problems can be difficult, because it's easy to overlook a simple configuration issue, and to look instead for some complicated (and usually nonexistent) cause.

Some of the most common hardware configuration problems occur when two cards installed in the same computer are configured to use the same interrupt, I/O port address, or DMA address. To resolve this type of problem, you must reconfigure one of the cards to use a nonconflicting setting.

Another common hardware configuration problem occurs when a card is physically configured in one way (via switches or jumpers), and the software driver for that card is configured with different settings. To resolve this type of problem, you must either change the hardware settings or the software driver settings so that both use the same settings.

Troubleshooting protocols can be a detailed, painstaking task.

TCP/IP, for example, is easy to configure improperly. Several settings must be typed on each computer that uses this protocol, including IP address, subnet mask, and default gateway. The best way to prevent configuration problems in a TCP/IP environment is to use a DHCP server to configure TCP/IP automatically on each computer on the network. If you don't use DHCP, you should manually verify that the settings are correctly entered on each computer that experiences a network communications problem.

NWLink IPX/SPX Compatible Transport also has several configuration settings, and thus is prone to human error during protocol configuration. Verify that all of the settings for this (and every) protocol are correctly entered on each computer that experiences a network communications problem.

Have You Mastered?

Now it's time to apply what you've learned in this chapter by testing your mastery of the material. These questions provide you with a means to determine if you are ready to move on to the next chapter or if you need to review the material again.

1. **You have installed a new hardware device in your Windows NT Workstation computer. You only want to use this hardware device automatically when you are in the office. What can you do to prevent this device from running all of the time?**

   ☐ A. Configure the startup properties for the hardware device as disabled.

   ☐ B. Configure the startup properties for the hardware device as system.

   ☐ C. Create a hardware profile and enable the device only in the profile for the office.

   ☐ D. Create a hardware profile called OFFICE and one called MOBILE. NT will do the rest.

The correct answer is **C**. A hardware profile contains configuration settings for which hardware device drivers will or will not be loaded during a session. If you have a network adapter that you use only in the office, the device driver does not need to be loaded when you are traveling around. For more information, see the "System Application" section.

2. **You are changing the domain that your Windows NT Workstation computer belongs to. What must you do in order to allow the computer to join the Windows NT domain?**

    ☐ A. Create a computer account in the domain.

    ☐ B. Create a user account for yourself.

    ☐ C. Create a workgroup and configure the NT Workstation to participate in the workgroup.

    ☐ D. Configure the network access order so that Microsoft Networks is first.

The correct answer is **A**. In order for a Windows NT computer to participate in a Windows NT domain, there must be a computer account created for the computer. Otherwise, there is no way to ensure that only authorized computers participate in a network. The network access order only affects the performance of the computer, not its ability to work in a domain. For more information, see the "Networking" section.

3. **You are configuring your Windows NT Workstation 4.0 computer. You have two network adapters, one connected to your corporate network and the other is connected to the Internet. What can you do to prevent people from accessing your shared folders over the Internet?**

    ☐ A. Change the network access order so Microsoft Networks is last.

    ☐ B. Place the computer in a Workgroup rather than an NT Domain.

    ☐ C. Disable the server service on the network adapter connected to the Internet.

    ☐ D. Disable the NetBEUI protocol on the network adapter connected to the Internet.

The correct answer is **C**. By disabling the server service, Windows NT does not broadcast nor accept connection requests for shared folders and shared printers. The network access order has nothing to do with accepting requests. Distracter D was thrown in for advanced users, because NetBEUI is not used for Internet connections. For more information, see the "Networking" section.

4. You are working on your Windows NT Workstation and you notice that someone appears to be accessing private files on your computer. You want to disconnect only the user accessing the private files. What should you do?

☐ A. Change the network access order.
☐ B. Disable the server service on the network adapter interface.
☐ C. Disable the workstation service on the network adapter interface.
☐ D. Use the Server icon in Control Panel to view the user connection and disconnect it.

The correct answer is **D**. Because you only want to disconnect the one user, the server icon in Control Panel is the best choice, as it allows you to view each user connection and what file they are accessing. Disabling the server service will disconnect all of the users, not just the unauthorized user. For more information, see the "Server Application" section.

5. You have been experiencing problems your modem when it is connecting to your Internet Service Provider. What can you do to view historical information on the modem connections?

☐ A. Use the Windows NT Event Viewer.
☐ B. Use the Windows NT Performance Monitor.
☐ C. Configure the modem to record a log file.
☐ D. Use the server icon in the Control Panel.

The correct answer is **C**. The only way to view historical information on the status and performance of modem connections is with a log file. Neither the Event Viewer nor the Performance Monitor can view the performance information of a modem. For more information, see the "Peripherals and Devices" section.

6. You are configuring your Windows NT Workstation computer. You want to increase the performance of the paging file on your computer. How should you configure the page file settings on

the computer?

- [ ] A. Configure one large page file on the partition that contains the Windows NT boot files.
- [ ] B. Configure one page file for each disk in the computer, including the Windows NT boot partition.
- [ ] C. Configure one page file for each disk in the computer except the Windows NT boot partition.
- [ ] D. Configure one large page file on a partition other than the Windows NT boot partition.

The correct answer is **C**. By spreading the page files over multiple disks, Windows NT can access the files in parallel, rather than waiting for a file to be read and then placed in the page file. Also, by not placing a page file on the boot partition, Windows NT has faster access to the boot and system files without having to contend with page file access. For more information, see the "System Application" section.

7. **You are configuring your Windows NT workstation computer that has 64MB of RAM. This computer shares files and printers with other computers on the network. You would like to ensure that this computer is configured for optimum system recovery so that it can provide a high up-time of resources to the network. How should you configure the page files on this computer?**

- [ ] A. Configure a 64MB page file on a partition other than the Windows NT boot partition.
- [ ] B. Configure a 64MB page file on the Windows NT boot partition.
- [ ] C. Configure a 32MB page file on a partition other than the Windows NT boot partition.
- [ ] D. Configure a 32MB page file on the Windows NT boot partition.

The correct answer is **B**. If the paging file is at least as large as the amount of RAM in the computer and is placed on the boot partition, Windows NT will use the paging file as a normal paging file.

Additionally, the paging file will enable Windows NT to write a memory.dmp file when the operating system crashes. For more information, see the "System Application" section.

8. **You are installing Windows NT workstation. After the installation you notice that it takes longer to access NetWare server resources than it does for Windows NT servers. You use NetWare servers more often than Windows NT servers. What can you do to improve the performance of accessing NetWare servers?**

    ☐ A. Change the application performance setting to increase foreground application speed.
    ☐ B. Configure the network bindings.
    ☐ C. Change the Network access order.
    ☐ D. Disable the Server service for the network adapter.

The correct answer is **C**. By configuring the Network access order, you determine which Network Operating System will be used first for each communications. Rather than waiting for the Microsoft Network to timeout and then using the NetWare network, you can configure the NetWare network to be used first. For more information, see the "Networking" section.

9. **Which of the protocols that ship with Windows NT Workstation is a fast, routable enterprise protocol that is used on the Internet and is supported by many operating systems, including Windows NT, Windows 95, Macintosh, UNIX, MS-DOS, and IBM mainframes?**

    ☐ A. NetBEUI
    ☐ B. TCP/IP
    ☐ C. NWLink IPX/SPX Compatible Transport
    ☐ D. DLC

The correct answer is **B**. The TCP/IP protocol is a scalable, routable protocol that has support or more platforms that any other protocol available. In addition, TCP/IP can be used across many different networks and topologies, including the Internet. For more information, see the "Networking" section.

Practice Your Skills

Here is a chance to apply your practical, hands-on experience and material from this chapter. These exercises are designed for you to apply not only the material in the book, but to gain greater experience and exposure to the product. These exercises are a critical part of understanding the product and gaining valuable experience for using the product and passing the certification exam. For each of the following problems, consider the given facts and determine what you think are the possible causes of the problem and what course of action you might take to resolve the problem.

1. Changing Domain membership

EXERCISE You are changing the network configuration on your Windows NT Workstation computer. You have been participating in a Windows NT workgroup and you are joining a Windows NT Domain. During the change, you enter your name and password to create a domain account for the computer. You are unable to complete the change. What is most likely the problem?

ANALYSIS Most of the time that this happens it is because the user name and password you specified oes not belong to the Domain Admins group or does not have Add a Computer to the Domain access rights. Usually specifying a domain admin account to use for the change will resolve the problem.

2. Troubleshooting the server service

EXERCISE You are troubleshooting communications problems between your Windows NT Workstation computer and other NT computers on the network. The other computers on the network use various protocols to communicate with each other, such as TCP/IP, NetBEUI, and the NWLink IPX/SPX Compatible Transport. What determines which protocol your Windows NT Workstation computer will use to respond to network requests from other computers?

ANALYSIS Windows NT uses the Server service for sharing resources on the network. When the Server service receives a request from a computer, the response is sent using the same protocol as the request was received on. So Network access order and bindings have no impact on which protocol will be used when responding, but these configuration parameters do affect the performance of the Workstation service that is used to originate requests to other computers.

3. Adding a CD-ROM drive

EXERCISE You have added an IDE CD-ROM drive to your Windows NT Workstation computer. After starting Windows NT, you look in the Windows Explorer and you do not see the CD-ROM drive. What should you do to determine if Windows NT saw the new CD-ROM and the controller it is attached to?

ANALYSIS The SCSI icon in the Control Panel shows a view of the SCSI and IDE devices that have been detected by Windows NT. If the device is not displayed, either the device is not operative or is not supported by Windows NT. If it is not supported by the default driver set, you can add the manufacturer's driver files to Windows NT in this dialog box as well.

4. Optimizing application performance

EXERCISE You are adding a database application to your Windows NT Workstation computer. You want to ensure that this application is running as fast as possible, even if it means applications run in the foreground are slowed down. What should you do?

ANALYSIS You should use the System icon in the Control Panel to set the Application Performance Boost to NONE. This will give background applications higher priority over applications run in the foreground, which are usually applications that the computer has started, such as Microsoft Office.

5. Configuring Page File settings

EXERCISE Your Windows NT Computer has three hard drives, configured so that the first drive is partitioned as C and D drives, and the remaining two drives each have a single partition, defined as drives E and F. Windows NT is installed in the D drive and the C drive is used to boot the computer. How should you configure the page file setting for Windows NT for the best performance?

ANALYSIS To achieve the best performance, avoid placing the page file on the boot partition, the C Drive, and configure a small page file on the remaining three drive partitions. Otherwise, the page file will be competing with Windows NT accessing the boot files, and will cause drive contention, which will slow down the computer.

Managing User and Group Accounts

Y OU NEED TO UNDERSTAND HOW to create and manage
user accounts to pass the NT Workstation exam. This
chapter looks at the steps involved in creating a user
account and configuring specific Windows NT user
account properties. Are you prepared for exam questions on local and global groups? Do you know what
the limitations are when using a local or global group? This chapter also
looks at built-in groups as well as user profiles.

Exam Material in This Chapter

Based on Microsoft Objectives

Managing Resources

- Creating and managing local user accounts and local group accounts to meet given requirements
- Setting up and modifying user profiles

Based on Author's Experience

- You need to understand that users must be assigned dialin permission before they are permitted to connect to a Windows NT Remote Access Server.
- Watch for exam questions about renaming user accounts and whether they retain local and network permissions.
- You need to know the limitation of local groups and which types of groups can contain others.
- You should understand the purpose of the six built-in account groups and their permissions.
- You should be familiar with user profiles, their purpose, and how they are created.

Are You Prepared?

Do you have what it takes? Try out these self-assessment questions to see if you have prepared for the material in this chapter or if you should review problem areas.

1. **What Windows NT feature can you use to increase the security level for users who connect to a Windows NT Remote Access Server?**

   □ A. Configure Call Back permissions as Preset To.
   □ B. Configure Call Back permissions as Set by Caller.
   □ C. Place the user accounts in the Everyone group.
   □ D. Define user account profiles.

2. **What happens to the network security permissions for a user account when it is renamed?**

   □ A. All of the network and user account rights are lost.
   □ B. All of the network permissions are lost, but the account rights are maintained.
   □ C. All of the permissions are retained.
   □ D. All of the network permissions are retained, but the account rights are lost.

3. **What can you do if you want to ensure that users will always receive the same desktop settings, no matter which computer they are using?**

   □ A. Configure a home directory.
   □ B. Configure a mandatory profile.
   □ C. Add the user account to the replicator group.
   □ D. Add the user account to the power users group.

Answers:

1. B   *Once users have authenticated themselves, call back
         security will hang up the connection and call users
         back. If the administrator presets the number, you can
         increase the security because even if a hacker guessed
         your username and password, it is very difficult to steal
         your phone number. If the caller is permitted to set a
         call-back number once they are connected, this does
         not increase the security, but it does alleviate long
         distance phone card charges sometimes! For more
         information, refer to the "Creating and Managing User
         Accounts" section of this chapter.*

2. C   *When a user account is renamed, all of the permissions
         and rights assigned to it are maintained. If the account
         is deleted and re-added, even with the same name, all
         of the permissions are lost forever. For more
         information, refer to the "Creating and Managing User
         Accounts" section of this chapter.*

3. B   *If a user account is configured to use a mandatory
         profile, the user will only be permitted to log on to the
         network if the profile can be located and loaded on her
         computer. If the profile cannot be located, the user will
         be denied access. For more information, refer to the
         "Managing User Profiles" section of this chapter.*

Creating and Managing User Accounts

User accounts are records that contain unique user information, such as user name, password, and any logon restrictions. User accounts enable users to log on to Windows NT computers or domains.

There are two types of user accounts: built-in user accounts, and user accounts that you create. You can configure various user account properties, including group memberships, profile, and the dialin permission.

Built-in User Accounts

There are two built-in user accounts in Windows NT: Administrator and Guest. Built-in accounts are created automatically during the installation of Windows NT.

The *Administrator* account has all of the rights and permissions needed to administer a Windows NT computer. The Administrator account can be used to perform numerous tasks, including creating and managing users and groups, managing file and folder permissions, and installing and managing printers and printer security. In addition, members of the Administrators local group have the right to take ownership of any file, folder, or printer. The Administrator account's rights and permissions are due solely to its membership in the Administrators local group.

 Membership in the Administrators local group is a prime target for exam questions. Be on the lookout for questions on a user's inability to perform a task. The most likely cause will be that the user is not in the Administrators local group.

The Administrator account, because of its powerful capabilities, can pose a security risk to your network if an unauthorized user is able to guess the password for the account. For this reason, you should consider renaming the Administrator account. (Renaming user accounts is covered later in this chapter.)

The *Guest* account is designed to permit limited access to network resources to the occasional user who doesn't have his own user account.

For example, a client visiting your office might want to connect a laptop computer to the network to print a document. The client can log on using the Guest account. You can specify which network resources are available to this account by assigning the appropriate file, folder, and printer permissions to the Guest account.

The Guest account is disabled by default. If your network contains sensitive data I recommend, for security reasons, you leave the Guest account disabled. Instead of using the Guest account, establish a user account for every person who needs access to network resources.

User Account Properties

User accounts have several options that can be configured. These options are called *user account properties.*

User account properties that you can configure on Windows NT Workstation computers include group memberships, profile, and the dialin permission.

User account properties are configured in the User Properties dialog box in User Manager.

Figure 5-1 shows the User Properties dialog box for Administrator in User Manager on a Windows NT Workstation computer. Notice the Groups, Profile, and Dialin command buttons along the bottom of the dialog box.

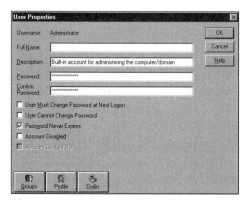

Figure 5-1 *Administrator's user properties on a Windows NT Workstation computer*

Groups

The Groups command button in the User Properties dialog box is used to configure which group(s) a user is a member of. Assigning users to groups is an efficient way to manage permissions for multiple users. (The subject of groups is covered in more detail later in this chapter.)

When you click the Groups command button in the User Properties dialog box, the Group Memberships dialog box appears. Figure 5-2 shows the Group Memberships dialog box for Administrator.

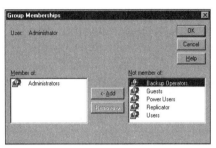

Figure 5-2 *Administrator's group memberships*

Profile

The Profile command button in the User Properties dialog box is used to configure the user's environment. You can configure the user profile path, logon script name, and home directory location.

When you click the Profile command button in the User Properties dialog box, the User Environment Profile dialog box appears. Figure 5-3 shows the User Environment Profile dialog box for Administrator.

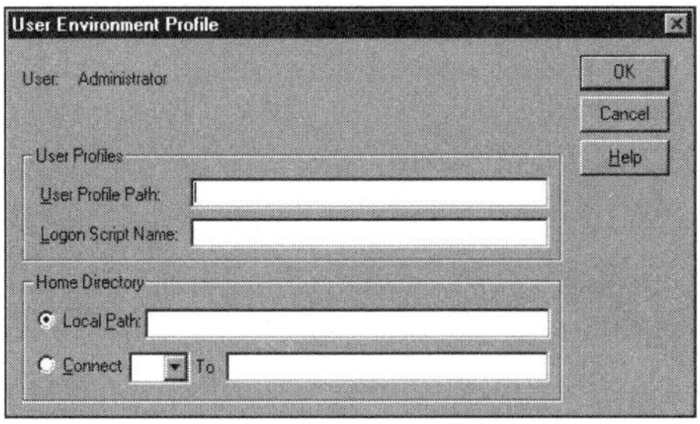

Figure 5-3 *Administrator's environment profile*

The user profile path is used to assign a location for the user's profile. A user's profile contains the user's unique desktop settings, such as screen color, screen saver, desktop icons, fonts, and so on. The default location for a user's profile is the `<winntroot>\Profiles\%USERNAME%` folder. User profile paths must include the complete path to the folder that contains the user's profile, in the format of `\\Server_name\Share_name\Folder\Subfolder`. If no path is entered in the User Profile Path text box, Windows NT uses the default location.

The Logon Script Name text box is an optional configuration that enables you to enter the user's logon script filename, if the user has one. *Logon scripts* are batch files that run on a user's computer during the logon process. Many Windows NT installations don't use logon scripts. If you choose to use logon scripts, enter the user's logon script filename in the Logon Script Name text box.

The Home Directory section of the User Environment Profile dialog box is used to configure either a local home directory on the user's computer, or a server-based home directory.

A *home directory* (either local or server-based) is a user's default directory for the Save As and File Open dialog boxes in most Windows-based applications. Using server-based home directories enables the network administrator to back up user-created data files easily, as the user-created files are stored by default on the server rather than on individual computers.

The most common way to assign a server-based home directory is to create a shared folder, named `Users`, on the server first. Then, assign the path `\\Server_name\Users\%USERNAME%` as each user's home directory location. When the `%USERNAME%` variable is used in a path, Windows NT creates a home directory/folder (that is named using the user's account name) in the `Users` shared folder.

Dialin

The Dialin command button in the User Properties dialog box is used to configure dialin permission for a user account. The dialin permission enables a user to log on by using a Dial-Up Networking connection.

When you click the Dialin command button in the User Properties dialog box, the Dialin Information dialog box, which is shown in Figure 5-4, appears. Notice that, by default, a user account is not granted the dialin permission.

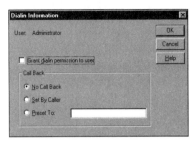

Figure 5-4 *Granting dialin permission to a user account*

The dialin permission should be granted to every user that needs access to the network by using a Dial-Up Networking connection. For example, traveling sales representatives need to access e-mail and other network resources from their laptop computers, and employees who occasionally work from home may need to dial in to access network resources from their home computers.

To grant a user the dialin permission, select the check box next to Grant dialin permission to user.

Dialin is a prime target for NT exams, as most environments use Remote Access Server. Look for a scenario where the user cannot connect because she does not have dialin permission, or Call Back is set and she is at a different phone number than Call Back was configured for.

There are three options in the Call Back section: No Call Back, Set By Caller, and Preset To. The default setting is No Call Back.

If you select No Call Back, the user can dial in to the server, but the user can't request that the server break the connection and call the user back. Selecting No Call Back ensures that the user dialing in — not the server — is billed for any long distance telephone charges.

If you select Set By Caller, the server prompts the user for a telephone number. The server breaks the connection and calls the user back using this number, and thus the server incurs the bulk of any long distance telephone charges.

If you select Preset To, you must enter a telephone number that the server will always use to call this user back when the user dials in. This setting reduces the risk of unauthorized access to network resources because the server always calls a preset telephone number, such as a user's home telephone number. An unauthorized user might be able to dial in and guess a password, but will not be able to direct the server to call back at any other number than the number specified in Preset To, and thus will not be able to connect to the network.

 True or False?

1. Any user account can belong to the administrators local group.
2. Users cannot specify a call-back number when connecting to a dialin server.
3. A Home directory can only exist on a Windows NT Workstation computer.
4. The Guest account is enabled by default.
5. The Admin and Guest accounts cannot be deleted.

Answers: *1. True 2. False 3. False 4. False 5. True*

Renaming and Deleting User Accounts

Occasionally you may want to rename or delete a user account. Renaming a user account retains all of the account properties, including group memberships, permissions, and rights for the new user of the account. You might want to rename a user account when a new staff member replaces an employee who has left the company.

Deleting a user account is just what it sounds like — the user account is permanently removed, and all of its group memberships, permissions, and rights are lost. Normally, you only delete a user account when you don't plan to use the account ever again.

The two built-in accounts, Administrator and Guest, can't be deleted, although they can be renamed.

Changing user accounts and retaining permissions

When you rename a user account, it retains its security ID used throughout the network. That means anything that the user had access to before, he still has access to after the renaming process. When you delete a user, the security ID is never reused, even for a new account with the same name. Once you delete a user account, all of the permissions required for the account must be reapplied.

Creating and Managing Groups

Using groups is a convenient and efficient way to assign rights and permissions to multiple users. *Groups* are collections of user accounts. We will be looking at three types of groups in this chapter: *local groups* and *built-in groups*.

Local Groups

Local groups are primarily used to control access to resources. In a typical Windows NT configuration, a local group is assigned permissions to a specific resource, such as a shared folder or a shared printer. Individual user accounts are made members of this local group. The result is that all members of the local group now have permissions to the resource. Using local groups simplifies the administration of resources because permissions can be assigned once, to a local group, instead of separately to each user account.

All user accounts and group accounts are stored in the directory database in which they are created. For example, if you create a local group on a Windows NT Workstation computer, it is stored in that NT Workstation computer's local directory database.

Local Groups

Local groups can be created on any Windows NT computer. A local group in the directory database on a Windows NT Workstation computer can be assigned permissions to resources *only* on that computer.

A local group in the directory database on a Windows NT Workstation computer (that is a member of a domain) can contain individual user accounts from the local directory database (see Figure 5-5). It can also contain user accounts and global groups from the directory database of the member domain, and user accounts and global groups from the directory database of any trusted domain.

A local group in the directory database on a Windows NT Workstation computer (that is not a member of a domain) can only contain individual user accounts from the local directory database.

Watch out for exam questions about adding local groups to other local groups — it cannot be done, you must use a global group.

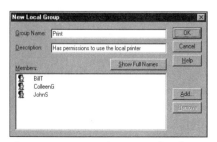

Figure 5-5 *Creating a new local group*

Built-in Groups

Built-in groups are groups with preset characteristics that are automatically created during the installation of Windows NT. On Windows NT Workstation computers, all built-in groups are local groups.

The members of built-in local groups have the rights and/or permissions to perform certain administrative tasks. You can assign users to the built-in local groups that most closely match the tasks users need to perform. If there isn't a built-in local group with the rights and/or permissions needed to perform a specific task or access a specific resource, you can create a local group and assign it the necessary rights and/or permissions to accomplish the task or access the resource.

You can assign permissions to and remove permissions from built-in groups. (An exception is the built-in Administrators group — this group always has full rights and permissions to administer the computer or domain.) You can also assign users to and remove users from built-in groups. Built-in groups cannot be renamed or deleted.

Table 5.1 lists the various built-in local groups on Windows NT Workstation computers, and gives a brief description of each group's purpose or function.

TABLE 5.1 Built-in Local Groups on Windows NT Workstation Computers

Built-in local group name	Description
Administrator	Has full administrative rights and permissions to administer the computer; initially contains the built-in Administrator user account.
Backup Operator	Has permissions to back up and restore files and folders on the computer.
Guest	Has no initial permissions; initially contains the built-in Guest user account.
Replicator	Used by the Windows NT Directory Replicator service.
User	Has no initial permissions; when new user accounts are created, they are automatically made members of this group.
Power User	Can create and modify user and group accounts, with the exception of the Administrator user account and the Administrators group; can share folders and printers.

True or False?

1. On Windows NT Workstation computers, all built-in groups are global groups.
2. Local groups can contain other local groups.
3. The Power Users group can create and modify user and group accounts.
4. You cannot assign permissions to and remove permissions from built-in groups.
5. Where possible, it is better to assign permissions to groups rather than users.

Answers: *1. False 2. False 3. True 4. False 5. True*

Managing User Profiles

In Windows NT, a *user profile* is a collection of settings and options that specify a user's desktop and all other user-definable settings for a user's work environment. The following sections discuss the contents of a user profile, how a user profile is created, customizing the Default User and the All Users profile folders, and roaming and mandatory user profiles.

User Profile Contents

Various settings are saved in a user profile. The contents of a user profile include the following:

- All user-specific settings for Windows NT Explorer, NotePad, Paint, HyperTerminal, Clock, Calculator, and other built-in Windows NT applications
- User-specific desktop settings, including: screen saver, background color, background pattern, wallpaper, and other display settings
- User-specific settings for applications written to run on Windows NT

- User-specific settings for network drive and printer connections

- User-specific settings for the Start menu, including program groups, applications, and recently accessed documents

A user profile is normally stored in a subfolder of the `<winntroot>\Profiles` folder on the local computer. Each user's profile is stored in a separate folder named after the user's account. For example, the Administrator's user profile is stored in the `<winntroot>\Profiles\Administrator` folder. Figure 5-6 shows, in Windows NT Explorer, the location and contents of the Administrator's profile folder.

Figure 5-6 *Contents of the Administrator's profile folder*

 All user profiles have the same contents as those shown for the Administrator.

How a User Profile Is Created

Windows NT automatically creates a user profile for every new user the first time the new user logs on. After that point, an Administrator can create and assign a user profile to an existing user (a user who has previously logged on and been assigned a user profile by Windows NT) by copying an existing user profile over that user's profile.

Roaming User Profiles

There is a way to assign a user profile to a new user in Windows NT — the Administrator can assign a new user a *server-based* (roaming) user profile. Roaming user profiles make it possible for the Administrator to copy and assign a user profile to a new user and have that profile be effective the first time the new user logs on.

As mentioned previously in this section, when a new user logs on for the first time, Windows NT creates a new user profile folder for the user. Windows NT accomplishes this by copying the entire contents of the Default User profile folder to a new folder named after the user's account. When Windows NT creates a new user's profile, the new user's initial profile is an exact copy of the Default User profile folder.

The Default User profile folder can also be customized by an Administrator, as described in the next section.

Customizing the Default User Profile Folder

Administrators can customize the Default User profile folder so new users, at first logon, have the appropriate desktop and work environment settings. For example, you might want to place a shortcut to a network application on the desktop of all new users. Or, you might want to add a shortcut that will appear in the Start menu for all new users.

You can customize the local Default User profile folder on a Windows NT computer, or you can create a domain-wide Default User profile folder for all Windows NT Workstation computers and member servers in a domain. Changes to the local Default User profile folder on a Windows NT computer affect only new users that log on to that computer. The domain-wide Default User profile folder affects all new domain users when they log on to Windows NT Workstation computers (that are domain members) and member servers.

To customize the local `Default User` profile folder on a Windows NT computer, an Administrator can either copy an existing user profile to the local `Default User` profile folder, or create shortcuts in the `Default User` profile subfolders.

To create a domain-wide `Default User` profile folder for all Windows NT Workstation computers and member servers in a domain, customize and copy an existing user profile to a subfolder named `Default User` in the `<winntroot>\System32\Repl\Import\Scripts` folder on the *primary domain controller* (PDC).

Profile files and directory replication

If you have configured directory replication on your PDC, copy the existing user profile to the `<winntroot>\System32\Repl\Export\Scripts\Default User` folder on the PDC, *not* to the `<winntroot>\System32\Repl\Import\Scripts\Default User` folder. If you copy it to the `Import\Scripts` folder and directory replication is configured, the Directory Replicator service will delete any files or folders in the `Import\Scripts` folder that do not exist in the `Export\Scripts` folder.

When choosing the user who is permitted to use this copied profile in the Choose User dialog box, select the Everyone group and ensure that the Everyone group is listed in the Permitted To Use section of the Copy To dialog box.

After a `Default User` profile folder is created on the `Netlogon` share on the PDC, the domain-wide `Default User` profile folder is available to all Windows NT computers that are members of the domain. When a Windows NT Workstation computer (that is a member of the domain) or a member server is rebooted, it copies the domain-wide `Default User` profile folder from the PDC to a subfolder named `Default User (Network)` in its local `Profiles` folder. This member

computer now has two Default User profile folders: one named
Default User and one named Default User (Network).

The domain-wide Default User profile folder is *not* copied
to the local Profiles folder on any domain controller in the
domain. It is only copied to the local Profiles folder on
nondomain controllers that are members of the domain.

Figure 5-7 shows the Profiles folder and its subfolders on a
Windows NT Workstation computer that is a member of the LAB
domain. Notice the Default User and Default User (Network)
folders.

Figure 5-7 *Two* Default User *profile folders on a member computer*

When a user logs on to a member computer that has two Default
User profile folders by using a *local user account*, and that user does
not have a profile folder on this local computer, Windows NT creates
a new user profile for the user on the local computer by using the
Default User profile folder.

When a user logs on to a member computer that has two Default
User profile folders by using a *user account from the domain*, and that
user does not have a profile folder on this local computer, Windows NT
creates a new user profile for the user on the local computer by using the
Default User (Network) profile folder.

Customizing the All Users Profile Folder

The All Users profile folder is a subfolder of the Profiles folder on all Windows NT computers. The All Users profile folder contains only two subfolders: Desktop and Start Menu. Figure 5-8 shows the All Users profile folder and its subfolders in Windows NT Explorer.

Figure 5-8 *The* All Users *profile folder*

The purpose of the All Users profile folder is to enable an administrator to create shortcuts and install applications that are made available to all — not just new — users of a particular Windows NT computer. Whenever a user logs on to a Windows NT computer, any shortcuts or applications placed in the Desktop and Start Menu subfolders of the local All Users profile folder appear on the user's desktop and/or Start Menu, as appropriate. Only members of the Administrators group on the local computer can customize the All Users profile folder.

Currently, there is no method to create a domain-wide All Users profile folder on a server. This means that an Administrator must customize the All Users profile folder on each individual Windows NT computer.

To customize the All Users profile folder, follow the same steps you would use to customize the Default User profile folder, except select the All Users profile folder in Windows NT Explorer instead of the Default User profile folder.

Mandatory User Profiles

Mandatory user profiles are user profiles that, when assigned to a user, cannot be changed by the user. A user can make changes to desktop and work environment settings during a single logon session, but these changes are *not* saved to the mandatory user profile when the user logs off. Each time the user logs on, the user's desktop and work environment settings revert to those contained in the mandatory user profile.

In most cases, an administrator permits users to change and customize their own user profiles. There are instances, however, when you might want to use mandatory user profiles:

- When problem users require a significant amount of administrator time
- When an administrator has a large number of users to administer

Occasionally, a problem user modifies his or her profile and needed shortcuts and applications are deleted, and the administrator must constantly fix the user's profile by reinstalling the necessary items. After repairing the user's profile, the administrator might choose to assign the user a mandatory user profile. To make an individual user's profile (either local or roaming) a mandatory user profile, rename the user's Ntuser.dat file in the user's profile folder as Ntuser.man. The mandatory profile becomes effective the next time the user logs on.

Sometimes an administrator needs to create a standardized desktop and work environment for a large number of users with similar job tasks. To accomplish this, the administrator can assign a single, customized mandatory profile to multiple user accounts.

KNOW THIS Using Mandatory profiles

If you assign a user a mandatory user profile and the profile cannot be accessed or found, the user will be unable to log on to the computer. Avoid using mandatory profiles for administrative accounts for this reason.

Have You Mastered?

Now it's time to apply what you've learned in this chapter by testing your mastery of the material. These questions provide you with a means to determine if you are ready to move on to the next chapter or if you need to review the material again.

1. **You are installing a new Windows NT Workstation computer. The first time you try to log on to the system, you use the Guest user account, but you are denied logon access. What is the most likely problem?**

   ☐ A. The Guest account is disabled.
   ☐ B. The Guest account has a user profile configured and it cannot be located.
   ☐ C. The computer belongs to a domain, and the local Guest account is not permitted to log on to the computer.
   ☐ D. The Guest account has a home directory configured and it cannot be located.

   The correct answer is **A**. When Windows NT Workstation is installed, the Guest account is disabled by default. This is to prevent unauthorized access to local and network resources without your consent. If the account had a user profile configured that could not be located, the user could still log on, unless it was a mandatory profile. If the home directory cannot be located, a user account will be permitted to log on as well. For more information, see the "Creating and Managing User Accounts" section of this chapter.

2. **What Windows NT feature can you use to increase the security of connections made to a Windows NT Remote Access Server?**

    ☐ A. Configure the user accounts for Call Back security set as **Set By Caller**.

    ☐ B. Configure the user accounts for Call Back security set as **Preset To**.

    ☐ C. Assign the user accounts a mandatory profile.

    ☐ D. Add the user accounts to the **Users** group.

The correct answer is **B**. If a user account is configured for Call Back security, the RAS server will hang up the connection and call the user back. If Call Back is configured as Preset To, the user must be at a predefined phone number, or the call back routine will not work. This increases the level of security because even if a hacker guessed a user name and password, he would be unable to receive the call back phone number. For more information, see the "Creating and Managing User Accounts" section of this chapter.

3. **Your Windows NT Workstation computer is a member of a Windows NT domain. You are working with John in the accounting department on a company project. When you try to add the Power Users group on John's computer to your local Power Users group, you are unable to see John's group. What is the most likely problem?**

    ☐ A. You are not a member of John's Administrators group.

    ☐ B. John is not a member of your Administrators group.

    ☐ C. A local group cannot contain local groups from another computer.

    ☐ D. John's Power Users group is a global group.

The correct answer is **C**. Because local groups are contained in the security database of a local computer, they are not accessible by other computers. The only way that members of John's group can be members of your Power Users group is to create a global group that contains the members of John's group. For more information, see the "Creating and Managing Groups" section of this chapter.

4. **You want to add an icon to the desktop for all of the users on your Windows NT Workstation computer. All of your users have roaming user profiles assigned to their accounts. Where should you place the icon?**

   ☐ A. In the `<winntroot>\Profiles\All Users\Desktop` folder on each computer.

   ☐ B. In the `Profiles\All Users\Desktop` folder on the server containing the roaming profiles.

   ☐ C. In the `<winntroot>\Profiles\Default User\Desktop` folder on each computer.

   ☐ D. In the `<winntroot>\Profiles\Default User\Desktop` folder on the server containing the roaming profiles.

The correct answer is **A**. Because there is no way to define a company-wide roaming All Users profile, you must make the change on each Windows NT computer. The Default User profile is only used when a user logs on to the computer and does not have a local or roaming profile already defined for her. For more information, see the "Managing User Profiles" section of this chapter.

5. **A Windows NT Workstation local group can contain which of the following user and group types? (Choose two.)**

   ☐ A. Local groups on other Windows NT computers.
   ☐ B. Global groups from the computer's domain.
   ☐ C. Local groups from the computer's security database.
   ☐ D. User accounts from other Windows NT computers.

The correct answers are **B** and **D**. Local groups cannot contain any other local group, including groups defined on the computer itself. For more information, see the "Creating and Managing Groups" section.

6. You want to create a location on the network that enables users to store their personal files. You want the users to have access to the location wherever they are on the network, and regardless of which computer they use. What should you do?

☐ A. Configure each user account with a home directory.

☐ B. Configure each user account with a mandatory profile.

☐ C. Create a user profile for each user and add them to the Replicator global group.

☐ D. Create a mandatory user profile for each user and add them to the Power Users group.

The correct answer is **A**. A Home directory is a special configuration that is used to connect users to a shared folder, or local folder, to store their personal files automatically. Each time a user logs on to a Windows NT computer, their home directory folder is automatically connected. If a profile is configured properly, it could be used to connect to a shared folder; however, if the location ever needs to be changed, updating the profiles would be very difficult (if not impossible) to accomplish. For more information, see the "Creating and Managing User Accounts" section.

7. You want to enable users to log on to any computer and use their personal user profile. What must you do in order to configure their existing profiles to be a roaming profile and to make it a mandatory profile? (Choose three.)

☐ A. Rename the users' Ntuser.dat profile as Ntuser.man.

☐ B. Rename the users' Ntuser.usr profile as Ntuser.dat.

☐ C. Use the Windows Explorer to copy the users' profiles to a shared folder.

☐ D. Use the System icon in control panel to change to profile type to roaming.

☐ E. Define a Home directory for each user account.

☐ F. Define a profile path for each user account.

The correct answers are **A**, **D**, and **F**. Because you want to retain the current profiles that have been defined on the computer, you must first change the profile type using the System icon in Control Panel. You can then change the profile file, `Ntuser.dat` to a `.man` file which makes it a mandatory profile. Then you can define a profile path for each user account. You cannot use the Windows Explorer to copy or move user profiles around. For more information, see the "Creating and Managing User Accounts" and "Creating and Managing Profiles" sections of this chapter.

Practice Your Skills

Here is a chance to apply your practical, hands-on experience and material from this chapter. These exercises are designed for you to apply not only the material in the book, but to gain greater experience and exposure to the product. These exercises are a critical part of understanding the product and gaining valuable experience in using the product and passing the certification exam. For each of the following problems, consider the given facts and determine what you think are the possible causes of the problem and what course of action you might take to resolve the problem.

1. Troubleshooting Remote Access Server

EXERCISE Every time you connect to your Windows NT Remote Access Server and authenticate yourself, the server hangs up. When you call back the phone number is busy. What is the most likely problem?

ANALYSIS Most likely, your account has Call Back security enabled. Because the server is disconnecting after you authenticate yourself, and the phone is busy when you call back, the server is likely attempting to reach you at a predefined phone number. Either change the Call Back security option or disable Call Back security.

2. Built-in group permissions

EXERCISE You have a Windows NT Workstation that is shared between everyone in the office. You want to enable some users to manage the system, including new users and changing passwords. You do not want to permit these users to change the system's Administrator account or its password. What should you do?

ANALYSIS The Power Users group permits members to add new accounts, share files and printers, but does not permit them to make changes to the Administrator account or the local Administrators group. This is a lot easier than trying to assign each user the specific user rights they would need to accomplish the tasks required.

3. Using local groups

EXERCISE Your Windows NT Workstation computer is a member of a Windows NT domain. What must you do so that you can add members of a local group on another computer to one of your local groups?

ANALYSIS Local groups can only be used on the computer containing the security database within which the local group is defined. As a result, you must create a global group, place members in the group, and then add the global group as a member of your local group.

4. Implementing mandatory profiles

EXERCISE You are considering implementing mandatory user profiles for your company. You have several different types of users in your company; some perform just data entry, while others help design software programs. What are some of the benefits and drawbacks to mandatory profiles?

ANALYSIS Mandatory profiles are best suited for environments where the workflow of the user is pre-
dictable, such as a data entry clerk who uses only two or three
applications. Mandatory profiles usually do not offer enough flexi-
bility for power users, such as engineers and programmers. As a
result, there may be a clash between you and your users if you
attempt to implement profiles that do not work with their job
requirements. When mandatory profiles are employed, users are
unable to make changes to the desktop settings; at the same
time, however, they are guaranteed a desktop that is always the
same, regardless of any "playing" they may have done previously.
The other disadvantage is that if a mandatory profile cannot be
located, the user will not be permitted to log on to the network.

Sharing and Securing File Systems

PREPARING FOR THE WORKSTATION exam wouldn't be complete without a look at security and sharing resources on a Windows NT Workstation computer. In this chapter we take a look at file and folder attributes, share permissions and assigning user and group permissions. We also examine how NTFS permissions are applied to new, moved, and copied files and folders; and how NTFS and share permissions interact. The chapter wraps up with troubleshooting common resource access and permission problems.

Exam Material in This Chapter

Based on Microsoft Objectives

Planning

- Planning strategies for sharing and securing resources

Managing Resources

- Setting up shared folders and permissions
- Setting permissions on NTFS partitions, folders, and files

Troubleshooting

- Choosing the appropriate course of action to take when a user cannot access a resource

Based on Author's Experience

- You need to know that user and group permissions are additive, and the *least* restrictive permission is the user's effective permission.
- You should know how NTFS and folder permissions are applied when they conflict.
- You must understand how to determine effective permissions when a user has explicit user permissions and group permissions.
- You should expect to see some questions on what happens to permissions when files and folders are moved between NTFS volumes.

Are You Prepared?

Do you have what it takes? Try out these self-assessment questions to see if you have prepared for the material in this chapter or if you should review problem areas.

1. **You are assigning a user access rights to a shared folder. You grant his account Full Control. The user belongs to the accounting group, which has been granted Read permissions for the folder, and also belongs to the Marketing group, which has been granted the No Access permission for the folder. What are the user's effective rights for the folder?**

   - ☐ A. Full Control
   - ☐ B. Read
   - ☐ C. No Access
   - ☐ D. Write
   - ☐ E. Special Access

2. **When you move a file from an NTFS volume to another NTFS volume, what happens to the file permissions?**

   - ☐ A. They stay the same.
   - ☐ B. They inherit the access permissions of the new folder containing it.
   - ☐ C. The Everyone group is automatically granted Full Control.
   - ☐ D. The Everyone group is automatically granted No Access.

3. **Your Windows NT Workstation computer has a Floppy disk (A:), two hard disks (C: and D:), and a CD-ROM drive (E:). What**

Administrative shares are automatically created when you boot Windows NT? (Choose all that apply.)

- ☐ A. Admin$
- ☐ B. C$
- ☐ C. D$
- ☐ D. E$
- ☐ E. A$
- ☐ F. yourcomputername$

1. C   *No Access always overrides all other share permissions. If a user has the Full Control permission, but is a member of a group that has the No Access permission, the user's effective permission is No Access. See the "Shared Folder Permissions" section.*

2. B   *When a file or folder is moved between NTFS volumes, the file permissions are set to match the permissions of the folder containing the file on the new NTFS volume. If the file is moved or copied within the same volume, the permissions remain the same. See the "NTFS Permissions for New, Moved, and Copied Files and Folders" section.*

3. A, B, *Administrative shares are automatically created for* and *each hard disk volume, but not for removable media* C *such as floppy disks and CD-ROMs. See the "Administrative Shares" section.*

File and Folder Attributes

Windows NT files and folders have various *attributes*, some of which the administrator can use to provide a limited amount of data protection (see Figure 6-1). For example, administrators often use the read-only file attribute to prevent accidental deletion of files, such as application files. Other file and folder attributes are applied by Windows NT system files automatically during installation.

File attributes can be used on both FAT and NTFS partitions, with the exception of the Compress attribute, which is only available on NTFS partitions.

Table 6.1 lists and describes the five Windows NT file and folder attributes.

TABLE 6.1 Windows NT File and Folder Attributes

Attribute	Description
Archive	Indicates that the file or folder has been modified since the last backup. Is applied by the operating system when a file or folder is saved or created, and is commonly removed by backup programs after the file or folder has been backed up. Is normally not changed by the administrator.
Compress	Indicates that Windows NT has compressed the file or folder. Is only available on NTFS partitions. Uses the same compression algorithm as the MS-DOS 6.0 DoubleSpace utility. Can be set on individual files. Is applied by administrators to control which files and folders will be compressed.
Hidden	Indicates that the file or folder can't be seen in a normal directory scan. Files or folders with this attribute can't be copied or deleted. Is applied to various files and folders by NT automatically during installation.

Continued

137

TABLE 6.1 *Continued*

Attribute	Description
Read-only	Indicates that the file or folder can only be read. It can't be written to or deleted. Is often applied by administrators to prevent accidental deletion of application files.
System	Indicates that the file or folder is used by the operating system. Files or folders with this attribute can't be seen in a normal directory scan. Files or folders with this attribute can't be copied or deleted. Is applied to various files and folders by NT automatically during installation.

 The archive attribute is prime target for exam questions, especially for backup and restore objectives.

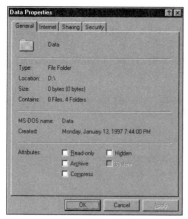

Figure 6-1 *Setting file or folder attributes*

File Attributes

Any user who can access a file or folder on a FAT partition can modify that file or folder's attributes. Any user who has the Write (W) NTFS permission (or any permission that includes the Write (W) permission) to a file or folder on an NTFS partition can modify that file or folder's attributes.

On NTFS volumes, when a file or folder has the Read-only attribute, and the file or folder also has the Write (W) NTFS permission for a user or group, the Read-only attribute takes precedence. The Read-only attribute must be removed before the file can be modified or deleted.

Shared Folders

In Windows NT, folders are *shared* to enable users to access network resources. Users cannot access a folder across the network until it is shared or placed within another folder that is shared. Once a folder is shared, users with the appropriate permissions can access the shared folder (and all folders and files that the shared folder contains) over the network (see Figure 6-2).

A shared folder appears in Windows NT Explorer and My Computer as a folder with a hand under it. A shared folder is often referred to as a *share*.

 Only members of the Administrators, Server Operators, and Power Users built-in local groups can share folders.

Only certain users can share folders. Members of the Administrators local group can share folders on any Windows NT computer; members of the Server Operators group can share folders on all Windows NT domain controllers; and members of the Power Users group can share folders on all Windows NT non-domain controllers, including Windows NT Workstation computers.

When a folder is shared, its *entire contents* (including all files and subfolders) are available to users who have the appropriate permissions to the share. Because all files and subfolders are accessible when a folder is shared, you should consider which groups and users need access to folders when you design your folder structure.

When sharing a folder, it's a good idea to assign it a share name that's easily recognized by users and one that appropriately describes the resources contained in the folder. Otherwise, users can become frustrated trying to find the specific network resources they need. Additionally, keep in mind when you assign a name to a shared folder that a long share name may *not* be readable by all client computers on your network. You can use Windows NT Explorer to share folders.

 TEST TRAP You can use Windows NT Explorer to share folders on a local Windows NT Workstation computer. However, you cannot use Windows NT Explorer to share folders on remote computers.

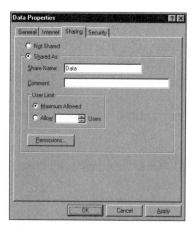

Figure 6-2 *Using Windows NT Explorer to share a folder*

If you want to restrict user access to the folders that you have shared, you can assign shared folder permissions.

Shared Folder Permissions

Shared folder permissions control user access to shared folders. Shared folder permissions only apply when users connect to the folder over the network — they do not apply when users access the folder from the local computer.

Shared folder permissions do not apply when users access the folder from the local computer.

Shared folder permissions (commonly called *share permissions*) apply to the shared folder, its files, and subfolders (in other words, to the *entire* directory tree under the shared folder).

Share permissions are the only folder and file security available on a FAT partition (with the exception of file attributes), and control only over-the-network access to share — local access is totally unrestricted on a FAT partition.

Table 6.2 lists and describes the Windows NT share permissions, from the most restrictive to the least restrictive.

TABLE 6.2 Windows NT Share Permissions

Permission	Description
No Access	Permits a user to connect to a share only, but prevents a user from accessing the shared folder and its contents.
Read	Permits a user to view file and folder names. Permits a user to change current folder to a subfolder of the share. Permits a user to view data in files; and to run application files.
Change	Permits a user to perform all tasks included in the Read permission. Permits a user to create files and folders within the share; to edit data files and save changes; and to delete files and folders within the share.
Full Control	Permits a user to perform all tasks included in the Change permission. Permits a user to change NTFS permissions (discussed later in this chapter) — this only applies to shares on NTFS partitions. Permits a user to take ownership of files and folders — this only applies to shares on NTFS partitions.

Shared folder permissions are prime targets for exam questions.

Share permissions are assigned by adding a user or group to the permissions list for the share (see Figure 6-3). From an administrative standpoint, it's much more efficient to add groups to the permissions list for a particular share than to add individual users. By default, the Everyone group is granted Full Control permission to all newly created shared folders.

When assigning permissions to a share, you should consider assigning the most restrictive permission that still allows users to accomplish the tasks they need to perform. For example, on shares that contain applications, consider assigning the Read permission so that users can't accidentally delete application files.

You can assign share permissions by using Windows NT Explorer.

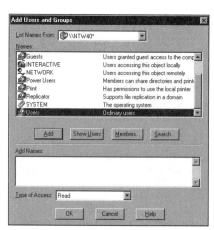

Figure 6-3 *Adding users and groups to the permissions list for the share*

Combining User and Group Permissions

It is not uncommon for a user to have permission to a share and to be a member of multiple groups that have different permissions to that share.

When this occurs, the user and group permissions are additive, and the *least* restrictive permission is the user's effective permission. For example, a user has the Read permission to a share, and a group that the user is a member of has the Change permission to the share. The user's effective share permission is Change.

The exception to this rule is the No Access permission. *No Access always overrides all other share permissions.* If a user has the Full Control permission, but is a member of a group that has the No Access permission, the user's effective permission is No Access. *No Access always means no access.*

Multiple Access Rights Rule

When a user belongs to multiple groups with different permissions to a shared folder, the user and group permissions are additive. The exception is that No Access permission overrides all other share permissions. If a user or a group the user belongs to has been assigned the No Access permission, the user's effective rights are No Access — period!

Administrative Shares

Every time you start Windows NT on a computer, NT automatically creates several hidden shares that only members of the Administrators group have permission to access. These shares are referred to as *administrative shares* because they are used by Administrators to perform administrative tasks.

The Windows NT administrative shares are: C$, D$, E$, and so on (one share for the root of each hard disk partition on the computer); and a share named Admin$, which corresponds to the folder in which NT is installed (<winntroot>). The $ at the end of each administrative share causes the share to be hidden from users when they browse the network.

Administrative shares make it possible for an Administrator to connect to any hard drive on a computer and access all of its files and folders, regardless of whether regular shares exist on that hard drive. In this way an Administrator can perform backup, restore, and other administrative functions on a Windows NT computer.

Any share can be configured as a hidden share by placing a $ at the end of its share name. However, hiding a share by appending a $ to the share name does *not* limit user access to the share. The hidden share retains its assigned share permissions. Only access to the hidden *administrative* shares is restricted, by default, to Administrators only.

POP QUIZ **True or False?**

1. The compress attribute is available on FAT and NTFS partitions.

2. Windows 95 computers can only see share names up to 12 characters long.

3. Only the Administrators group can create shared folders.

4. No Access always overrides all other share permissions.

5. By default, the Everyone group is granted Read permission to all newly created shared folders.

Answers: *1. False 2. True 3. False 4. True 5. False*

NTFS File and Folder Security

When files and folders are stored on an NTFS volume, NTFS permissions can be assigned to provide a greater level of security than share permissions, because:

- NTFS permissions, unlike share permissions, can be assigned to individual files as well as folders. This gives an administrator a much finer level of control over shared files and folders than is possible by using only share permissions.

- NTFS permissions apply to local users as well as to users who connect to a shared folder over the network. This fills

the large security loophole left when files and folders on
FAT partitions are secured only by share permissions.

The following sections discuss NTFS permissions, including how
they are assigned to files and folders, how NTFS permissions are applied,
and how NTFS and share permissions interact.

NTFS Permissions

NTFS permissions, which can only be assigned to files and folders on
NTFS volumes, protect data from authorized access when users connect
to the share locally or over the network.

The NTFS permissions that can be assigned, and how each permission applies to folders and files, are shown in Table 6.3.

TABLE 6.3 Windows NT NTFS Permissions

Permission	When applied to a folder, a user is able to . . .	When applied to a file, as user is able to . . .
Read (R)	View folder attributes, permissions, and owner; view names of files and subfolders.	View file attributes, permissions, owner, and file contents.
Write (W)	View folder attributes, permissions, and owner; change folder attributes; add files and subfolders.	View file attributes, permissions, and owner; change file attributes; change file contents.
Execute (X)	View folder attributes, permissions, and owner; change the current folder to a subfolder.	View file attributes, permissions, and owner; run the file if it is an executable program.
Delete (D)	Delete the folder.	Delete the file.
Change Permissions (P)	Assign NTFS permissions to the folder.	Assign NTFS permissions to the file.
Take Ownership (O)	Take ownership of the folder.	Take ownership of the file.

Table 6.4 shows the standard NTFS directory permissions. The permissions specified within the first set of parentheses following the permission name apply to the *folder*, and the permissions specified within the second set of parentheses following the permission name apply to *files* within the folder.

TABLE 6.4 Standard NTFS Directory (Folder) Permissions

Standard Permission	Description
No Access (None) (None)	Prevents access to the folder, and to any file in the folder. When the permission is initially assigned, the administrator can choose whether to apply the permission to existing files and subfolders.
List (RX) (Not Specified)	Assigns the Read and Execute permissions to the folder, but no permissions are assigned to any files in the folder.
Read (RX) (RX)	Assigns the Read and Execute permissions to the folder and to *new* files created in the folder. When the permission is initially assigned, the administrator can choose whether to apply the permission to all *existing* files and subfolders.
Add (WX) (Not Specified)	Assigns the Write and Execute permissions to the folder, but no permissions are assigned to any files in the folder.
Add & Read (RWX) (RX)	Assigns the Read, Write, and Execute permissions to the folder, and assigns the Read and Execute permissions to *new* files created in the folder. When the permission is initially assigned, the administrator can choose whether to apply the permission to all *existing* files and subfolders.

Standard Permission	Description
Change (RWXD) (RWXD)	Assigns the Read, Write, Execute, and Delete permissions to the folder and to *new* files created in the folder. When the permission is initially assigned, the administrator can choose whether to apply the permission to all *existing* files and subfolders.
Full Control (All) (All)	Assigns all NTFS permissions (Read, Write, Execute, Delete, Change Permissions, and Take Ownership) to the folder and to *new* files created in the folder. When the permission is initially assigned, the administrator can choose whether to apply the permission to all *existing* files and subfolders.

Table 6.5 shows the standard NTFS file permissions. NTFS file permissions apply only to the individual file they are assigned to. Other files in the same folder are *not* affected.

TABLE 6.5 Standard NTFS File Permissions

Standard File Permission	Description
No Access (None)	Prevents access to the file.
Read (RX)	Assigns the Read and Execute permissions to the file.
Change (RWXD)	Assigns the Read, Write, Execute, and Delete permissions to the file.
Full Control (All)	Assigns all NTFS permissions (Read, Write, Execute, Delete, Change Permissions, and Take Ownership) to the file.

Sometimes a user has a different set of NTFS permissions to a file than to the folder that contains the file. When the user wants to access a file, and the NTFS file and folder permissions conflict, the file permissions are applied. For example, if a user has the Change (RWXD)

(RWXD) permission to the folder, and has the Read (RX) permission to the file, the user's effective permission to the file is Read (RX).

If a user has permission to access a file, but does *not* have permission to access the folder that contains the file, the user can access the file by typing the file's full path name (in an application, in the Run dialog box, or at the command prompt). The user can't see the file when browsing in Windows NT Explorer.

Be sure to remember this for the test: File permissions take precedence over folder permissions.

As with share permissions, it is not uncommon for a user to have one set of NTFS permissions to a file or folder, and to be a member of multiple groups that have different NTFS permissions to the file or folder. When this occurs, the user and group permissions are additive, and the *least* restrictive combination of permissions applies. The exception to this rule is the No Access permission. *No Access always overrides all other NTFS permissions.*

Think through the scenarios presented in the exam questions. There is usually at least one piece of information that should make it obvious what the answer is.

NTFS permissions are assigned by adding a user or group to the *access control list* (ACL) for the file or folder. From an administrative standpoint, it's much more efficient to add groups to the ACL for a particular file or folder than to add individual users. By default, the Everyone group is granted the Full Control (All) (All) NTFS permission to the root of all newly created NTFS volumes.

NTFS Permissions for New, Moved, and Copied Files and Folders

When files are created in a folder on an NTFS volume, the new files inherit the NTFS permissions of the folder in which they are created. For example, if you create a new file in the Public folder, and the Public folder has the Change (RWXD) (RWXD) NTFS permission for the

Everyone group, the new file inherits the Change (RWXD) permission for the Everyone group.

Permissions for New Files

The permissions in the *second* set of parentheses following the NTFS folder permission name are the permissions that are assigned to the new *file*. So, if you create a new file in the Data folder, and the Data folder has the Add & Read (RWX) (RX) NTFS permission for the Users group, the file inherits the Read (RX) permission for the Users group.

When new subfolders are created on an NTFS volume, they inherit the NTFS permissions of the folder that contains them. For example, if you create a new subfolder in the Data folder, and the Data folder has the Add & Read (RWX) (RX) NTFS permission for the Everyone group, the new subfolder inherits the Add & Read (RWX) (RX) permission for the Everyone group.

NTFS Permission Inheritance

- When you create a file or folder on an NTFS volume, the file or folder inherits the permissions of the folder in which they were created.

- When you move or copy files or folders to a different NTFS volume, the files' or folders' permissions will be set to match the folder that contains them.

- When you move or copy files or folders within the same NTFS volume, the files' or folders' permissions do not change.

When files or folders are moved or copied, their NTFS permissions often change. Normally, when files or folders are moved or copied, they inherit the NTFS permissions of the destination folder. The only exception to this rule is when files or folders are *moved* to a new folder on the *same*

NTFS volume — in this case, the moved files or folders retain their original NTFS permissions.

Because FAT partitions can't support NTFS permissions, any files that you copy or move to a FAT partition lose all their NTFS permissions, along with the security that those permissions provided.

NTFS and Share Permissions

When users access a share on an NTFS volume over the network, *both* NTFS and share permissions are used to determine the user's effective permission to the file or folder in the share. This means that if *either* the NTFS or the share permissions deny a user access, access is denied.

True or False?

1. File permissions take precedence over folder permissions.

2. A user can set permissions for a file if the user has the Change Permissions NTFS permission to the file.

3. When you move files between NTFS partitions, the file permissions stay the same.

4. A user can set permissions for a file only if the user is the owner of the file.

5. Shared folder permissions take precedence over NTFS file permissions.

Answers: *1. True 2. True 3. False 4. False 5. False*

When NTFS and share permissions differ, the *most* restrictive permission becomes the user's effective permission to the file or folder in the share.

Troubleshooting Common Resource Access and Permission Problems

When a user can't access a resource (that he or she is supposed to be able to access), the administrator must determine why this is happening and correct the problem. Most resource access problems are caused by incorrectly configured and/or conflicting permissions.

Here are some recommended troubleshooting tips to help you to determine why a user can't access a shared network resource:

- **Look for conflicting share and NTFS permissions.** Determine which groups the user is a member of (including groups in other domains), and determine the user's effective share permission and effective NTFS permissions to the resource.

- **Look for the No Access permission.** If the user, or any group of which the user is a member, has been assigned the No Access permission to the share or has been assigned the No Access NTFS permission to the resource, the user will not be able to access the resource.

- If you have just assigned the user permission to the resource, and the user can't access the resource, **try having the user log off and log on again**, so the user's access token will be updated.

Have You Mastered?

Now it's time to apply what you've learned in this chapter by testing your mastery of the material. These questions provide you with a means to determine if you are ready to move on to the next chapter or if you need to review the material again.

1. **You are managing a group of folders on a Windows NT Workstation computer. When you look at the attributes that are available for the files, you notice the Compress attribute is not shown. Why not?**

   ☐ A. You have insufficient permissions to configure the Compress attribute.
   ☐ B. The folders are on a FAT partition.
   ☐ C. The folders are on a NTFS partition.
   ☐ D. The folders are in a Windows NT stripe set.

   The correct answer is **B**. The Compress attribute is available only on NTFS partitions, because only NTFS partitions have the ability to compress at the folder or file level. For more information, see the "File and Folder Attributes" section.

2. **You belong to three Windows NT groups, whose respective share permissions are Change, Read, and Full Control. What is your effective share permission?**

   ☐ A. Change
   ☐ B. Read
   ☐ C. Full Control
   ☐ D. Special Access

The correct answer is **C**. User and group access permissions are additive, and the least restrictive access is your effective access permission. So in this case your effective access permission for the share is Full Control. For more information, see the "Combining User and Group Permissions" section.

3. **You belong to three Windows NT groups, whose respective share permissions are No Access, Read, and Full Control. What is your effective share permission?**

   ☐ A. No Access
   ☐ B. Read
   ☐ C. Full Control
   ☐ D. Special Access

The correct answer is **A**. This is the exception to the rule, even though user and group permissions are additive, if No Access is specified for the user or a group, the effective permission for the share is No Access. For more information, see the "Combining User and Group Permissions" section.

4. **You are the network administrator for a network consisting of Windows NT Server computers and Windows NT Workstation computers. You need to update a few files on the C drive in one of the Windows NT Workstation computers. What can you do to access the hard drive of the Windows NT Workstation computer from your computer?**

   ☐ A. Connect to the Windows NT Workstation computer's `Admin$` share.
   ☐ B. Connect to the Windows NT Workstation computer's `C$` share.
   ☐ C. You cannot remotely access the hard drive of a Windows NT Workstation computer.
   ☐ D. Tell the user of the Windows NT Workstation computer to share the C drive, as it is not shared by default.

The correct answer is **B**. By default, Windows NT automatically creates an administrative share for every hard drive partition in your computer. The administrative shares are named after their logical drive letter assignment and the $ sign is appended to hide the share from network browsers. For more information, see the "Administrative Shares" section.

5. **You are configuring the security settings and user group assignments for your Windows NT domain network. You want to allow users to create shared folders on their workstations, but you do not want them to be able to make changes to the Administrators local group. What groups can you place the users in? (Choose all that apply.)**

   ☐ A. Administrators
   ☐ B. Power Users
   ☐ C. Server Operators
   ☐ D. Users

The correct answers are **A** and **B**. The Administrators and Power Users groups will allow users to create shared folders on a Windows NT Workstation. However, if the users were placed in the Administrators group, there would be nothing to prevent them from making changes to the group or even changing the administrators password. The Users group has no permissions to add shared folders or printers on a Windows NT Workstation computer. For more information, see the "Shared Folders" section.

6. **You are configuring the share permissions for a project folder on your Windows NT Workstation computer. You want to allow everyone in the Marketing department to have Read access to the folder. You want everyone in the Engineering department to have Full Control to the folder. You configure the share permissions by granting the Marketing user group Read access and the Engineering user group Full Control. When users in the Engineering department attempt to make changes to the folder**

they get an access denied message, but they are able to read the files in the folder. What is the most likely problem?

- ☐ A. The folder is on a FAT partition that has FAT permissions set as Read only.
- ☐ B. The users are only members of the Marketing user group.
- ☐ C. The users are members of both the Marketing and Engineering user groups.
- ☐ D. The folder is on an NTFS partition that has NTFS permissions set as Read only.

The correct answer is **D**. When NTFS file permissions and share permissions are different, the most restrictive access permissions become the users effective permissions. In this case the NTFS permissions were set as Read only, so no matter what share permissions were granted, the file system would only allow read access. For more information, see the "NTFS and Share Permissions" section.

7. You are moving a marketing ad campaign project folder from your Windows NT Workstation computer to a Windows NT Server computer. On your computer the folder had NTFS permissions that allowed only the marketing department Full Control; the Everyone group was granted No Access. The folder that will contain the project folder on the Windows NT Server computer has NTFS permissions that grant Change permissions to the Everyone group. What are the NTFS permissions for the folder after it has been moved?

- ☐ A. The permissions will stay the same, the marketing group will have Full Control and the Everyone group will have No Access.
- ☐ B. The permissions will be set back to the default with the Everyone group having Full Control.
- ☐ C. The permissions will be set to match the new folder's permissions with the Everyone group having Change permissions.
- ☐ D. The permissions will be set so that only the Administrators group has Full Control.

The correct answer is C. When files or folders are moved off of a partition, to another partition or another computer, the file permissions inherit the permissions of the folder containing the moved files or folders. If the files/folders are moved within the same partition the file permissions will remain the same. For more information, see the "NTFS Permissions for New, Moved, and Copied Files and Folders" section.

Practice Your Skills

Here is a chance to apply your practical, hands-on experience and material from this chapter. These exercises are designed for you to apply not only the material in the book, but to gain greater experience and exposure to the product. These exercises are a critical part of understanding the product and gaining valuable experience for using the product and passing the certification exam. For each of the following problems, consider the given facts and determine what you think are the possible causes of the problem and what course of action you might take to resolve the problem.

1. Sharing folders

EXERCISE You are the network administrator for a Windows NT domain network. You receive a phone call from a user who says he is unable to share a folder on his Windows NT Workstation computer. You walk him through the steps, but he is still unable to share the folder. What is the most likely problem?

ANALYSIS The user is probably not a member of the Administrators or Power Users groups on his Windows NT Workstation computer. You need to either add him to one of these groups on his computer or you need to create the share while logged in with your administrative account.

2. Limiting access to a shared folder

EXERCISE You are configuring the permissions for a shared folder on your network. You have assigned the Marketing and Sales user groups Change permissions for the share. You need to prevent the interns in the Marketing and Sales department from accessing the files in the shared folder. What can you do to prevent these few users from accessing the files?

ANALYSIS The No Access share permission over-rides all other assigned permissions. So you can configure the share permissions and grant the user accounts for the interns the No Access permission.

3. Moving files to a new hard disk

EXERCISE You are in the process of adding a new hard disk to your Windows NT Workstation computer. You want to move your project data files from the older, smaller hard disk to the new, larger hard disk. What is the largest problem you are likely to encounter after moving the files?

ANALYSIS Since the new hard disk will be in addition to the existing one, when the files are moved, all of the NTFS file permissions will be lost. When the files are placed on the new hard disk, the files will inherit the permission settings set on the hard disk, or the folder containing the files. Before moving the files, document the NTFS file permission configuration and recreate the permissions after the files have been moved.

Managing Printing

S YOU CONTINUE YOUR PREPARATION for the Workstation exam it is important to look into managing printers. In this chapter I show you how to create and connect to printers, as well as use drag-and-drop printers. I then cover the different print monitors that Windows NT Workstation provides to access print devices and print queues on a variety of hardware and software configurations. Next, it's on to a look at printer permissions and configuring printer properties. The chapter wraps up with an examination of some troubleshooting steps for common print problems.

Exam Material in This Chapter

Based on Microsoft Objectives

Managing Resources

- Installing and configuring printers in a given environment

Troubleshooting

- Choosing the appropriate course of action to take when a print job fails

Based on Author's Experience

- You should be aware of the benefits of using *enhanced metafile* (EMF) or RAW printer spool configurations.

- You need to be familiar with the process of connecting to and using drag-and-drop printers.

- You must understand the difference between the various print monitors, the platforms they support, and general configuration settings for each monitor.

- You should be familiar with the benefits of using the NetWare print monitor.

- You may see some questions about using separator pages.

- You definitely need to understand printer permissions and what happens when a user is assigned conflicting permission settings.

Are You Prepared?

Do you have what it takes? Try out these self-assessment questions to see if you're prepared for the material in this chapter or if you should review problem areas.

1. Your network consists of three network segments connected together with a router. You want to create a shared Windows NT Workstation printer for your network users. The print device has an HP JetDirect Network Card installed. What port monitor should you use to connect to the printer?

☐ A. Localmon
☐ B. Hpmon
☐ C. TCP/IP
☐ D. NetWare

2. A user belongs to the Marketing user group, which has been granted Print permission. The user also belongs to the Interns user group, which has been assigned the No Access permission. What is the user's effective permission for the printer?

☐ A. Print permission
☐ B. No Access permission
☐ C. Manage Documents permission
☐ D. Read only permission

3. You are connecting a dual-language print device to your Windows NT Workstation computer. The printer supports the PCL and Postscript printer languages. The printer cannot automatically detect the language of an incoming print job.

What can you do to switch between the printer languages as needed?

- ☐ A. Create two printers, one with Postscript drivers and the other with PCL drivers.
- ☐ B. Create two printers and assign a separator page that switches between the languages.
- ☐ C Assign all the printer users the Manage Documents permission.
- ☐ D Assign all printer users the Full Control permission.

Answers:

1. C   *TCP/IP. Most of the new JetDirect cards support TCP/IP and DLC, but the network is connected with a router, so DLC cannot be used because it's a nonroutable protocol. See the "Print Monitors" section.*

2. B   *Printer permissions behave just like share permissions; they are additive, except if the user has been assigned No Access. The users effective permissions are No Access, as it overrides all other permissions. See the "Printer Security" section.*

3. B   *Windows NT can use separator pages that contain instructions to have printers switch between PCL and Postscript printer languages. Just creating two printers with different drivers does not solve the problem. See the "Printer Properties" section.*

Printing Terminology

In Windows NT, the term *printer* does not represent a physical device that produces printed output. Rather, a printer is the software interface between the Windows NT operating system and the device that produces printed output.

In Windows NT, the term *print device* refers to the physical device that produces printed output — more commonly referred to as a "printer."

 Remember: A *printer* is software, and a *print* (or *printing*) *device* is hardware. Be sure you understand the Windows NT printing terminology to avoid confusion when taking the exam.

EMFs in Network Printing

Using Windows NT *enhanced metafiles* (EMFs) can significantly increase the performance of printing across a network for the following reasons:

- Windows NT creates an EMF faster than it can create a RAW format file.
- Windows NT splits the overhead of the print process between the local computer (which creates the EMF) and the network-connected computer (which converts the EMF to the RAW format).

This means that the user who creates the print job experiences faster printing than if the RAW format file was created locally on the user's computer.

Creating and Connecting to Printers

Two ways are available to install and configure a printer in Windows NT: You can either create a printer, or you can connect to a shared network printer.

Creating a printer involves installing and configuring all the drivers needed to use a locally managed print device. Connecting to a shared network printer involves installing and configuring all the drivers needed to use a print device managed by another computer on the network. You can either connect to a shared network printer by using the Add Printer Wizard in the `Printers` folder, or you can use drag-and-drop printing to connect to a shared network printer.

Drag-and-Drop Printing

Drag-and-drop printing is an easy way to connect to a shared network printer, because drag-and-drop printing requires less user interaction than using the Add Printer Wizard interactively.

To use drag-and-drop printing to connect to a shared network printer, you must first use My Computer to locate a file you want to print. Next use Network Neighborhood to locate the shared network printer (or NetWare print queue) you want to use.

Figure 7-1 shows two windows open on the desktop. Note that one window shows the shares available on a network computer named Bdclab and that the other window contains files in the `Windows` folder. (If you prefer, instead of using My Computer and Network Neighborhood, you can accomplish the same thing by opening two copies of Windows NT Explorer, and then tiling the windows.)

To connect to the shared network printer and print your document, drag the file from the open window and drop it on the shared network printer in the other window. Figure 7-1 shows a document being dropped on the shared printer.

Windows NT displays an information dialog box, which is shown in Figure 7-2. In essence, Windows NT must connect to the shared network printer and install drivers on your local Windows NT computer before the document can be printed.

If you click No, Windows NT automatically cancels your print job. If you click Yes, Windows NT automatically connects to the shared network printer, installs local printer drivers, opens the application the document was created in, prints the document, and closes the application.

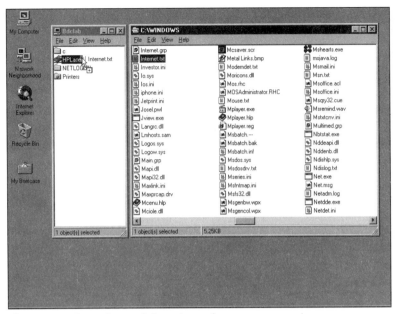

Figure 7-1 *Dragging and dropping a document on a printer*

Figure 7-2 *Instructing NT to install local drivers for a shared network printer*

If you click Yes and the Windows NT computer that hosts the shared network printer does *not* have printer drivers for your version of Windows NT or for your hardware platform (such as Intel, DEC Alpha, MIPS R4000, or PowerPC), or if you are dragging and dropping a document to a NetWare print queue, Windows NT prompts you to select and install appropriate printer drivers before it completes the drag-and-drop printing.

Print Monitors

Print monitors are software components that run in kernel mode. In Windows NT, print monitors send ready-to-print print jobs to a print device, either locally or across the network. Print monitors are also called *port monitors.*

When you create a printer, you select the port to which the print device is connected. Each port is associated with one specific print monitor.

The most commonly used print monitors are Localmon, Hpmon, Appletalk, TCP/IP, and NetWare.

Localmon

The *Localmon print monitor* sends print jobs to print devices connected to hardware ports on a local Windows NT computer (local hardware ports include LPT1: and COM1:). Localmon is the only print monitor installed by default during the installation of Windows NT. All other print monitors require you to install additional Windows NT services and/or protocols.

Hpmon

The *Hpmon print monitor* sends print jobs to a network print device via a Hewlett-Packard JetDirect adapter. The HP JetDirect adapter may either be installed in the print device or function as a separate external unit.

Hpmon uses the DLC protocol to communicate with HP JetDirect adapters. Most HP JetDirect adapters support multiple protocols, including TCP/IP, IPX, AppleTalk, and DLC. However, Hpmon can only communicate by using the DLC protocol, which is a nonroutable protocol. A Windows NT computer that uses Hpmon can only communicate with HP JetDirect adapters located on the same network segment. In other words, the DLC protocol is not forwarded by a network router to another network segment.

If your network supports bridging, however, you can use DLC to communicate to an HP JetDirect adapter on any network segment connected by a bridge.

The Hpmon print monitor is not installed by default during the installation of Windows NT. Hpmon is installed automatically when you install the DLC protocol. You must install DLC before you can connect to an HP JetDirect adapter using Hpmon.

Watch for exam questions that deal with printing to network-attached printers, such as HP printers. Make sure you read the scenario carefully, and determine if the question deals with the Hpmon port or the TCP/IP port.

Hpmon Connection Type

If a printer isn't shared and you select a continuous connection, only a single user has access to the HP JetDirect adapter for printing. In this situation, you should generally select a job-based connection.

However, if you share the printer associated with the Hpmon port, selecting a continuous connection can make sense. This computer then functions as a print server and manages all print jobs sent to the shared printer. In this situation, all computers on the network that have access to the shared printer have access to the HP JetDirect adapter for printing.

AppleTalk

The *AppleTalk print monitor* sends print jobs to network print devices that support the AppleTalk protocol, which is usually associated with Apple Macintosh computers. Before you can connect to an AppleTalk print device, you must install the AppleTalk protocol on your Windows NT Workstation computer.

AppleTalk is a routable protocol. A Windows NT computer that uses the AppleTalk print monitor can communicate with any AppleTalk print device on any segment of a routed AppleTalk network.

Don't expect to see too many AppleTalk printer questions in the exam.

TCP/IP

The *TCP/IP print monitor* sends print jobs to network print devices that both support TCP/IP *and* function as *line printer daemon* (LPD) print servers. TCP/IP and LPD are normally associated with UNIX computers.

Daemon is a UNIX term. A UNIX daemon performs the same function as a Windows NT service. Basically, a UNIX daemon is a program that runs in the background and performs an operating system service.

Line printer daemon (LPD) is the print server software used in TCP/IP printing. The client print software used in TCP/IP printing is called *line printer remote* (LPR). To connect to a TCP/IP print server that uses LPD, use a TCP/IP print client that uses LPR.

Before you can connect to a TCP/IP print device, you must install TCP/IP and the Microsoft TCP/IP Printing service on your Windows NT computer. To share printers on a Windows NT computer as TCP/IP printers, you must also start the TCP/IP Print Server service. The TCP/IP Print Server service is configured for manual startup by default, so you should configure this service to start automatically.

TCP/IP is a routable protocol. A Windows NT computer that uses the TCP/IP print monitor can communicate with any TCP/IP print device on any segment of a routed TCP/IP network.

Figure 7-3 shows the Add LPD compatible printer dialog box. Notice the IP address of the device providing the LPD service (in this case, an HP JetDirect adapter) and the name of the printer have been entered.

Add LPR compatible printer		
Name or address of server providing lpd:	131.107.2.245	OK
Name of printer or print queue on that server:	hplj5mp	Cancel
		Help

Figure 7-3 *Configuring an LPR port*

Read the exam question scenarios closely to determine which print monitor port the question is about.

The Hpmon port monitor uses the DLC protocol to connect with network-attached print devices. DLC is not routable and is often the subject of many network topology questions involving a router.

The TCP/IP port monitor uses TCP/IP to connect with network-attached print devices. It has a large application, as more vendors support TCP/IP than DLC, and it is a routable protocol.

NetWare

The *NetWare print monitor* sends print jobs to a print queue on a Novell NetWare server. The NetWare server then sends the print job from the print queue to the print device.

A *print queue* is the NetWare term for a shared printer. A NetWare print queue is designed to handle print jobs that are ready to send to the print device and that need no additional conversion or formatting.

Before you can connect to a NetWare print queue, you must install NWLink IPX/SPX Compatible Transport on your Windows NT Workstation computer. In addition, you must install *Client Service for NetWare* (CSNW). NWLink IPX/SPX Compatible Transport is a routable protocol. A Windows NT computer that uses the NetWare print monitor can communicate with any NetWare server on any segment of a routed NetWare network.

Before you can connect to a NetWare print queue, you must install NWLink IPX/SPX Compatible Transport on your Windows NT Workstation computer. In addition, you must install *Client Service for NetWare* (CSNW).

POP QUIZ — True or False?

1. A printer must be specially configured to support drag-and-drop printing.
2. Using the RAW spool format yields faster print performance.
3. The term *print device* refers to the physical device that produces printed output.
4. The Hpmon port monitor can use either the DLC or TCP/IP protocol to connect to print devices.
5. The user must install the Microsoft TCP/IP Printing service to use the TCP/IP port monitor.

Answers: *1. False 2. False 3. True 4. False 5. True*

Print Server Properties

A *print server* is a computer (or network device) that manages print jobs and print devices. The Windows NT Spooler service performs many of the functions of a print server. You can configure several of the Spooler service's properties (which Windows NT calls *print server properties*) including the spool folder, forms, and ports.

Changing the Spool Folder

The *spool folder* is used by the Windows NT Spooler service as a temporary storage area for print jobs waiting to be sent to a print device. The default location for the spool folder is <winntroot>\System32\Spool\ Printers.

If the partition that contains the spool folder does not have enough free space to store print jobs, you may experience print job failures. On a busy Windows NT computer with multiple shared printers, for example, you might need between 25MB and several hundred megabytes of free space for the spool folder, depending on the number, type, and size of print jobs spooled on this server.

Look for exam questions with this scenario: There is a small amount of free space left on the system partition and you need to make sure the disk doesn't fill up. One of the answers may be to move the spool folder to another partition with more space.

If you experience print job failures due to a lack of free space for your spool folder, you can specify that a different folder on another partition (that has more free space) be used as your spool folder.

To change your spool folder, click the Advanced tab in the Print Server Properties dialog box. Next, edit the contents of the Spool Folder text box. You can specify any folder in any partition as your spool folder, in the format of *Drive_letter:\Folder\Subfolder*.

Figure 7-4 shows the Advanced tab in the Print Server Properties dialog box. Note the default spool folder location and the additional options you can configure on this tab.

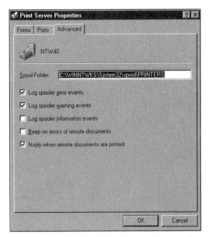

Figure 7-4 *Configuring advanced print server properties*

Here is a scenario you may find in the exam: You have changed the spool folder on a Windows NT computer, only to find users can no longer print to shared network printers on this computer.

To solve this problem, you must assign permissions so that all users who print to any shared printer on the Windows NT computer have the Change permission to the spool folder. Users that don't have the Change permission to the spool folder won't be able to print to any shared network printer on the Windows NT computer.

Printer Properties

In Windows NT you can configure options for a printer in the printer's Properties dialog box. This dialog box is printer specific and is titled *Printer_name* Properties.

Assigning a Separator Page

You can configure Windows NT so that a *separator page* is printed at the beginning of every document. Using separator pages at the beginning of print jobs enables users to locate their print jobs at the print device easily. Separator pages are sometimes called *banner pages*.

You can assign a separator page to a printer by using the Properties dialog box for your printer. When you open this dialog box, you should see three default separator page files: Pcl.sep, Pscript.sep, and Sysprint.sep. The Pcl.sep separator page file switches a dual-language print device to PCL printing and causes a separator page to be printed at the beginning of each print job.

Switching print languages

You can use the pcl.sep page file with print devices that have PCL and Postscript installed but are unable to automatically detect the language of incoming print jobs. Otherwise, the print devices use the language that was configured on their panel or configuration software and print out random characters.

The `Pscript.sep` separator page file switches a dual-language print device to PostScript printing, but does *not* cause a separator page to be printed at the beginning of each print job. The `Sysprint.sep` separator page file causes a separator page to be printed at the beginning of each print job and is only compatible with PostScript print devices.

You can create additional separator page files by editing an existing separator page file and saving it with a different name.

Printer Security

You can use Windows NT printer security to control access to a printer by assigning printer permissions to users and groups. Printer security is configured on the Security tab in a printer's Properties dialog box. In addition, you can take ownership of a printer and configure Windows NT to audit printer usage in this dialog box.

Figure 7-5 shows the Security tab in a printer's Properties dialog box. Note the Permissions, Auditing, and Ownership command buttons.

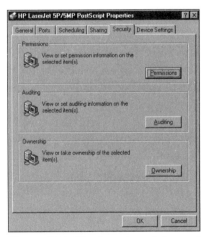

Figure 7-5 *The Security tab in a printer's Properties dialog box*

Printer permissions

Printer permissions control which tasks a user can perform on a specific printer. Table 7.1 lists and describes the Windows NT printer permissions.

TABLE 7.1 Windows NT Printer Permissions

Printer Permission	Description and Functionality
No Access	A user or group that has the No Access permission cannot access the printer.
Print	The Print permission allows users to create print jobs and also to delete their own print jobs.
Manage Documents	The Manage Documents permission allows users to pause, restart, delete, and control job settings for their own print jobs. The Manage Documents permission does not allow users to print to the printer.
Full Control	A user or group that has the Full Control permission can do everything that a user with the Print and Manage Documents permissions can do, and in addition can assign printer permissions, delete printers, share printers, and change printer properties.

You can assign printer permissions to users and groups. User and group permissions are additive. In other words, if a user has the Print permission and a group that the user is a member of has Full Control permission, the user has Full Control permission.

There is one exception to this rule. If a user or any group that a user is a member of has the No Access permission, the user's effective permission is always No Access. For example, a user may have the Full Control permission, but a group that the user is a member of may have the No Access permission. The user's effective permission is No Access, and the user cannot access the printer.

Print permissions behave exactly like Share permissions because they are both shared resources on a Windows NT computer.

To assign printer permissions to users and groups, click the Permissions command button on the Security tab in the Properties dialog box for the printer you want to configure. Figure 7-6 shows the default printer permissions assigned to a newly created printer in the

Printer Permissions dialog box. Note that by default the Everyone group has the Print permission, which effectively enables all users to create and delete their own print jobs on this printer.

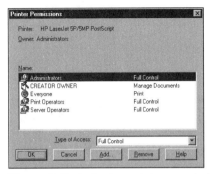

Figure 7-6 *Assigning printer permissions*

To modify permissions in this dialog box, highlight a user or group, and then select the permission you want to assign to this user or group from the Type of Access drop-down list box. Next, click OK, and then click OK in your printer's Properties dialog box.

To add a user or group to the Name list box, click the Add command button in the Printer Permissions dialog box. The Add Users and Groups dialog box appears. Select the user(s) and/or group(s) you want to add, and then click the Add command button. Click OK to return to the Printer Permissions dialog box. Click OK in the Printer Permissions dialog box, and click OK in your printer's Properties dialog box.

To remove a user or group from the Name list box, highlight the user or group and press Delete. Click OK, and then click OK in your printer's Properties dialog box.

True or False?

1. As far as printer permissions go, user and group permissions are not additive.

2. If a user has the Manage Documents permission, they can also print to the printer.

3. You can relocate the printer spool directory.

Continued

> **4.** If a user is granted No Access for a printer, they can still use the printer if they belong to a group that does have access.
>
> **5.** You can assign a separator page to switch between languages on a print device.
>
> **Answers:** *1. False 2. False 3. True 4. False 5. True*

Troubleshooting Common Printing Problems

Printing problems can occur on a Windows NT network for several reasons. Some of the most common printing problems involve users who do not have the permissions they need to access the printer, or users who have the Full Control permission or the Manage Document permission accidentally deleting documents that belong to other users. When troubleshooting printer problems, a good first step is to ensure users have appropriate printer permissions.

Some common printing problems, along with their probable causes and recommended solutions, are listed below.

Problem #1 Print jobs are not being sent from the printer to the print device. A print job with a size of 0 bytes is at the top of the print job list for the printer. Other documents are also listed in the print job list, and users can still send print jobs to the printer. There is plenty of free space on the partition that contains your spool folder.

The most likely cause of this problem is a stalled print spooler. Stop and restart the Spooler service, and printing should resume.

Problem #2 No print events are listed in the Security Log in Event Viewer. You recently configured success auditing for print events in the Properties dialog box for the printer. Several days have passed, and hundreds of documents have been printed.

The most likely cause of this problem is the success option for auditing file and object access has *not* been configured in User Manager. Auditing of printers requires that auditing of file and object access be

configured. To resolve the problem, configure the necessary options in
User Manager.

Problem #3 A printer that uses the Hpmon print monitor has
stopped sending print jobs to its assigned print device.

This problem usually occurs when another computer on the network
is configured to use Hpmon to connect to the print device by using a
continuous connection. If you want more than one printer to be able to
access a print device by using Hpmon, configure a job-based connection
for all printers.

Problem #4 You are unable to connect a Windows NT computer to a
print device that uses TCP/IP and LPD.

Of the many possible causes for this problem, the most common is
an incorrect configuration of a TCP/IP parameter on either the Windows
NT computer or on the print device that uses TCP/IP and LPD. Ensure
the IP address, subnet mask, and default gateway parameters on both the
Windows NT computer and the print device that uses TCP/IP and LPD
are set correctly.

Problem #5 You experience a paper jam in the middle of an important print job. You want to reprint the entire print job, but it is not possible to reprint the job from the application that created it because you
deleted the document after you created the print job.

The cause of the paper jam is not important here, but being able to
reprint the entire print job is. To solve this problem, I recommend that
you follow these steps:

1. Immediately double-click the printer in the `Printers` folder.

2. The Printers dialog box appears. Select Document ⇨ Pause. This
   pauses the print job.

3. Clear the paper jam at the print device.

   Select Document ⇨ Restart to reprint the entire print job. (Do
   not select Resume from the Document menu, because this only
   prints the print job from wherever the printer jammed to the
   end of the document, and the pages jammed in the print device
   will likely be lost.)

Problem #6 You receive spooler messages indicating your print job has been spooled with a size of 0 bytes.

The most probable cause of this problem is the partition that contains the printer's spool folder does not have enough free space to print the document in question. You should delete some files from this partition or move the spool folder to a different partition that has more free space.

Have You Mastered?

Now it's time to apply what you've learned in this chapter by testing your mastery of the material. These questions provide you with a means of determining if you are ready to move on to the next chapter or if you need to review the material again.

1. **You use your Windows NT Workstation to print large presentation documents. You want to increase the speed at which your computer spools and sends off your print jobs to the print server. What can you do to increase your print performance?**

   ☐ A. Configure your spool settings to use EMF.
   ☐ B. Configure your spool settings to use RAW.
   ☐ C. Print your documents using drag-and-drop.
   ☐ D. Print your document using an application and not drag-and-drop.

   The correct answer is A. The EMF spool setting configures your computer to perform only half of the print rendering and then ships it to the print server, which completes the print processing. The methods in which you submit your print job, such as drag-and-drop, have little to do with print performance. For more information, see the "EMFs in Network Printing" section.

2. **You are in the process of migrating your NetWare network to a Windows NT network. You want to allow users who have been migrated to Windows NT to still be able to print to printers connected to NetWare servers. What must you do on Windows**

NT print server computers that are to forward print jobs to NetWare servers? (Choose two.)

☐ A. Install Client Service for NetWare.
☐ B. Install NWLink IPX/SPX Compatible Transport.
☐ C. Configure a separator page.
☐ D. Configure the spool format as RAW.

The correct answers are A and B. Before a Windows NT computer can forward print jobs to a NetWare print queue, the computer must have these two components installed. You do not need to have a separator page defined, nor does the spool format need to be changed to forward to a NetWare queue. For more information, see the "Print Monitors" section.

3. **You have installed a print device on your network using a JetDirect card. You want to allow some users to print directly to the print device and bypass the print server. You want the other users to use your Windows NT Workstation computer as a print server for the print device. The JetDirect card only supports the DLC protocol. How should you configure the printer on the print server to allow some users to print directly to the print device?**

☐ A. Configure the Hpmon print monitor properties as Continuous.
☐ B. Configure the Hpmon print monitor properties as Job Based.
☐ C. Grant the users who should print directly to the print device Full Control for the printer.
☐ D. This cannot be done using the JetDirect card and Hpmon print monitor.

The correct answer is B. If the Hpmon print monitor is configured as Job Based, a connection to the JetDirect card is only made when a print job is waiting. If Continuous is selected, the print server connects to the JetDirect card and prevents any other devices from connecting to the print device. For more information, see the "Print Monitors" section.

4. **You have been experiencing poor performance on your Windows NT Workstation computer. You regularly print large presentation and CAD design documents. While the documents are being spooled to print, the computer slows down appreciably and applications often timeout. What can you do to increase the performance of your computer while it is printing documents? (Choose two.)**

   ☐ A. Move the spool directory off of the system partition.
   ☐ B. Assign separator pages to all the printers.
   ☐ C. Change the spool format to EMF.
   ☐ D. Change the spool format to RAW.

The correct answers are **A** and **C**. If the printers are heavily used, the constant spooling and deleting of print jobs can slow down disk access, especially on the system partition. Additionally, the EMF format is more efficient because the print job is only partially processed before it is sent to a print server. For more information, see the "Print Server Properties" section.

5. **You are the network administrator for your company's Windows NT domain. The manager of the Research department has called you because she is unable to print to the departmental color printer. You check the printer permissions and see that she has been granted the Manage Documents permission. What must you do to allow the manager to use the printer?**

   ☐ A. Revoke the Manage Documents permission and grant her Print permission.
   ☐ B. Grant her Print permission.
   ☐ C. Add her to the Power Users user group.
   ☐ D. Delete all of the existing documents in the printer queue.

The correct answer is **B**. The Manage Documents permission does not allow a user to print to the printer, it only allows them to manage the print queue and user documents sent to the printer. Additionally, while answer A would also work, the question used the word "must; therefore, because you do not necessarily have to revoke Manage Documents permission, answer A is not correct in this scenario. For more information, see the "Printer Security" section.

Practice Your Skills

Here is a chance to apply your practical hands-on experience and material from this chapter. These exercises are designed not only to reinforce the material you've learned, but also to enable you to gain greater experience and exposure to the product. These exercises are a critical part of understanding the product and gaining valuable experience for using the product and passing the certification exam. For each of the following problems, consider the given facts and determine what you think are the possible causes of the problem and what course of action you might take to resolve the problem.

1. Reprinting a document

EXERCISE Halfway through a print job you discover the print device's paper tray contains letterhead paper, and you need your document printed on white paper. You want to reprint the entire job, but you have already deleted your document from the spreadsheet application you were using. What can you do?

ANALYSIS If the print job is still in the printer queue, you can pause your print job, change the paper in the print device, and restart the print job from the beginning. If the job has already been spooled to the print device, the queue will be empty and you cannot reprint the job unless you still have the file.

2. Choosing print monitors

EXERCISE Your network consists of several types of client computers and various operating systems, ranging from MS-DOS to UNIX. You want to install print devices that will support the largest variety of platforms as possible. Which of the Windows NT print monitors have the greatest pervasiveness for network support?

ANALYSIS In general, you will find that TCP/IP, and DLC to a lesser extent, are the most pervasive support platforms for network-attached printers. If you purchase a print device or network print servers that support either of these protocols, you will probably be able to meet the printing needs of your users.

3. Configuring printer properties

EXERCISE You are creating a standard configuration for a Windows NT Workstation computer, with a 500MB C drive formatted as FAT and a NTFS D drive configured for the remaining space. Why would it be a good idea to move the printer spool directory?

ANALYSIS Windows NT places the spool directory in a subfolder of the Windows NT system directory, which is usually on the C drive. If space is limited, it is very likely that a large print job, combined with your system and data files, will fill up your C drive. Without any free space Windows NT may have terrible performance or crash.

4. Using Separator Pages

EXERCISE What are the advantages of using a separator page on large, high-speed printers used by numerous users?

ANALYSIS Not only do separator pages make it easier for users when printing to high-speed devices because it visibly identifies who's printing, it also separates print jobs from one another. Additionally, separator pages can be used to switch between print device languages such as PCL or post-script.

Accessing NetWare Servers

Y OU ARE LIKELY TO RUN INTO a number of NetWare-
client-related questions on your Windows NT
Workstation exam. In this chapter I look at the most
common components of NetWare connectivity. The
chapter starts with a look at the NWLink IPX/SPX
Compatible Transport protocol that is used to commu-
nicate with NetWare servers. I also take a look at the Client Service for
NetWare to show its function and use in most environments. Preparing
for the Windows NT Workstation exam includes knowing these
NetWare-related topics. So dig in, and let's get started.

Exam Material in This Chapter

Based on Microsoft Objectives

Connectivity

- Adding and configuring the network components of Windows NT Workstation
- Using various methods to access network resources
- Implementing Windows NT Workstation as a client in a NetWare environment

Based on Author's Experience

- You should understand the process of configuring Frame Types for NWLink IPX/SPX Compatible Transport.
- You will definitely need to know how to troubleshoot NWLink IPX/SPX Compatible Transport configuration problems.
- You should expect some questions on the exam about configuring and using Client Service for NetWare.
- You need to know what types of commands should be eliminated from NetWare logon scripts for clients using Client Service for NetWare.

Are You Prepared?

Do you have what it takes? Try out these self-assessment questions to see if you have prepared for the material in this chapter or if you should review problem areas.

1. You are adding a Windows NT Workstation computer to a network that has NetWare 4.*x* server computers. Each of the servers run different frame types. How should you configure the frame type setting for the Windows NT Workstation network adapter?

   ☐ A. Use auto frame type.
   ☐ B. Add each frame type to the network adapter.
   ☐ C. Choose one frame type and configure a default tree for Client Service for NetWare.
   ☐ D. Add a network adapter card for each frame type and use auto frame type.

2. Your Windows NT Workstation computer has Client Service for NetWare and NWLink IPX/SPX Compatible Transport installed. When you log on to the NetWare server using a MS-DOS based NetWare client, your logon script runs fine. When you log on to the NetWare server using your Windows NT Workstation computer, the logon script does not run at all. What should you do?

   ☐ A. Change the Internal network number for your network adapter.
   ☐ B. Change the External network number for your network adapter.

☐ C. Configure Client Service for NetWare to enable logon scripts.

☐ D. Configure Client Service for NetWare to specify a preferred server.

3. **You are installing Client Service for NetWare and NWLink IPX/SPX Compatible Transport on your Windows NT Workstation computer. You want to log on to and access resources on a NetWare 4.x server. What should you configure in Client Service for NetWare?**

☐ A. Preferred server

☐ B. Default Tree and Context

☐ C. Frame Type

☐ D. You cannot use Client Service for NetWare to connect to a NetWare 4.x server

1. B   *A network adapter card can have more than one frame type configured, allowing it to work on networks with multiple frame types in use. See the "Frame Types" section.*

2. C   *By default, Client Service for NetWare does not process logon scripts when clients log on to NetWare servers. If their user account has a logon script and it is processed on another platform type, the logon script options are probably not configured properly on the Windows NT Workstation computer. See the "Client Service for NetWare" section.*

3. B   *When logging onto a NetWare 4.x server, you must define a default tree and context. See the "Client Service for NetWare" section.*

Windows NT in a NetWare Environment

Microsoft includes components with Windows NT Workstation that enable Windows NT Workstation computers to coexist with Novell NetWare servers and client computers on the same network.

In a nutshell, these features enable Windows NT Workstation computers to utilize the resources on NetWare servers in a heterogeneous networking environment. These components can be used for long-term integration in a mixed network operating system environment, or for the short term during a migration from NetWare to Windows NT.

When you consider the large number of existing Novell NetWare networks, particularly when Windows NT was first released, it's not too surprising that Microsoft has developed and included these components with Windows NT. Solutions that enable both Windows NT and NetWare to be used on the same network were critical to Windows NT's wide acceptance in the network operating system arena.

Microsoft has addressed this challenge by developing a protocol and a service that increase the interoperability of Windows NT with NetWare:

- NWLink IPX/SPX Compatible Transport
- Client Service for NetWare (CSNW)

TEST TIP If you don't regularly use a NetWare server on your network, plan to review this chapter just before you take the Workstation exam. The details in this chapter are *very* important!

NWLink IPX/SPX Compatible Transport

NWLink IPX/SPX Compatible Transport is a routable transport protocol typically used in a combined Windows NT and NetWare environment. NWLink IPX/SPX Compatible Transport is Microsoft's version of Novell's IPX/SPX protocol. (*IPX/SPX* is the protocol used on most

Novell NetWare networks.) NWLink provides protocol compatibility between Windows NT and NetWare computers. In addition to its functionality in a NetWare environment, NWLink also fully supports Microsoft networking.

NWLink IPX/SPX Compatible Transport, which is included with Windows NT Workstation, must be installed on NT Workstation computers in order to enable them to communicate over the network with NetWare computers.

There are two important topics that need to be discussed before moving on to the installation of NWLink IPX/SPX Compatible Transport: frame types and network numbers. Because frame types and network numbers must be configured during installation, it's important to have a solid grasp of these basic network concepts.

Frame Types

Frame types (also called *frame formats*) are accepted, standardized structures for transmitting data packets over a network. All frame types include certain common components, such as source address, destination address, data field, and cyclic redundancy check — but the various frame types include different combinations of additional fields beyond the common components.

Windows NT and NWLink IPX/SPX Compatible Transport support nine different frame types, which are described in Table 8.1.

TABLE 8.1 NWLink IPX/SPX Compatible Transport Frame Types

Frame Type	Default/Common Usage	Network Adapters That Support This Frame Type
Ethernet 802.2	Default frame type for NetWare 3.12 and later NetWare versions on Ethernet networks.	Ethernet
Ethernet 802.3	Default frame type for NetWare 3.11 and earlier NetWare versions on Ethernet networks.	Ethernet

Frame Type	Default/Common Usage	Network Adapters That Support This Frame Type
Ethernet II	Commonly associated with the TCP/IP protocol; not commonly used with NWLink IPX/SPX Compatible Transport.	Ethernet
Ethernet SNAP	Commonly associated with the AppleTalk protocol; not commonly used with NWLink IPX/SPX Compatible Transport.	Ethernet, FDDI
ARCNET	Default frame type for all versions of NetWare on ARCNET networks.	ARCNET
Token-Ring	Default frame type for all versions of NetWare on Token Ring networks.	Token Ring
Token-Ring SNAP	Commonly associated with the AppleTalk protocol; not commonly used with NWLink IPX/SPX Compatible Transport.	Token Ring
FDDI	Default frame type for NetWare 3.12 and later NetWare versions on FDDI networks.	FDDI
FDDI 802.3	Default frame type for NetWare 3.11 and earlier NetWare versions on FDDI networks.	FDDI

Before you select a frame type when installing and configuring NWLink IPX/SPX Compatible Transport, you should determine which frame type(s) are already in use on the network. You should select a frame type that *matches* the frame type already in use, or use the Windows NT auto frame type detection feature to automatically select a frame type. You can assign more than one frame type to an individual network adapter.

If you do not know what frame type is being used, use the auto frame type.

Frame type mismatching is a common cause of communications problems on networks that use NWLink IPX/SPX Compatible Transport.

Network Numbers

Network numbers are 32-bit binary numbers that uniquely identify a NWLink IPX/SPX Compatible Transport network segment for routing purposes. Because network numbers uniquely identify a network segment, they are used by IPX routers to correctly forward data packets from one network segment to another.

Network numbers are only assigned to Windows NT computers that use NWLink IPX/SPX Compatible Transport. Network numbers are assigned during the installation and configuration of NWLink IPX/SPX Compatible Transport.

Network numbers are commonly presented in an eight-digit hexadecimal format. (In a hexadecimal format, the numbers 0 through 9 and the letters A through F can be used.) Don't confuse a network number with a TCP/IP network ID or a computer's MAC (hardware) address.

Two Types of Network Numbers

There are two types of network numbers: *external network numbers* (network numbers that are assigned to network adapters) and *internal network numbers*. A Windows NT computer that uses NWLink IPX/SPX Compatible Transport can have one or more external network number(s) and an internal network number, as well.

When NWLink IPX/SPX Compatible Transport is used, an external network number is assigned to each network adapter installed in a computer. An external network number uniquely identifies the network segment to which the network adapter is connected. (If more than one frame type is assigned to a network adapter, each frame type is assigned its own external network number.) Windows NT can automatically detect and use the external network number in use on a network segment. However, you can manually assign any unique eight-digit external network number to a network adapter during the configuration of NWLink IPX/SPX Compatible Transport. External network numbers are sometimes referred to simply as network numbers.

Remember this for the exam — you can assign multiple frame types and network numbers to an individual network adapter.

An internal network number must be assigned to a Windows NT computer that uses NWLink IPX/SPX Compatible Transport when more than one network adapter is installed in it. (If there is only one network adapter installed in a computer, Windows NT does not require you to assign an internal network number, although you can assign an internal network number if you want.) An internal network number is an additional unique eight-digit network number that is used by the computer's operating system — an internal network number does *not* correspond to a specific network adapter installed in the computer. A Windows NT computer has only one internal network number, regardless of the number of network adapters installed in it.

True or False?

1. NWLink IPX/SPX Compatible Transport does not fully support Microsoft networking.
2. A Windows NT computer can have more than one Internal IPX/SPX network number.
3. A Windows NT Computer can only have one frame type per network adapter card.
4. Each network card in a Windows NT computer running IPX/SPX should have its own network number.

Answers: *1. False 2. False 3. False 4. True*

Client Service for NetWare (CSNW)

Client Service for NetWare (CSNW) is a Windows NT Workstation service that, when installed and configured on a Windows NT Workstation computer, enables users to access resources, such as files, folders, and printers, on a NetWare server. CSNW enables access to resources on NetWare 4.*x* servers as well as NetWare 3.*x* servers.

CSNW is included with Windows NT Workstation. CSNW requires the use of NWLink IPX/SPX Compatible Transport.

CSNW makes it possible for users of Windows NT Workstation computers to log in to NetWare 4.*x NetWare Directory Services* (NDS), and to browse and access resources in the NDS tree. (NDS is a distributed security database on NetWare 4.*x* servers that enables storage of user names, computer names, and resources in a hierarchical tree structure.) However, you can't manage NDS from a Windows NT Workstation computer running CSNW. To manage NDS, you must run Novell's client software for Windows NT on the Windows NT Workstation computer instead of CSNW.

Additionally, CSNW enables users to run NetWare login scripts during the Windows NT Workstation logon process.

CSNW also supports the use of long filenames on NetWare 3.12 and NetWare 4.1 servers that have the OS/2 name space (`OS2.nam`) installed, and on NetWare 4.11 servers that have the `Long.nam` name space installed.

CSNW can be installed on any Windows NT Workstation computer, and should be installed whenever users of the computer want to access resources on NetWare servers.

Configuring Client Service for NetWare (CSNW)

You can either configure CSNW the first time you log on after installing CSNW, or you can configure CSNW at a later time by using the CSNW application in Control Panel (see Figure 8-1).

When configuring CSNW, you should be prepared to enter either the name of a preferred NetWare 3.*x* server you want to use or your tree and context for a NetWare 4.*x* server.

Figure 8-1 *Configuring Client Service for NetWare*

To configure CSNW, you must select from one of two primary options: Preferred Server, or Default Tree and Context. You can also select print and login script options in this dialog box:

- **Preferred Server:** Select the option button next to Preferred Server if you primarily access resources on NetWare 3.*x* servers. Then select the NetWare server of your choice from the Select Preferred Server drop-down list box.

- **Default Tree and Context:** Select the option button next to Default Tree and Context if you primarily access resources on NetWare 4.*x* servers. Then enter the tree name and context that contain your NetWare 4.*x* user account in the Tree and Context text boxes.

- **Print Options:** If you print to a printer on a NetWare server, you can configure the Print Options section of the Client Service for NetWare dialog box.

There are three options you can select:

- **Add Form Feed:** Selecting this check box causes an additional form feed to be sent at the end of each print job. Deselect this check box if an additional blank page is printing at the end of each of your print jobs. By default, this check box is not selected.

- **Notify When Printed:** Selecting this check box causes a pop-up message to appear on your screen after a print job is sent by the NetWare server to the print device. Clear this check box if you no longer want to receive these messages. This check box is selected by default.

- **Print Banner:** Selecting this check box causes an additional sheet of paper that identifies the user that initiated the print job (called a *banner page*) to be printed at the beginning of each print job. If you want to save paper, deselect this check box. This check box is selected by default.

- **Login Script Options:** Selecting the check box next to Run Login Script in this section causes the NetWare login script to run during the Windows NT logon process.

Using CSNW to Access Resources on NetWare Servers

Resources on NetWare 3.x servers and NetWare 4.x servers are accessed by using two different types of UNC path names.

To access resources on NetWare 3.x servers from a Windows NT Workstation computer that is running CSNW, you can use standard UNC path names in the format:

`\\server_name\share_name`

For example, to connect to a volume named SYS on a NetWare 3.*x* server named NWSERVER, use the following UNC path name:

\\nwserver\sys

You can use these UNC path names when:

- Connecting to a printer by using the Add Printer Wizard
- Connecting to a shared folder in Windows NT Explorer

To access resources on NetWare 4.*x* servers from a Windows NT Workstation computer that is running CSNW, you can use UNC path names in the format:

*tree_name**volume_name.organizational_unit.organization_name**folder_name*

For example, to connect to the Public folder in a volume named NWSERVER_SYS (on a NetWare 4.*x* server) in the Sales organizational unit in the Widgets organization in a tree named CORP, use the following UNC path name:

\\corp\nwserver_sys.sales.widgets\public

You can use these UNC path names when:

- Connecting to a printer by using the Add Printer Wizard
- Connecting to a shared folder in Windows NT Explorer

True or False?

1. The default tree and context are primarily used to access NetWare 4.*x* resources.

2. You cannot run NetWare logon scripts when using Client Services for NetWare.

3. You can log onto NetWare 4.*x* servers using Client Services for NetWare.

Answers: *1. False 2. False 3. True*

Troubleshooting Common Problems

There are a few common NetWare connectivity problems. Most NetWare connectivity problems are caused by incorrectly configuring NWLink IPX/SPX Compatible Transport or CSNW on the computer that is experiencing the problem. Most user-reported problems relate to an inability to connect a Windows NT Workstation computer to resources on NetWare servers.

The most common configuration errors are a frame type mismatch and/or a network number mismatch. Both the NT client and the NetWare server normally must use the same frame type. Additionally, these computers must use the same network number if they are located on the same network segment. To find out what frame type and network number are being used on the NetWare server, type **config** at the : prompt on the NetWare server. Normally, you can use the NT autodetect feature for frame type selection on an NT computer. However, if you are unable to connect to a resource while using the autodetect feature, try manually configuring the frame type and network number on the NT computer to match those of the NetWare server. Remember, NetWare 3.11 and earlier versions use the Ethernet 802.3 frame type by default on Ethernet networks. NetWare 3.12 and later versions use the Ethernet 802.2 frame type by default on Ethernet networks.

Have You Mastered?

Now it's time to apply what you've learned in this chapter by testing your mastery of the material. These questions provide you with a means to determine if you are ready to move onto the next chapter or if you need to review the material again.

1. **You are installing Client Service for NetWare and the NWLink IPX/SPX Compatible Transport on your Windows NT Workstation computer. Your computer has one network adapter and you will be connecting to a NetWare 3.x server. What information must you have to configure these two components? (Choose all that apply.)**

   - ☐ A. An external network number
   - ☐ B. An internal network number
   - ☐ C. Frame type
   - ☐ D. Default Context
   - ☐ E. Default Tree
   - ☐ F. Preferred Server

   The correct answers are A, C, and F. Because the computer only has one network adapter, you are only required to have an external network address. You also need the Frame type for the network segment the computer is connected to and what preferred server should be used to log on to. For more information, see the "Windows NT in a NetWare Environment" section.

2. **Your network consists of ten subnets connected with routers. You have configured the router to enable forwarding of NetBIOS**

broadcast traffic. Which protocols can be used to browse over multiple subnets on this network? (Choose two.)

- ☐ A. NetBEUI
- ☐ B. TCP/IP
- ☐ C. NWLink IPX/SPX Compatible Transport

The correct answers are B and C. NetBEUI is a nonroutable protocol period. Even with NetBIOS forwarding enabled, routers are still unable to forward NetBEUI traffic. As a result, only TCP/IP and NWLink IPX/SPX Compatible Transport can be used to browse multisubnet networks. For more information, see the "NWLink IPX/SPX Compatible Transport" section.

3. You are adding a Windows NT Workstation computer to the network. You want to log on to and access resources on your NetWare 4.x server. Which entries must you configure for Client Services for NetWare? (Choose two.)

- ☐ A. Preferred Server
- ☐ B. Default Tree
- ☐ C. Logon Script Option
- ☐ D. Default Context
- ☐ E. Print Options

The correct answers are B and D. When logging on to and using NetWare 4.x servers, you must specify your default tree and context. A preferred server only needs to be defined for computers logging into a NetWare 3.x server. For more information, see the "Client Service for NetWare" section.

4. You are adding a Windows NT Workstation computer to the network. You want to access resources on a NetWare 3.x server. You are configuring NWLink IPX/SPX Compatible Transport. What NWLink IPX/SPX Compatible Transport property should be the same on all of the servers on the network?

- ☐ A. External network number
- ☐ B. Internal network number

☐ C. Frame type
☐ D. Default Tree

The correct answer is **C**. For NWLink IPX/SPX Compatible
Transport to communicate between computers, the computers must
support the same frame type. Some computers will support more
than one frame type on each network adapter, others do not. For
more information, see the "NWLink IPX/SPX Compatible
Transport" section.

Practice Your Skills

Here is a chance to apply your practical hands-on experience and material from this chapter. These exercises are designed for you to apply not only the material in the book, but to gain greater experience and exposure to the product. These exercises are a critical part of understanding the product and gaining valuable experience for using the product and passing the certification exam. For each of the following problems, consider the given facts and determine what you think are the possible causes of the problem and what course of action you might take to resolve the problem.

1. Unable to access NetWare 3.x servers

EXERCISE You have just added a new Windows NT Workstation 4.0 computer to your network. You have installed the Client Service for NetWare and the NWLink IPX/SPX Compatible Transport to the computer. You are able to see other Windows NT Workstation computers via IPX/SPX, but you cannot locate any NetWare 3.x servers. What is the most likely problem?

ANALYSIS Because you are able to see other computers using NWLink IPX/SPX Compatible Transport, the problem is probably that the wrong frame type was configured for the adapter. The NetWare servers are probably running a frame type other than what you have configured your adapter for. Check the NetWare server frame type and update the configuration on the Windows NT Workstation computer.

2. Error while logging on to a NetWare server

EXERCISE You are logging on to a NetWare server and during the process the NetWare logon script window opens and displays several messages. At one point, the computer stops responding and you are unable to continue with the logon process. This process repeats when you reboot and log on to the NetWare server again. What is the most likely problem?

ANALYSIS Although Client Service for NetWare supports several NetWare features, it is unable to process some commands commonly found in logon scripts. Of those, commands that load TSRs or attempt to load the MS-DOS Command interpreter often cause problems when logon scripts are processed on a Windows NT Workstation computer. As a result, you should ensure that clients logging into NetWare from Windows NT Workstation computer do not run these commands.

Networking Using TCP/IP

ONE OF THE MORE COMPLEX SECTIONS of the Windows NT Workstation exam is TCP/IP. In this chapter, I cover the most common subjects you are likely to see on the exam. After a brief overview of TCP/IP, I explore IP address configurations and addressing methods. The chapter then prepares you for exam questions on Microsoft Peer Web Services by looking at its features, configurations, and capabilities. To ensure that you are fully prepared for the Windows NT Workstation exam, the chapter wraps up with a look at troubleshooting the most common TCP/IP connectivity problems.

Exam Material in This Chapter

Based on Microsoft Objectives

Connectivity

- Add and configure the network components of Windows NT Workstation
- Use various configurations to install Windows NT Workstation as a TCP/IP client
- Configure Microsoft Peer Web Services in a given situation

Based on Author's Experience

- You must have an understanding of TCP/IP addressing as it relates to network and host ID portions.
- You need to understand the role of a subnet mask and what it represents to a Windows NT Workstation computer.
- You must be familiar with the rules of assigning TCP/IP addresses to computers (for example, all devices must have a unique TCP/IP address).
- You should be aware of the benefits of using DHCP or manually assigning TCP/IP addresses.
- You need to understand the purpose of a default router and the problems that can occur from not using one.
- You should know services are provided in Microsoft Peer Web Services.
- You must know the connection limit for Microsoft PWS.

Are You Prepared?

Do you have what it takes? Try out these self-assessment questions to see if you have prepared for the material in this chapter or if you should review problem areas.

1. **Your Internet Service Provider has assigned you a TCP/IP address to use to access the Internet from your corporate network. The address assigned to you is 10.10.222.200 and has a subnet mask of 255.255.0.0. What portion of the address is the network ID?**

    ☐ A. 10
    ☐ B. 10.10
    ☐ C. 10.10.222
    ☐ D. 10.10.0.0

2. **You are working on your company's electronic newsletter. You have designed and posted the newsletter to the WWW service on your Peer Web Service. How many simultaneous connections can you support with this service?**

    ☐ A. 10
    ☐ B. 50
    ☐ C. 255
    ☐ D. Unlimited

3. **You are installing Microsoft Peer Web Services on your Windows NT Workstation computer. Which Internet services are provided in Microsoft PWS? (Choose three.)**

    ☐ A. Gopher

☐ B. Archive
☐ C. WWW
☐ D. FTP
☐ E. LDAP

Answers:

1. B   *The subnet mask indicates which portion of a TCP/IP address is the network and host ID portions. In this scenario, the subnet mask of 255.255.0.0 shows that the first two octets are the network ID – 10.10. See the "IP Addressing" section of this chapter.*

2. A   *Peer Web Services allows up to 10 simultaneous connections. See the "Microsoft Peer Web Services" section of this chapter.*

3. A, C, and D   *Microsoft Peer Web Services provides WWW, FTP, and Gopher services. Archive and LDAP are not provided in PWS, although they may be provided in third-party products. See the section entitled "Publishing on the Internet" later in this chapter.*

Overview of TCP/IP

The *Transmission Control Protocol/Internet Protocol* (TCP/IP) is a widely used transport protocol that provides robust capabilities for Windows NT networking.

TCP/IP is a fast, routable enterprise protocol that is used on the Internet. TCP/IP is supported by many other operating systems, including Windows 95, Macintosh, UNIX, MS-DOS, and IBM mainframes. TCP/IP is typically the recommended protocol for large, heterogeneous networks.

A good place to begin a basic discussion of TCP/IP is with IP addressing — including subnet masks and default gateway addresses.

IP Addressing

An *IP address* is a 32-bit binary number, broken into four 8-bit sections (often called *octets*), that uniquely identifies a computer or other network device on a network that uses TCP/IP. IP addresses must be unique — *no two computers or other network devices on an internetwork should have the same IP address.*

Unique Addresses

A network must have unique TCP/IP addresses for every device on the network. You are likely to see questions on the exam to test this point.

If two computers have the same IP address, one or both of the computers may be incapable of communicating over the network. An IP address is *not* the same as a network adapter's hardware (or MAC) address.

Although an IP address is a 32-bit binary number, it is normally represented in a dotted decimal format. Each 8-bit octet is represented by a whole number between 0 and 255. The following numbers are sample IP addresses:

192.168.59.5

172.31.151.1

An IP address contains two important identifiers: a *network ID* and a *host ID*. One portion of each IP address identifies the network segment on which a computer (or other network device) is located. This portion is called the network ID. The length of the network ID within an IP address is variable and is specified by the subnet mask used in conjunction with the IP address.

The second portion of each IP address identifies the individual computer or network device. This portion is called the host ID.

To ensure that unique IP addresses are used, if you plan to connect your network to the Internet, you should contact your Internet Service Provider or InterNIC to obtain a range of valid IP addresses for your network.

Remember these clues for the exam:

All computers located on the same network segment have the same network ID.

Each computer or other network device on a given network segment must have a unique host ID.

Subnet Masks

A *subnet mask* specifies which portion of an IP address represents the network ID and which portion represents the host ID. A subnet mask lets TCP/IP determine whether network traffic destined for a given IP address should be transmitted on the local subnet, or whether it should be routed to a remote subnet.

A subnet mask should be the same for all devices on a given network segment.

A subnet mask is a 32-bit binary number, broken into four octets that is normally represented in a dotted decimal format. Each 8-bit section (or octet) is represented by a whole number between 0 and 255.

A common subnet mask is 255.255.255.0. This particular subnet mask specifies that TCP/IP will use the first three octets of an IP address as the network ID, and will use the last octet as the host ID.

Another common subnet mask is 255.255.0.0. This subnet mask specifies that TCP/IP will use the first two octets of an IP address as the network ID, and use the last two octets as the host ID. (Without getting into too much binary math, an octet number of 255 specifies the entire octet is part of the network ID; and an octet number of 0 specifies the entire octet is part of the host ID. Numbers between 0 and 255 specify that part of the octet corresponds to the network ID and the remaining part corresponds to the host ID.)

If subnet masks are incorrectly configured, network communications problems due to routing errors may occur. For example, TCP/IP may incorrectly determine that a computer on the local subnet is located on a remote subnet and attempt to route a packet to the remote subnet. In this instance, the computer on the local subnet would never receive the packet intended for it.

Default Gateway Addresses

A *default gateway address* specifies the IP address of a router on the local network segment. When a computer that uses TCP/IP determines that the computer it wants to communicate with is located on a remote subnet, it sends all network messages intended for the remote computer to the default gateway address, instead of directly to the destination computer. Then the router on the local subnet, specified by the default gateway address, forwards the messages to the destination computer on the remote subnet (either directly or via other routers).

Watch out for scenarios on the test in which the client computer does not have a default router assigned. The Default router will always be the network adapter on the local subnet.

If a computer's default gateway address does *not* specify a router on the local subnet, that computer will be *incapable* of communicating with computers or other network devices located on other network segments.

When a router is used to connect two network segments, it has two network cards and two IP addresses. Figure 9-1 illustrates how default gateway addresses are used to specify the IP address of a router on the local subnet.

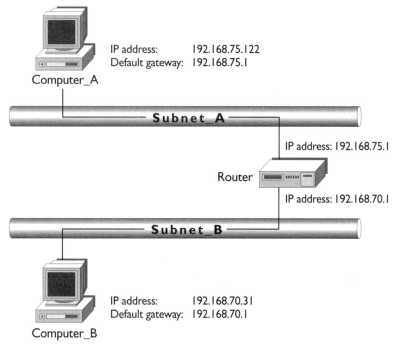

Figure 9-1 *Default gateway addresses specify local router*

Notice in Figure 9-1, the default gateway address of Computer_A matches the IP address of its local router, and the default gateway address of Computer_B matches the IP address of its local router.

 True or False?

1. Each network adapter should have its own subnet mask address.

2. A TCP/IP address represents a host ID address followed by a Network ID address.

3. The default router address should be the address of the router's network adapter on the local subnet.

4. Each network adapter should have a unique host ID address.

5. By default, a host uses the network adapter's MAC address as its TCP/IP address.

Answers: *1. False 2. False 3. True 4. True 5. False*

Assigning IP Addresses

IP addresses must be configured on each computer when TCP/IP is installed. You can assign an IP address to a Windows NT computer in one of two ways: by configuring a computer to obtain an IP address automatically from a DHCP server, or by manually specifying a computer's IP address configuration.

IP addresses are assigned to Windows NT computers in the Microsoft TCP/IP Properties dialog box.

Using a DHCP Server

The most convenient method for assigning IP addresses to multiple computers, in terms of administration time required, is to configure each of the computers to obtain its IP address from a *Dynamic Host Configuration Protocol* (DHCP) server.

Assigning IP addresses by using a DHCP server is the preferred method because

- Using a DHCP server makes it possible for you to manage IP addresses centrally, thus ensuring addresses are valid and are *not* duplicated.

- Using a DHCP server reduces the amount of administration time required to manage and maintain IP addresses for each computer on the network.

- Using a DHCP server reduces the likelihood of human error when IP addresses are assigned because there is no need to enter an IP address manually on every individual computer.

- Using a DHCP server enables you to regain the use of an IP address no longer assigned to a host when the DHCP lease period for this IP address expires.

For the exam, make sure you understand the benefits of using a DHCP server.

Before you can assign an IP address to a Windows NT computer by using a DHCP server, you must first install and configure a DHCP server on your network. After a DHCP server is installed and configured, you can configure client computers to obtain their IP addresses from the DHCP server.

Manual IP Addressing

If you don't have a DHCP server, you must assign IP addresses manually. This method is both more time-consuming than using a DHCP server and more error prone because an IP address must be typed on each individual computer manually.

Figure 9-2 shows a manually configured IP address for a Windows NT Workstation computer.

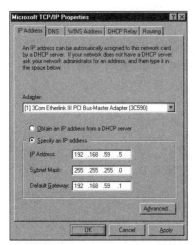

Figure 9-2 *Assigning an IP address manually*

Publishing on the Internet

Publishing World Wide Web pages on the Internet is becoming more popular every day. Many companies and organizations, from small, home-based businesses to multimillion dollar corporations, use the Web to advertise their products and services. Web pages can be made available to anyone who has an Internet connection and a Web browser, such as Internet Explorer or Netscape Navigator. Microsoft's Windows NT Workstation tool for publishing on the Internet is Microsoft Peer Web Services.

Microsoft Peer Web Services

Microsoft Peer Web Services (generally called *Peer Web Services* for short) is a Windows NT Workstation service that provides World Wide Web (WWW), File Transfer Protocol (FTP), and Gopher publishing services. Peer Web Services is optimized as a small-scale intranet publishing service — it supports a maximum of 10 simultaneous connections.

Peer Web Services uses *Hypertext Transfer Protocol* (HTTP) to publish WWW documents on the Internet. FTP enables users to transfer files between computers on the Internet. The FTP service included with Peer Web Services replaces the FTP service included in previous versions of Windows NT Workstation.

 Gopher is a complicated publishing service that is no longer extensively used and is not included in the objectives for the Workstation exam.

Peer Web Services requires the use of TCP/IP. You *must* have TCP/IP installed in your Windows NT Workstation computer to install and use Peer Web Services. No additional hardware is required to install and use Peer Web Services on an internal intranet. A Windows NT Workstation computer that runs Peer Web Services is sometimes called a *Peer Web Server*.

Connecting to the Internet

If you want to connect your Peer Web Server to the Internet instead of just using it on your company's internal network (intranet), additional hardware is required.

Different hardware is required for different types of Internet connections. When determining the type of Internet connection to use, you should consider how many people will access your Peer Web Server, the frequency and duration of those accesses, and the size of documents and files being accessed.

Table 9.1 shows some of the Internet connection types, their speeds, and the additional hardware each requires.

TABLE 9.1 Internet Connection Types

Connection Type	Speed	Additional Hardware Required
Modem	28.8 – 56Kbps	A modem and standard telephone line
ISDN	64 – 128Kbps	An ISDN adapter card with either an internal or external network terminating unit (NT1), and an ISDN line
Digital Leased Line	56Kbps – 44.7Mbps	A router, a DSU/CSU, a network adapter, and a digital leased line — 56Kbps, fractional T1, T1, or T3

Installation and configuration

Before installing and configuring Peer Web Services, you should install Windows NT Workstation and TCP/IP. If you plan to use an Internet connection, you may also want to install and configure the connection, including the additional hardware required, before you install Peer Web Services. You can install Peer Web Services either during the Windows NT Workstation installation process or at a later time.

Another Microsoft Peer Web Services Setup dialog box appears, as shown in Figure 9-3. Notice the options that can be installed with Peer Web Services.

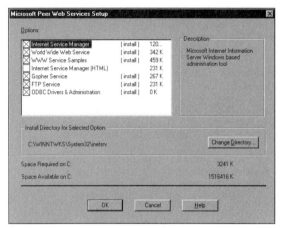

Figure 9-3 *Selecting Peer Web Services options*

 You need to stop or remove any other WWW or FTP software when you are installing Peer Web Services.

The Publishing Directories dialog box appears, as shown in Figure 9-4. Note the default publishing directories.

Figure 9-4 *Configuring publishing directories for the WWW, FTP, and Gopher services*

Microsoft Peer Web Services is now installed, and all its services have been started. You needn't restart your computer at this time.

True or False?

1. Microsoft Peer Web Services provides WWW, FTP, and Archive services.
2. Microsoft Peer Web Services allows up to 10 simultaneous connections.
3. You must have TCP/IP installed before installing Microsoft Peer Web Services.
4. You must install DHCP client software to use a DHCP server.
5. A client can keep a DHCP address as long as it wants without restriction.

Answers: *1. False 2. True 3. True 4. False 5. False*

Internet Service Manager

Once you have installed Peer Web Services, you can use Internet Service Manager to manage this service. *Internet Service Manager* can be used to configure Peer Web Services services, to configure Peer Web Services security, and to start and stop the individual Peer Web Services services.

You can modify the properties for WWW Services on remote computers using the Internet Service Manager. The WWW Service Properties dialog box is shown in Figure 9-5. Note the configurable options on the Service tab.

The configuration options for the WWW service are on the Service tab. Many of the options on this tab are security features. The most commonly configured options are

- **Anonymous Logon:** This section should be configured if the check box next to Allow Anonymous is selected in the Password Authentication section. When a user name and password are entered in the Anonymous Logon section, the user rights and permissions assigned to this user name are applied to all anonymous users of the WWW service. In this way, Peer Web Services security is integrated with Windows NT security. The default user name listed is IUSR_*Computer_name*.

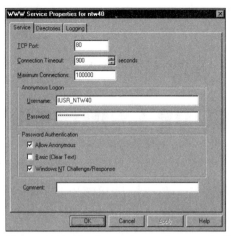

Figure 9-5 *Configuration options on the WWW Service Properties Service tab*

- **Password Authentication:** The three options in this section are Allow Anonymous, Basic (Clear Text), and Windows NT Challenge/Response.

- **Allow Anonymous:** If you select the check box next to Allow Anonymous, anyone with Internet access can access the WWW service on your computer anonymously. These users will not be required to supply a user name and password. If you clear the check box next to Allow Anonymous, all users will be required to supply a user name and a password to access the WWW service.

- **Basic (Clear Text):** If you select the check box next to Basic (Clear Text), user names and passwords can be sent over the Internet in an unencrypted format. Selecting this option is not normally desirable because it compromises the security of your computer. If this check box is cleared, unencrypted user names and passwords will not be accepted by the WWW service. The Basic (Clear Text) option is not selected by default.

- **Windows NT Challenge/Response:** If you select the check box next to Windows NT Challenge/Response, user names and passwords can be sent over the Internet in an encrypted format. If this check box is cleared, encrypted user names and passwords will not be accepted by the WWW service. This security feature is selected by default and should be used in high-security environments.

Troubleshooting Common Problems

Most TCP/IP connectivity problems are caused by incorrectly configured TCP/IP settings on the computer that has the problem.

TCP/IP connectivity problems commonly reported by users include the following:

- A user is unable to access a computer located on another subnet.
- A user is unable to access the Internet.
- A user is unable to access computers on both the local and remote subnets.
- TCP/IP fails to initialize on the user's computer.

When troubleshooting a TCP/IP connectivity problem, carefully check the TCP/IP settings on the computer experiencing the problem, including: IP address, subnet mask, and default gateway.

- **IP address:** Make sure the computer's IP address is *not* a duplicate of another IP address used on the network, and that it is an appropriate IP address for the local subnet (the network ID portion of the IP address must be the same for all computers on the local subnet).
- **Subnet mask:** Ensure the computer's subnet mask is the same subnet mask used by all computers and routers located on that subnet.
- **Default gateway:** Ensure the computer's default gateway address matches the IP address of a router on the local subnet.

Two command-line utilities exist that can help you when you're troubleshooting TCP/IP connectivity problems: `Ipconfig.exe` and `ping.exe`.

`Ipconfig.exe` displays the computer's current IP configuration settings, including IP address, subnet mask, and default gateway. To use `Ipconfig.exe`, select Start ➪ Programs ➪ Command Prompt. At the command prompt, type **ipconfig /all** and press Enter.

It is important to understand that the ping command can be used to determine if there are any communication failures or errors between two network computers. This is often the target of many TCP/IP troubleshooting questions on the test.

`Ping.exe` verifies network communications between the local computer and any other computer specified on the network. To use `ping.exe`, select Start ➪ Programs ➪ Command Prompt. At the command prompt, type **ping *ip_address*** and press Enter. (The IP address entered is the IP address of the computer with which you are attempting to communicate.) If your computer is capable of communicating with the remote computer specified, `ping.exe` will display four replies from the remote computer's IP address. The following is an example of a successful ping response:

```
Reply from 192.168.59.5: bytes=32 time<10ms TTL=128
Reply from 192.168.59.5: bytes=32 time<10ms TTL=128
Reply from 192.168.59.5: bytes=32 time<10ms TTL=128
Reply from 192.168.59.5: bytes=32 time<10ms TTL=128
```

If your computer is incapable of communicating with the remote computer specified, `ping.exe` usually displays `Request timed out` four times.

You can ping your own computer's IP address to determine whether TCP/IP is correctly configured and initialized on your local computer. If TCP/IP is properly configured on your local computer, `ping.exe` will display four replies from your local computer's IP address.

Have You Mastered?

Now it's time to apply what you've learned in this chapter by testing your mastery of the material. These questions provide you with a means to determine if you are ready to move on to the next chapter or if you need to review the material again.

1. **You are installing TCP/IP on a Windows NT Workstation computer. Which pieces of information must you have in order to configure TCP/IP to communicate with computers on the local subnet? (Choose two.)**

   ☐ A.   TCP/IP host address
   ☐ B.   Subnet mask
   ☐ C.   Default router
   ☐ D.   Frame type
   ☐ E.   Internal network number

   The correct answers are **A** and **B**. Because you only need to communicate with computers on the local subnet, you do not need a default router. Additionally, TCP/IP is not configured for a specific Frame type or internal network number as is IPX/SPX. For more information, see the "IP Addressing" section of this chapter.

2. **You are configuring Microsoft Peer Web Service on your Windows NT Workstation computer. What can you do to increase the level of security used when users connected to the WWW service? (Choose two.)**

   ☐ A.   Use Clear Text logon authentication.
   ☐ B.   Use Certificates for logon authentication.

☐ C. Use Windows NT Challenge/Response logon authentication.
☐ D. Configure a subnet mask.

The correct answers are **A** and **C**. By enabling Clear Text or Windows NT Challenge/Response, you can prevent users from connecting to the Web site anonymously. Additionally, you can assign permissions to users that enable them to access only certain parts of the Web site, thus increasing the security of the information on the Web site. Certificates cannot be used with PWS to provide authentication. For more information, see the section entitled "Microsoft Peer Web Services."

3. **You are installing 20 Windows NT Workstation computers onto a single subnet on your network. Your network consists of 30 subnets connected with routers. You are installing TCP/IP on each of the Windows NT Workstation computers. What TCP/IP configuration information will probably be the same on all of the computers? (Choose two.)**

☐ A. TCP/IP Address
☐ B. Subnet mask
☐ C. Default router
☐ D. Host name

The correct answers are **B** and **C**. Because the Windows NT Workstation computers are on the same subnet, they will likely have the same subnet mask and default router defined for them. Whereas the TCP/IP address and host name are unique to each computer, regardless of where it resides on a network. For more information, see the "IP Addressing" section.

4. **You are troubleshooting a communications problem on a Windows NT Workstation computer. The computer can access other computers and devices on the local subnet, but is**

incapable of accessing resources on other parts of the network and the Internet. What is the first thing you should verify?

☐ A. TCP/IP Address
☐ B. Subnet mask
☐ C. Default router
☐ D. Host name

The correct answer is **C**. If a computer is capable of accessing resources on a local subnet and cannot communicate across subnets, the problem is likely to be an incorrect default router setting. Without a default router defined, the workstation has no means to pass traffic to computers that reside on remote subnets. For more information, see the "Default Gateway Addresses" section of this chapter.

5. **Your Windows NT Workstation is configured to use a DHCP server from which to receive TCP/IP configuration settings. You need to determine the IP address that the server has assigned to your computer. What can you do to view your IP address that was assigned to your computer?**

☐ A. Use Network in Control Panel to view the TCP/IP protocol configuration.
☐ B. Use the `ipconfig /all` command.
☐ C. Use the Internet Service Manager to view your TCP/IP configuration.
☐ D. Use the `ping /all` command.

The correct answer is **B**. The command line `ipconfig` application can be used to display the current TCP/IP configuration for each network adapter in a computer. This application will show the TCP/IP address, subnet mask, and default gateway, among other things, for each adapter. Network in the Control Panel will not show the current TCP/IP assignments, it will only indicate that the computer is configured to use DHCP. For more information, refer back to the "Troubleshooting Common Problems" section.

6. You are experiencing difficulty connecting to a TCP/IP host computer on a remote subnet on your network. Previously you had no problems working with this remote host, but recently you have not been able to reach the host. What can you do to determine if there is a communications problem between your Windows NT Workstation computer and the remote host?

    ☐ A. Change your computer's subnet mask to match that of the remote host.
    ☐ B. Change your computer's default gateway to match that of the remote host.
    ☐ C. Use the `ipconfig` command.
    ☐ D. Use the `ping` command.

The correct answer is **D**. The ping command can be used in conjunction with the remote host name or TCP/IP address to determine if there is a communications failure. The ping command will trace the route to the remote host and report back if any errors are encountered or if the host was unreachable. The configuration settings on the Windows NT workstation won't necessarily solve the problem, especially when the scenario stated that the two computers had been communicating previously. For more information, refer back to the "Troubleshooting Common Problems" section.

7. You are configuring Microsoft Peer Web Services on your Windows NT Workstation computer. Which authentication type will prevent user names and passwords from being readable as they are transmitted to the Web server?

    ☐ A. Basic logon authentication
    ☐ B. Anonymous logon authentication
    ☐ C. Windows NT Challenge/Response logon authentication
    ☐ D. Certificate logon authentication

The correct answer is **C**. The Windows NT Challenge/Response logon authentication process prevents passwords from being transmitted in an unencrypted format. Both basic and anonymous authentications transmit user name and passwords in clear/readable text. Certificate authentication is not available with Microsoft Peer Web Services. For more information, see the "Microsoft Peer Web Services" section.

8. You are installing Microsoft Peer Web Services on your Windows NT Workstation computer. What must you do before you can install Microsoft Peer Web Services?

    ☐ A. Install the TCP/IP protocol.
    ☐ B. Remove all of the installed protocols except TCP/IP.
    ☐ C. Install the Microsoft Internet Services Manager.
    ☐ D. Connect to the Internet.

The correct answer is **A.** Before you can install Microsoft Peer Web Server, you must have TCP/IP installed and configured on your computer. Microsoft PWS will work fine with other protocols installed on the computer, but PWS will not be available through protocols other than TCP/IP. Additionally, the Internet Services Manager is a component that is installed with Microsoft Peer Web Services. For more information, see the "Microsoft Peer Web Services" section of this chapter.

Practice Your Skills

Here is a chance to apply your practical, hands-on experience and material from this chapter. These exercises are designed for you to apply not only the material in the book, but to gain greater experience and exposure to the product. These exercises are a critical part of understanding the product and gaining valuable experience for using the product and passing the certification exam. For each of the following problems, consider the given facts and determine what you think are possible causes of the problem and what course of action you might take to resolve the problem.

1. Choosing a protocol for a large network

EXERCISE You are designing a large enterprise-wide network. What makes TCP/IP such a good choice for large, routed networks supporting thousands of computers?

ANALYSIS The TCP/IP protocol is a high-speed routable protocol that scales to fit very large and complex networks. In addition to its capability to overcome network outages and downed links, TCP/IP is supported on more computing platforms that any other protocol. These factors combined with its capability to provide services to clients over a single protocol, make TCP/IP the logical choice for today's complex enterprise networks.

2. The importance of the subnet mask

EXERCISE You are installing Windows NT Workstation computers on a network that contains several subnets connected with routers. When you configure the TCP/IP protocol, why is it important to know what the subnet mask should be for the Windows NT Workstation computers?

ANALYSIS The subnet mask indicates to the Windows NT Workstation computer which portion of the host TCP/IP address is the network ID address and which is the host ID address. The subnet mask not only allows the client to know its own host address, but also to know that of the local subnet, and the addresses that are local to its subnet. When the computer determines that a destination address is not local, it forwards the traffic to the default router and indicates where it should be sent.

3. Using DHCP Servers

EXERCISE You are in the process of deploying a large number of Windows NT Workstation computers. You will be using the NWLink IPX/SPX Compatible Transport and TCP/IP on the computers. What are some advantages of using a DHCP server to provide TCP/IP configuration to the clients rather than manually configuring the clients?

ANALYSIS The DHCP server can automate the process of delivering TCP/IP configuration settings to a client computer. Each time the computer starts, it checks in with a DHCP server and requests an address, or verifies the last address assigned to it and retrieves configuration settings for default gateway, subnet mask, and so on. In addition, the DHCP server can specify the period of time for which the configuration is valid. This permits networks with thousands of client computers to share an IP address; when a client is shutdown and its lease on the address expires, another computer can assume the lease.

However, if the lease is not expired, or the lease period is too long, the address will not be recycled to other computers.

4. Installing Microsoft Peer Web Services

EXERCISE You are installing Microsoft Peer Web Services on your Windows NT Workstation computer. As you design and test your Web sites on the PWS service, what are some important things to remember?

ANALYSIS First of all, Microsoft Peer Web Services only supports a maximum of 10 simultaneous connections. Now that isn't 10 users, as most HTTP sessions use two or more connections, so the maximum number of simultaneous users is apt to be more like three to four users. Additionally, some of the security features found in Microsoft Internet Information Server are not available in Peer Web Services. As a result, the authentication process may perform differently than it will once the Web site is posted to an IIS server.

5. Managing Microsoft Peer Web Services

EXERCISE Your Windows NT Workstation computer has Microsoft Peer Web Services installed. You are adding a new hard disk to your computer and you would like to move the Web site directory to the new hard disk. What must you do?

ANALYSIS The Microsoft Internet Services Manager can be used to relocate the home directory to the new hard disk. You will then need to copy the Web site files to the new folder, as the Internet Services Manager only changes the directory that is looked in for the Web site files — it does not move your Web files to the new directory.

Dial-Up
Networking

ONE OF THE MOST POPULAR FEATURES of Windows NT Workstation computers is Remote Access. As a result, a number of questions on the Windows NT Workstation exam cover this topic. To prepare you, this chapter takes a look at Remote Access Server (RAS). Here I show you the various connection protocols available, as well as their benefits and configuration processes. You also have the opportunity to examine the RAS NetBIOS gateway feature and take a quick look at installing and configuring RAS. The chapter wraps up with a look at configuring Dial-Up Networking, which is the client component of Remote Access Server, and some common troubleshooting tips for RAS problems.

Exam Material in This Chapter

Based on Microsoft Objectives

Connectivity

- Configure and install Dial-Up Networking in a given situation

Based on Author's Experience

- You need to know the connection limit for Remote Access Server when it is installed on a Windows NT Workstation computer.

- You definitely need to understand the limitation of SLIP as it pertains to Windows NT Workstation computers.

- You should be familiar with the protocols supported by PPP connections and what configuration options are available for PPP connections.

- You should have a basic understanding of Multilink connections.

- You should expect a few questions on how network protocols are handled by RAS servers when a Windows NT Workstation computer dials in.

Are You Prepared?

Do you have what it takes? Try out these self-assessment questions to see if you have prepared for the material in this chapter or if you should review problem areas.

1. **You are installing Dial-Up Networking on your Windows NT Workstation computer. You want to use the highest level of security possible when connecting to your company's Windows NT Remote Access Server over the Internet. What should you do to ensure this?**

   ☐ A. Use a PPTP connection.

   ☐ B. Use a SLIP connection.

   ☐ C. Configure the RAS server to require encrypted passwords.

   ☐ D. Use only the NWLink IPX/SPX Compatible Transport for the connection.

2. **You are using your Windows NT Workstation computer to dial into your corporate Windows NT Remote Access Server. Every time you connect and authenticate yourself, the server hangs up. What is the most likely problem?**

   ☐ A. The server is configured for PPTP connections.

   ☐ B. The server is configured for Call Back security.

   ☐ C. Your computer is using a protocol not supported on the RAS server.

   ☐ D. Your computer is using a static IP address.

3. You are installing Remote Access Server on your Windows NT Workstation computer. You want to have outside consultants connect to the network and access your mail system through this computer. One of the consultants has called you because she is unable to connect to your computer from her UNIX system. What is the most likely problem?

    □ A. The server is configured for PPTP connections.

    □ B. The server does not have the TCP/IP protocol installed.

    □ C. The consultant's computer is using SLIP to connect to the server.

    □ D. The consultant's computer has a TCP/IP address that conflicts with an address on your corporate network.

Answers:

1. A   *The Point-to-Point Tunneling Protocol enables you to have a connection to your corporate RAS server while connected over the Internet. This provides you with the means for leveraging the global dispersion of ISPs and for using the infrastructure to provide a secure method of communications. See the "Connection Protocols Supported by RAS" section.*

2. B   *If Call Back security is enabled for your userid, once you have authenticated yourself, the RAS server hangs up and calls your computer back at a predetermined phone number, or if configured, at a number you specify during your authentication. See the "Configuring Security Properties" section.*

3. C   *Microsoft Windows NT does not support using a Windows NT computer as a SLIP host. SLIP is an older form of PPP common among UNIX systems. A Windows NT computer can dial into a SLIP host, but not vice versa. See the "Connection Protocols Supported by RAS" section.*

RAS Overview

Remote Access Service (RAS) is a Windows NT service that enables dial-up network connections between a RAS server and a Dial-Up Networking client computer. RAS includes software components for both the RAS server and the Dial-Up Networking client in a single Windows NT service.

 TEST TIP
RAS and Dial-Up Networking are complex topics. Even Administrators who manage RAS servers on a daily basis are well advised to study the details and nuances presented in this chapter before taking the Workstation exam. Become familiar with the various dialog boxes and configuration options. I recommend you review this chapter just prior to taking the exam.

RAS enables users of remote computers to use the network as though they were directly connected to it. Once the dial-up connection is established, there is no difference in network functionality, except the speed of the link is often much slower than a direct connection to the LAN.

RAS is an important networking function for today's highly mobile workforce. With RAS and Dial-Up Networking, users can connect to their company's network from home, from a hotel room, or from a client's remote office.

Although Windows NT Server RAS supports up to 256 simultaneous dial in connections, Windows NT Workstation RAS only supports a single dial in connection. For this reason, a Windows NT Workstation computer is not typically used as a RAS server.

 TEST TRAP
Windows NT Workstation supports only one dial in connection at a time. You may see an exam question in which users are unable to connect to a RAS server; if the server is a Windows NT Workstation computer, the problem may be due to a user already being connected to the server.

Client computers that run MS-DOS, Windows 3.1*x*, Windows for Workgroups, Windows 95, and Windows NT can be configured as Dial-Up

Networking or RAS client computers. These clients can all connect to a Windows NT RAS server.

RAS supports multiple connection types, connection protocols, and transport protocols.

Connection Protocols Supported by RAS

RAS communications can be carried out over several connection protocols. These protocols provide the data-link connectivity for Dial-Up Networking in much the same way Ethernet, ARCNET, or Token Ring provide the data-link connectivity on a local area network. Each of these protocols has different features and capabilities. The connection protocols commonly used by RAS include Serial Line Internet Protocol (SLIP), Point-to-Point Protocol (PPP), Point-to-Point Multilink Protocol, and Point-to-Point Tunneling Protocol (PPTP).

Serial Line Internet Protocol

The *Serial Line Internet Protocol* (SLIP) is an older connection protocol, commonly associated with UNIX computers, that only supports one transport protocol — TCP/IP. SLIP connections don't support NWLink IPX/SPX Compatible Transport or NetBEUI.

 Unlike PPP, which supports multiple protocols over its connection, SLIP connections can only carry TCP/IP. In addition, PPP is able to carry multiple protocols simultaneously. So even if you were using TCP/IP, PPP would still be the better choice because of simultaneous protocol transmissions and other features.

The version of SLIP supported by Windows NT 4.0 requires a static IP address configuration at the client computer — dynamic IP addressing is not supported. Additionally, password encryption is not supported by this version of SLIP. A script file is usually required to automate the connection process when SLIP is used.

Windows NT RAS can't be used as a SLIP server. Only the Dial-Up Networking portion of RAS (the client side) supports SLIP. This means only dial out SLIP connections are supported, such as when a Dial-Up Networking client computer dials out to connect to a UNIX SLIP server. (The Dial-Up Networking client computer, in this case, can be either a Windows NT Server or Windows NT Workstation computer that has RAS installed on it.)

Point-to-Point Protocol

Point-to-Point Protocol (PPP) is a newer connection protocol designed to overcome the limitations of SLIP. PPP is currently the industry standard remote connection protocol, and is recommended for use by Microsoft.

PPP is supported over both dial in and dial out connections. Windows NT computers that have RAS installed on them can function either as Dial-Up Networking clients or as RAS servers when using PPP.

PPP

PPP connections support multiple transport protocols, including TCP/IP, NWLINK IPX/SPX Compatible Transport, and NetBEUI. Additionally, PPP supports dynamic server-based IP addressing (such as DHCP).

PPP supports password encryption, and the PPP connection process does not usually require a script file.

Point-to-Point Multilink Protocol

Point-to-Point Multilink Protocol is an extension of PPP. Point-to-Point Multilink Protocol combines the bandwidth from multiple physical connections into a single logical connection. This means multiple modem, ISDN, or X.25 connections can be bundled together to form a single logical connection with a much higher bandwidth than a single connection can support.

Point-to-Point Multilink enables multiple connections to be bound together to provide a high aggregate bandwidth connection. The server must be configured to support this option.

To implement Point-to-Point Multilink Protocol, multiple modems and telephone lines (or multiple ISDN adapter cards and lines; or multiple X.25 adapters, PADs, and connections) are required at *both* the RAS server and at the Dial-Up Networking client locations. Additionally, both sides of the connection must be configured to use Point-to-Point Multilink Protocol.

Point-to-Point Tunneling Protocol

Point-to-Point Tunneling Protocol (PPTP) permits a virtual encrypted connection between two computers over an existing TCP/IP network connection. The existing TCP/IP network connection can be over a LAN or over a Dial-Up Networking TCP/IP connection (including the Internet). All standard transport protocols are supported within the PPTP connection, including NWLink IPX/SPX Compatible Transport, NetBEUI, and TCP/IP.

 PPTP connections are used over existing connections such as a LAN or Dial-Up Networking connection. This underlying connection must be in place before the PPTP connection can be established.

A primary reason for choosing to use PPTP is it supports the RAS encryption feature over standard, unencrypted TCP/IP networks, such as the Internet.

Transport Protocols Supported by RAS

All Windows NT standard transport protocols are supported by RAS. Client computers can connect to a RAS server by using one of the following:

- NetBEUI
- TCP/IP
- IPX — including NWLink IPX/SPX Compatible Transport

Remember that the DLC protocol is not supported for RAS connections, whereas NetBEUI, TCP/IP, and NWLink IPX/SPX Compatible Transport are supported.

Client computers can use one or more of these transport protocols on a RAS connection. For example, a client computer that needs to access a NetWare server and a UNIX host via a RAS server can use both NWLink IPX/SPX Compatible Transport and TCP/IP during a single RAS session.

The RAS server acts as a router for client computers that use TCP/IP or IPX, enabling these clients to access other computers on the network via the RAS server's routing functionality. Access to NetBIOS-based resources (such as shared folders and printers, Lotus Notes servers, SQL Servers, and SNA Servers) and protocol-specific resources (such as NetWare servers and World Wide Web servers) is possible because of the RAS server's routing capability. The RAS server can only route protocols installed on the RAS server.

A RAS server acts as a NetBIOS gateway for client computers that use the NetBEUI protocol.

RAS NetBIOS Gateway

The *RAS NetBIOS gateway* is a function of the RAS server. The RAS NetBIOS gateway enables client computers that use NetBEUI to access shared resources on other servers located on the RAS server's local network. These other servers can use TCP/IP, NWLink IPX/SPX Compatible Transport, or NetBEUI. In a nutshell, the RAS NetBIOS gateway performs protocol translation for the remote NetBEUI client computer so that computer can access shared resources on the RAS server's local network.

 Only NetBIOS-based services (such as shared folders and printers, Lotus Notes servers, SQL Servers, and SNA Servers) can be accessed by NetBEUI client computers via the RAS NetBIOS gateway. Protocol-specific services (such as NetWare servers and World Wide Web servers) can't be accessed by NetBEUI client computers via the RAS NetBIOS gateway.

Installing and Configuring RAS

Before installing RAS, you should install and configure all the transport protocols you plan to use on the RAS server. Also, you should install and configure at least one connection device, such as a modem, ISDN adapter card, or X.25 adapter card, in the Windows NT computer on which you plan to install RAS. Alternatively, you can install the Point-to-Point Tunneling Protocol (PPTP).

Configuring Ports

Configuring modems and ports is an integral part of the RAS installation and configuration process. Each RAS modem or port can be configured to either receive calls, make calls, or do both, as shown in Figure 10-1.

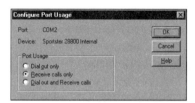

Figure 10-1 *Configuring dial in/dial out port settings*

Note the three port usage options available:

- **Dial out only:** If you select the option button next to Dial out only, the port is *only* available for use by the Dial-Up Networking client. Selecting this option button for *all* ports effectively selects a client-only role for this computer. This computer isn't able to function as a RAS server if this option button is selected for all ports.

- **Receive calls only:** If you select the option button next to Receive calls only, the port will *only* be available for use by the RAS server. Selecting this option button for *all* ports effectively selects a RAS server-only role for this computer. This computer won't be able to function as a Dial-Up

Networking client if this option button is selected for all ports.

- **Dial out and Receive calls:** If you select the option button next to Dial out and Receive calls, the port becomes available for use by both the RAS server and the Dial-Up Networking client. This computer is then able to function both as a RAS server and as a Dial-Up Networking client.

Each port is configured individually. If one port is configured to dial out only, another can be configured to receive calls only or to dial out and receive calls.

Configuring Protocols and Encryption

The next part of the RAS installation and configuration process involves configuring protocols and encryption. The Network Configuration dialog box, shown in Figure 10-2, is the primary RAS configuration dialog box. Notice the Dial out Protocols and Server Settings sections. In this dialog box, select dial out protocols (if you configured any ports for dial out usage), configure dial in protocols and RAS server settings (if you configured any ports for dial in usage), and select RAS encryption features.

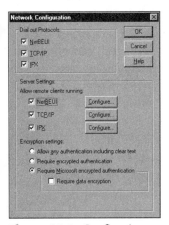

Figure 10-2 *Configuring protocols and security*

Configuration options selected in the Network Configuration dialog box are global settings that apply to *all* ports. No individual port protocol or encryption settings are available.

You can configure the RAS properties using the following settings:

- **Dial out Protocols:** If you configured any ports for dial out usage, you can select any or all of three dial out protocols: NetBEUI, TCP/IP, and/or IPX (NWLink IPX/SPX Compatible Transport). If you *didn't* configure any ports for dial out usage, these options are grayed out and not available. All installed protocols are selected by default.

- **Server Settings: Allow remote clients running:** If you configured any ports for dial in (RAS server) usage, you can select any or all of three dial in protocols: NetBEUI, TCP/IP, and/or IPX (NWLink IPX/SPX Compatible Transport). If you didn't configure any ports for dial in usage, the Server Settings configuration section is not displayed. All installed protocols are selected by default.

You can configure individual protocol-specific options for each of the three protocols in this section. (Configuring each of these protocols is discussed in detail later in this chapter.)

- **Server Settings: Encryption settings:** Select one of the three possible password authentication encryption options:

  - **Allow any authentication including clear text:** If you select the option button next to Allow any authentication including clear text, the RAS server authenticates user passwords in clear text or in any encryption format supported by the RAS server. Selecting this option button, in effect, enables the Dial-Up Networking client to determine the level of password encryption.

  - **Require encrypted authentication:** If you select the option button next to Require encrypted authentication, Dial-Up Networking clients are required to send encrypted user passwords in any encryption format supported by the RAS server. The RAS server won't authenticate user passwords sent in clear text.

- **Require Microsoft encrypted authentication:** If you select the option button next to Require Microsoft encrypted authentication, Dial-Up Networking clients must send user passwords encrypted using Microsoft encrypted authentication. The RAS server won't authenticate user passwords sent in clear text or in any encryption format other than Microsoft encrypted authentication. This is the most secure password authentication option and is selected by default. If this option button is selected, the Require data encryption check box is available.

- **Require data encryption:** If you select this check box, in addition to requiring Microsoft encrypted password authentication, the RAS server requires that all data sent to the RAS server from the Dial-Up Networking client be transmitted in an encrypted format. This check box is not selected by default. Currently, only Windows NT Dial-Up Networking clients support data encryption. If you want to use the RAS server to establish secure, private PPTP connections, make sure you select the option button next to Require Microsoft encrypted authentication *and* the check box next to Require data encryption.

Configuring TCP/IP

If you selected TCP/IP as a dial out protocol, it must be configured using the RAS Server TCP/IP Configuration dialog box, which is shown in Figure 10-3.

Notice the options to configure IP address assignment for remote Dial-Up Networking clients:

- **Entire network:** If you select the option button next to Entire network, the RAS server functions as a router for Dial-Up Networking client computers, and remote TCP/IP clients are capable of accessing resources on all servers that use TCP/IP on the RAS server's local network.

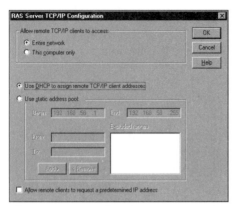

Figure 10-3 *Configuring RAS server TCP/IP options*

- **This computer only:** If you select the option button next
  to This computer only, the RAS server does not function as
  a router for Dial-Up Networking client computers, and
  remote TCP/IP clients are only able to access resources
  located on the RAS server. This option is sometimes used
  in high security environments to prevent unauthorized
  access to other computers on the corporate network.

- **Use DHCP to assign remote TCP/IP client addresses:** If
  you select the option button next to Use DHCP to assign
  remote TCP/IP client addresses, the RAS server requests an
  IP address for the remote TCP/IP client from the DHCP
  server on its local network when the remote TCP/IP client
  connects to the RAS server. This option should be selected
  if a DHCP server is available.

- **Use static address pool:** If you select the option button
  next to Use static address pool, the RAS server assigns an IP
  address to the remote TCP/IP client from the range of IP
  addresses specified in the Begin and End text boxes.

Configuring NWLink IPX/SPX Compatible Transport

If you selected IPX (NWLink IPX/SPX Compatible Transport) as a dial
out protocol, it must be configured. The RAS Server IPX Configuration
dialog box is shown in Figure 10-4.

Figure 10-4 *Configuring RAS
server IPX options*

Notice the network number configuration options:

- **Allocate network numbers automatically:** If you select the
  option button next to Allocate network numbers
  automatically, the RAS server assigns a network number
  not currently in use to a remote IPX client computer when
  it connects to the RAS server.

- **Allocate network numbers:** If you select the option button
  next to Allocate network numbers, the RAS server assigns a
  network number from the specified range of numbers
  listed in the From and To text boxes to a remote IPX client
  computer when it connects to the RAS server. You must
  specify a range of network numbers in the From and To
  text boxes if you select this option button.

Two additional check boxes are available in this section, regardless of
the network number allocation method you select:

- **Assign same network number to all IPX clients:** If you
  select the check box next to Assign same network number
  to all IPX clients, the RAS server assigns the same network
  number to all remote IPX client computers.

- **Allow remote clients to request IPX node number:** Select
  the check box next to Allow remote clients to request IPX
  node number when remote IPX clients have been configured
  so that their Dial-Up Networking software requests a specific
  IPX node number from the RAS server.

True or False?

1. You can configure individual port protocol or encryption settings.

2. RAS can only use a static pool of TCP/IP addresses for dial-in clients.

3. A RAS port can be configured for dial out or receive, but not both.

4. RAS can act as a NetBIOS gateway for NetBEUI dial-in clients.

5. PPTP sessions require an existing TCP/IP connection to be available.

Answers: *1. False 2. False 3. False 4. True 5. True*

Dial-Up Networking Connections

Dial-Up Networking is the client/dial out component of RAS. The Dial-Up Networking accessory is installed during the RAS installation. Dial-Up Networking enables Windows NT computers to connect to dial-up servers and to establish network connections through those servers. Dial-up servers include Windows NT RAS servers, UNIX computers configured as SLIP or PPP servers, and any other computers, routers, or front-end processors configured as SLIP or PPP servers.

Before the Dial-Up Networking functionality on a Windows NT computer can be used, RAS must be installed and configured, and at least one of the computer's RAS ports must be configured for dial out usage. Additionally, you must create at least one phonebook entry that contains various dialing information and instructions. Phonebook entries are created by using the Windows NT Dial-Up Networking accessory, and are explained in detail in the next section.

Compatible RAS Hosts

Windows NT Workstation can use Dial-Up Networking to access the following type of hosts:

- Windows NT RAS Servers
- Hosts configured to support SLIP or PPP connections, such as routers, async servers, and UNIX hosts

Configuring Phonebook Entries

Phonebook entries contain all the information and instructions required by Dial-Up Networking to connect to a dial-up server.

The Basic tab in the New Phonebook Entry dialog box is used to configure the phonebook entry name, the phone number to be used, and the modem/port to be used to establish the connection to the dial-up server. The Basic tab contains several configurable options:

- **Entry name:** Type in a name that describes the connection in the Entry name text box. The default name is MyDialUpServer. Entry name is a mandatory setting.

- **Comment:** You can enter a comment about the phonebook entry in the Comment text box, if you want to. This entry is optional.

- **Phone number:** In the Phone number text box, type in the phone number to be dialed to access the dial-up server. Alternate phone numbers for the dial-up server can be entered by clicking the Alternates command button. If this dial-up connection is to use PPTP, enter the IP address of the RAS server instead of a phone number in the Phone number text box. (Remember, PPTP tunnels its connection *inside* of an existing TCP/IP network connection.)

- **Use Telephony dialing properties:** If you select the check box next to Use Telephony dialing properties, Dial-Up Networking uses your location telephony settings (area code, number to dial to get an outside line, and so on) when dialing the phone number entered in the Phone number text box to establish a connection. If you don't select this check box, the location telephony settings aren't used — only the phone number listed in the Phone number text box is used.

- **Dial using:** Select the modem, other connection device, or PPTP RAS port you want to use for this connection from the Dial using drop-down list box. After you highlight your selection, click the Configure command button to configure the modem, device, or port. Modems can also be configured by using the Modems application in the Control Panel.

- **Use another port if busy:** Select the check box next to Use another port if busy if you want Dial-Up Networking to use a different port to establish a connection when the primary port you selected is busy.

Configuring a Multilink connection

When you need more throughput than a single line can provide, you might consider using multiple lines to establish a Point-to-Point Multilink Protocol connection.

The Multiple Line Configuration dialog box is shown in Figure 10-5. Notice the text in the dialog box that states multiple lines simultaneously connected to a PPP Multilink server behave like a single, faster connection. Select two or more modems, devices, or ports from those listed, and individually configure a phone number for each by highlighting the modem, device, or port and clicking the Phone numbers command button.

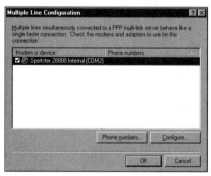

Figure 10-5 *Selecting the modems, devices, or ports to be used in a Multilink connection*

Call Back security should normally *not* be configured on RAS servers that support Multilink connections. The reason for this is only one phone number can be stored in the call back configuration, and if the RAS server breaks the connection and calls this number back, only a single line is then used for the connection. This effectively eliminates any Multilink functionality.

Multilink Connections

To establish a Multilink connection, both the Dial-Up Networking client and the RAS server must be configured to support Multilink. Although both Windows NT Workstation and Windows NT Server Dial-Up Networking can support dial out Multilink connections, only Windows NT Server (with RAS installed) can support dial in Multilink connections.

Configuring server properties

To configure server properties, including dial-up server type and network protocols, use the Server tab in the New Phonebook Entry dialog box. The Server tab is shown in Figure 10-6.

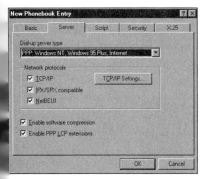

Figure 10-6 *Configuring dial-up server type and network protocols*

Before connecting to your host, you need to configure RAS to communicate properly with the remote host.

- **Dial-up server type:** Select the type of dial-up server you want to connect to from the Dial-up server type drop-down list box.

- **Network protocols:** Select the transport protocols you want to use for this dial-up connection. Protocols available include TCP/IP, (NWLink) IPX/SPX compatible (Transport), and NetBEUI. You can select more than one protocol. All installed protocols are selected by default.

- **TCP/IP Settings:** If you select TCP/IP, click the TCP/IP Settings command button to configure TCP/IP settings for this connection. Here you can specify if you want either a server-assigned IP address or specify a manual IP address configuration.

- **Enable software compression:** Select the check box next to Enable software compression if you want the Dial-Up Networking software to compress all data before it is transmitted to the RAS server. You should disable modem compression if you select this option. This check box is selected by default.

- **Enable PPP LCP extensions:** Select the check box next to Enable PPP LCP extensions if you want to enable the newer PPP features. Deselect this check box only if you are unable to connect with it selected. This check box is selected by default.

Configuring security properties

To configure security, including password authentication and encryption options, use the Security tab in the New Phonebook Entry dialog box. The Security tab is shown in Figure 10-7. Notice the authentication and encryption options are similar to the Server Settings configured for dial in connections during the installation of RAS.

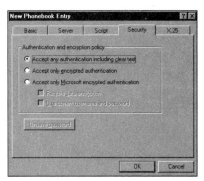

Figure 10-7 *Configuring password authentication and encryption options*

Options selected in this dialog box are applied to the Dial-Up Networking client only, not to the RAS server.

- **Accept any authentication including clear text:** If you select the option button next to Accept any authentication including clear text, Dial-Up Networking connects to a dial-up server using the lowest password authentication option accepted by the server. For example, if the dial-up server is configured to enable any authentication, including clear text, and this option is selected, Dial-Up Networking transmits the password to the dial-up server by using clear text.

- **Accept only encrypted authentication:** If you select the option button next to Accept only encrypted authentication, Dial-Up Networking is not able to connect to a dial-up server that does not support some form of encrypted authentication.

- **Accept only Microsoft encrypted authentication:** If you select the option button next to Accept only Microsoft encrypted authentication, Dial-Up Networking is not able to establish a connection with a dial-up server unless that server supports Microsoft encrypted authentication. You must select this option if you want to use data encryption.

If you select this option, two additional check boxes become available:

- **Require data encryption:** If you select the check box next to Require data encryption, the Dial-Up Networking client encrypts all data sent over this connection. You should select this check box if you are configuring a PPTP connection. This check box is only available if you selected the option button next to Accept only Microsoft encrypted authentication.

- **Use current username and password:** If you select the check box next to Use current username and password, Dial-Up Networking does not prompt you for a user name or password when establishing a connection with the dial-up server. This check box is only available if you selected the option button next to Accept only Microsoft encrypted authentication.

POP QUIZ **True or False?**

1. You should avoid using Call Back security when using Multilink connections.
2. Windows NT can connect to a host configured for SLIP connections only.
3. Scripts are usually required for PPP connections.
4. A phonebook entry contains all the configuration settings for a Dial-Up Networking connection.
5. You can only use one protocol for each Dial-Up Networking connection.

Answers: *1. True 2. True 3. False 4. True 5. False*

Troubleshooting Common Problems

Most common RAS problems reported by users involve an inability to connect to a RAS server, a third-party SLIP server, or a front-end processor from a Dial-Up Networking client computer. The following is a listing of common causes of RAS problems and recommended solutions:

- **Modem configuration or compatibility problem:** If you suspect your modem is the problem, first determine the type of modem to which you are attempting to connect, and then reconfigure your modem settings to the most compatible option, or as recommended by your ISP. If you are using an unsupported modem (for example, one not on the HCL), verify that your settings in the `Modem.inf` file are appropriate for your modem. If you have selected RAS software compression, ensure your modem is not configured to compress data. If you are still unable to connect, you can configure your modem to record a log file of all attempted connections. To configure a modem log file, use the Modems application in Control Panel to access your modem's Properties dialog box. Select the Connection tab and then the Advanced Connection Settings dialog box.

- **Password authentication problem:** If you suspect a password authentication problem, configure Dial-Up Networking to accept any authentication, including clear text, and/or configure the RAS server to enable any authentication, including clear text. (Note: Clear text passwords are usually required by SLIP servers.)

- **TCP/IP configuration problem:** If you suspect a TCP/IP configuration problem, contact the manager of the dial-up server you are attempting to connect to and determine the dial-up server's TCP/IP configuration. Configure Dial-Up Networking so that the client's TCP/IP configuration settings match those of the dial-up server.

- **Dial-Up Networking configuration problem:** Verify that you have chosen the appropriate dial-up server type (SLIP or PPP connection type) by contacting the manager of the dial-up server, if necessary.

- **Script problem:** If you are using a script, and your modem makes contact with the dial-up server but you are *not* able to successfully complete a connection to the dial-up server, try editing your script file or using a pop-up terminal window instead of the script file.

Have You Mastered?

Now it's time to apply what you've learned in this chapter by testing your mastery of the material. These questions provide you with a means of determining if you are ready to move on to the next chapter or if you need to review the material again.

1. **You are configuring your Windows NT Workstation computer to connect to a Windows NT RAS server computer. Which protocols are supported over a PPP connection and which enable you to access computers at the RAS Server site? (Choose all that apply.)**

   ☐ A. TCP/IP
   ☐ B. NetBEUI
   ☐ C. DLC 16bit
   ☐ D. DLC 32bit
   ☐ E. NWLink IPX/SPX Compatible Transport
   ☐ F. XNS/NB

   The correct answers are **A, B,** and **E.** Remote Access Server does not support DLC (in any flavor) or XNS/NB. Windows NT RAS servers do fully support TCP/IP, NetBEUI, and NWLink IPX/SPX Compatible Transport. For more information, see the "Connection Protocols Supported by RAS" section.

2. **You are installing Remote Access Server on your Windows NT Workstation computer so that people in your office can connect to the network using RAS on your computer. How many people can be connected simultaneously to your computer?**

☐ A. 1
☐ B. 5
☐ C. 10
☐ D. 256

The correct answer is **A**. Remote Access Server on a Windows NT Workstation computer does not support more than one simultaneous connection. If you need more connections, you need to use Windows NT Server, which supports up to 256 connections. For more information, see the "RAS Overview" section.

3. **You are connecting to your corporate network using Dial-Up Networking. You need to access HTTP and NetWare servers on the remote network using TCP/IP and NWLink IPX/SPX Compatible Transport. What Dial-Up Networking connection type must you use?**

☐ A. PPTP
☐ B. SLIP
☐ C. PPP
☐ D. ISDN

The correct answer is **A**. The Point-to-Point Protocol enables multiple protocols to be tunneled through the connection to the remote host. PPTP provides an encrypted connection over PPP and does not handle protocol-specific issues, and SLIP can only use TCP/IP. For more information, see the "Connection Protocols Supported by RAS" section.

4. **Because NetBEUI is a nonroutable protocol, how does Windows NT Remote Access Server treat PPP connections that are using NetBEUI?**

☐ A. The client computer is only allowed to access the RAS server.
☐ B. The RAS server refuses connections made using NetBEUI.
☐ C. The RAS server provides a NetBIOS gateway.

☐ D. The RAS server translates the NetBEUI traffic into NWLink IPX/SPX Compatible Transport packets.

The correct answer is **C**. The Remote Access Server automatically provides a gateway to NetBEUI users, enabling them to access the entire network through NetBIOS lookups. For more information, see the "RAS NetBIOS Gateway" section.

5. **You are configuring a Dial-Up Networking connection to your Internet service provider. You have two modems attached to your Windows NT Workstation computer. You configure your connection to Multilink. When you initiate the Dial-Up Networking connection, Multilink is unable to bind the two modems together. What is the most likely problem?**

☐ A. You do not have permission to use Multilink.
☐ B. The ISP host does not support Multilink.
☐ C. Your modems do not support Multilink.
☐ D. You are using a PPP connection.

The correct answer is **B**. Most Internet service providers do not use Windows NT RAS-compatible devices, so the likelihood of finding one that does support Multilink is slim. Furthermore, many ISPs specifically prohibit Multilink because it drastically reduces the number of available phone lines with which to connect. For more information, see the "Configuring a Multilink connection" section.

6. **You use Windows NT Dial-Up Networking to connect to your Internet service provider using PPP. When you connect, you are able to access Web servers at the ISP office, but you are unable to reach Web servers on the Internet. What configuration setting should you change?**

☐ A. Configure TCP/IP to use the default router on the remote network.
☐ B. Configure TCP/IP to disable PPP LCP extensions.

☐ C. Do not use a Multilink connection.

☐ D. Use TCP/IP instead of NWLink IPX/SPX Compatible Transport.

The correct answer is **A**. When you are able to connect to a RAS server and access hosts local to the RAS server, but are unable to reach other hosts, the problem is usually a TCP/IP default router configuration error. By using the default router on the remote network, the PPP connection uses the default router assigned by the RAS server. The use of LCP extensions or Multilink does not affect your ability to reach remote hosts once connected. For more information, see the "Configuring Protocols and Encryption" section.

7. **You are installing Remote Access Server on your Windows NT Workstation computer. Your computer has TCP/IP and NWLink IPX/SPX Compatible Transport installed. Users access your RAS computer using Dial-Up Networking and TCP/IP or NWLink IPX/SPX Compatible Transport. How does RAS handle the TCP/IP and NWLink IPX/SPX Compatible Transport traffic?**

☐ A. Remote Access Server acts as a router for the protocols.

☐ B. Remote Access Server acts as a bridge for the protocols.

☐ C. Remote Access Server acts as a gateway for the protocols.

☐ D. Remote Access Server acts as a repeater for the protocols.

The correct answer is **A**. Remote Access Server routes the two protocols, making the Dial-Up Networking connection a virtual subnet. Remote Access Server then routes between its local subnet and the Dial-Up Networking subnet. If a connection uses the NetBEUI protocol, RAS acts as a NetBIOS gateway for that protocol. For more information, see the "Configuring Protocols and Encryption" section.

8. **You are installing Remote Access Server on your Windows NT Workstation computer. You will be using a Windows NT Workstation computer to dial into your Remote Access Server using PPP. Which security features should you implement to have the highest level of security available? (Choose two.)**

☐ A. Accept only Microsoft encrypted authentication.
☐ B. Accept any authentication including clear text.
☐ C. Accept only encrypted authentication.
☐ D. Require data encryption.
☐ E. Enable software compression.
☐ F. Enable PPP LCP extensions.

The correct answers are **A** and **D**. Because you will be using a Microsoft-compatible platform to initiate a Dial-Up Networking connection, you can use a higher level of security than that provided by an open Remote Access Server configuration. The use of Microsoft encrypted authentication provides the highest level of encrypted user name and password authentication available. If you were using a non-Microsoft platform to make a PPP connection, this feature would most likely prevent a successful connection. For more information, see the "Configuring security properties" section.

Practice Your Skills

Here is a chance to apply your practical hands-on experience and material from this chapter. These exercises are designed not only to reinforce the material you've learned, but also to enable you to gain greater experience and exposure to the product. These exercises are a critical part of understanding the product and gaining valuable experience for using the product and passing the certification exam. For each of the following problems, consider the given facts and determine what you think are the possible causes of the problem and what course of action you might take to resolve the problem.

1. Choosing a remote connection protocol

EXERCISE You are configuring your Windows NT Workstation to use Dial-Up Networking to connect to a remote host. The remote host supports SLIP and PPP connections. What are the benefits of using PPP instead of SLIP?

ANALYSIS PPP connections support multiple transport protocols, including TCP/IP, NWLINK IPX/SPX Compatible Transport, and NetBEUI. PPP also supports dynamic server-based IP addressing (such as DHCP). PPP also supports password encryption, and the PPP connection process does not usually require a script file. SLIP connections can only use TCP/IP and usually require logon scripts to process the authentication.

2. Configuring RAS Server properties

EXERCISE You are installing Remote Access Server on your Windows NT Workstation. You plan on having users connect to your computer using PPP on a variety of platforms. What RAS options should you carefully evaluate to ensure Remote Access Server can support the largest variety of clients?

ANALYSIS Remote Access Server includes a number features and options that may be unsupported on non-Microsoft platforms. Enabling Microsoft encrypted authentication may prevent non-Microsoft clients from properly authenticating themselves. In addition, the use of Call Back security is also supported on a limited set of clients. When you install Remote Access Server, the default settings for PPP generally provide the largest support for mixed platform environments.

3. Using Call Back Security

EXERCISE You have installed Remote Access Server on your Windows NT Workstation. You are configuring the security features of Remote Access Server. What are some of the benefits of using Call Back security?

ANALYSIS The use of Call Back security can be leveraged in two ways. First, Call Back security can be configured with a preset phone number for calling a user back before continuing the Dial-Up Networking connection. The benefit of this type of configuration is it reduces the opportunity for unauthorized access to the network; even if a person got a hold of a user name and password, unless that person was at the proper phone number, he or she could not complete the connection. The second configuration enables the caller to specify a phone number for calling them back. This enables you to shift the cost of remote access connection from the user to your Remote Access Server, usually with better phone rates.

4. Troubleshooting failed PPP connections

EXERCISE You use Dial-Up Networking on your Windows NT Workstation computer to access remote access servers using PPP. What are some basic troubleshooting steps you can take when PPP connections fail?

ANALYSIS Dial-Up Networking has a number of PPP configurations that can be used to resolve connection failures. The most common problem is incorrectly configured TCP/IP settings. Most hosts that support PPP assign all o the TCP/IP settings required. Second, the use of PPP LCP extensions sometimes causes problems on older PPP hosts. By disabling these extensions, you may be able to resolve the problem. Third, the use of encrypted user names and passwords often prove problematic when connecting to non-Microsoft PPP hosts.

Running Applications on Windows NT

Now that you've learned about how to get a Windows NT Workstation running and configured, it's time to look at running applications. On the exam you are likely to be asked which types of applications are supported by Windows NT Workstation and how to configure an application to achieve optimal performance. In this chapter we look at the various support application types, as well as assigning application priorities and memory space configurations. Did you know that Win16 applications can be run in separate memory locations so that if one crashes, it will not cause an error in other Win16 applications? The chapter wraps up with a look at application priority boosting and troubleshooting common application problems.

Exam Material in This Chapter

Based on Microsoft Objectives

Running Applications

- Starting applications on Intel and RISC platforms in various operating system environments
- Starting applications at various priorities

Troubleshooting

- Choosing the appropriate course of action to take when an application fails

Based on Author's Experience

- You need to understand the limitations of running Win16 applications and what can happen when they crash.
- You definitely need to understand how Windows NT Workstation can run Win16 applications in separate NTVDMs.
- You must know which application types are supported by Windows NT Workstation.
- You should expect a few questions about application priorities and how they are assigned.
- You must be able to troubleshoot application failures caused by priority settings and memory space configurations.

Are You Prepared?

Do you have what it takes? Try out these self-assessment questions to see if you have prepared for the material in this chapter or if you should review problem areas.

1. **You are running a client-server application on your Windows NT computer. You need to provide the fastest performance and response times possible for the application. What application priority can you assign to the application to prevent it from being written out to the paging file?**

   ☐ A. Real-time
   ☐ B. High
   ☐ C. Separate
   ☐ D. Min

2. **You are running a Win16 application on your Windows NT Workstation computer. You want to make sure that if this application fails, it will not disrupt any other Win16 applications that are running on the computer. What can you do?**

   ☐ A. Assign the application a **low** priority.
   ☐ B. Assign the application a **high** priority.
   ☐ C. Run the application using the /separate command-line switch.
   ☐ D. Run the application using the /min command-line switch.

3. **You are installing applications on your Windows NT Workstation computer. By default, which application types can be**

preemptively multitasked in Windows NT Workstation? (Choose all that apply.)

☐ A. MS-DOS
☐ B. Win16
☐ C. Win32
☐ D. POSIX

Answers:

1. A   *Using the Real-time priority assignment prevents Windows NT Workstation from swapping an application to the page file and provides the highest possible performance. The downside is that other applications on the computer may have insufficient processor access as a result. See the "Application Priorities" section.*

2. C   *Windows NT Workstation allows Win16 applications to be run in a separate NTVDM through the use of the /separate command-line switch. This prevents rogue Win16 applications from disrupting other Win16 applications. See the "Win16 Environment" section.*

3. A, C, *Windows NT Workstation can preemptively multitask all*
   and   *of these application types except Win16. Win16*
   D   *applications run as a single thread process, unless they are run in a separate NTVDM using the /separate command-line switch. See the "Application Environments" section.*

Application Environments

Windows NT 4.0 is designed to run applications created for several different types of operating system environments. Windows NT supports these different application types by using multiple environment *subsystems*. These subsystems each include the *application programming interface* (API) of the operating system or environment that the subsystem is designed to support. The subsystems enable applications to run in the Windows NT environment as if they were running in the operating system environment they were designed for.

Application Environments

The application types and operating system environments supported by Windows NT 4.0 include:

- MS-DOS applications (MS-DOS environment)
- 16-bit Windows applications, such as those written for Windows 3.*x* and Windows for Workgroups (Win16 environment)
- 32-bit Windows applications, such as those written for Windows NT and Windows 95 (Win32 environment)
- POSIX applications (POSIX environment)
- OS/2 applications, such as those written for OS/2 1.*x* (OS/2 environment)

MS-DOS Environment

Applications designed for the MS-DOS environment are typically legacy applications that use a character-based, command-line interface. A *character-based, command-line interface* is one that relies on keyboard input rather than mouse input. Additionally, the screen display does *not* necessarily match the printed output — it's not *What You See Is What You Get* (WYSIWYG).

Windows NT 4.0 includes support for MS-DOS applications via a subsystem called an *NT Virtual DOS Machine* (NTVDM). An NTVDM emulates an Intel 486 computer running the MS-DOS operating system. NTVDM support is included for all hardware platforms supported by Windows NT 4.0, including Intel 486 and higher, DEC Alpha, PowerPC, and MIPS R4000.

MS-DOS applications that make direct calls to hardware are *not* supported by Windows NT.

Most MS-DOS applications are supported by Windows NT in an NTVDM.

MS-DOS Application Support

Each MS-DOS application runs in its own separate NT Virtual DOS Machine (NTVDM). Because each application runs in its own separate NTVDM, if an MS-DOS application crashes, other applications are *not* affected.

Windows NT 4.0 enables multiple NTVDMs to be run. Because each MS-DOS application runs in a separate NTVDM, Windows NT can preemptively multitask multiple MS-DOS applications. In *preemptive multitasking*, the operating system allocates processor time between applications. Because Windows NT — not the application — allocates processor time between multiple applications, one application can be preempted by the operating system, and another application allowed to run. When multiple applications are alternately paused and allocated processor time, they appear to run simultaneously to the user.

NTVDMs have three threads. (A *thread* is the smallest unit of processing that can be scheduled by the Windows NT Schedule service.) Two of these threads are used to maintain the NTVDM environment. The third thread is used by the application. An application that runs in an NTVDM is referred to as a *singled-threaded application* (because only one thread is used by the application).

All applications require at least one thread, the smallest unit of processing that can be scheduled by the Windows NT Schedule service.

Some MS-DOS applications require environmental settings that would normally be configured in the MS-DOS computer's `Autoexec.bat` or `Config.sys` files. For example, a path to the application may need to be specified, or a *terminate-and-stay-resident* (TSR) program may need to be loaded prior to starting the application. To provide the same environmental settings in a Windows NT environment, you can edit the `Autoexec.nt` and/or `Config.nt` files to include any necessary instructions. Settings contained in the `Autoexec.nt` and `Config.nt` files are executed each time an NTVDM is started. These files are edited in the same manner as you would edit an `Autoexec.bat` or `Config.sys` file. The `Autoexec.nt` and `Config.nt` files are stored in the `<winntroot>\System32` folder.

Win16 Environment

Win16 environment applications consist of 16-bit Windows applications designed for Windows 3.*x* and Windows for Workgroups. These applications are graphical applications that accept input from both a mouse and keyboard. Often the screen display matches the printed output (WYSIWYG).

Windows NT provides support for 16-bit Windows applications via a special subsystem called *WOW*, for *Win16-on-Win32*. The WOW subsystem emulates an Intel 486 computer running MS-DOS and Windows 3.1. The WOW subsystem runs in an NTVDM called the *Win16 NTVDM*.

Because NTVDMs are supported on all Windows NT platforms, Windows NT supports Win16 applications on all hardware platforms supported by Windows NT.

Windows NT supports most 16-bit Windows applications. However, 16-bit Windows applications that make undocumented calls to the operating system or that require specific device drivers that make direct calls to hardware may not run correctly on Windows NT.

Running a Win16 application in a separate NTVDM is referred to as *running Win16 applications in separate memory spaces.*

By default, when multiple Win16 applications are run at the same time, they all run in a single Win16 NTVDM. This means that, by default, all Win16 applications share the same memory space and the Win16 NTVDM's single thread. Because the Win16 applications share the same memory space, if one application crashes, other Win16 applications may also crash. Because multiple Win16 applications share a single NTVDM's thread, Windows NT *can't* preemptively multitask multiple Win16 applications. To prevent a rogue Win16 application from crashing all of your other Win16 applications, and to allow Win16 applications to be preemptively multitasked, Windows NT permits Win16 applications to be run in separate NTVDMs.

Multitasking Win16 Applications

You can use separate NTVDMs to run Win16 applications in separate memory spaces. This allows the applications to be preemptively multitasked and to prevent applications from causing errors in other applications when they crash.

Running Win16 applications in separate memory spaces

Windows NT allows the user to run a 16-bit Windows application in its own separate memory space. When a Win16 application is configured to run in its own separate memory space, Windows NT assigns that application its own Win 16 NTVDM when the application is run.

Running Win16 applications in separate memory spaces has advantages and disadvantages. Advantages include:

- When a Win16 application running in a separate memory space crashes, other applications are *not* affected.
- Windows NT can preemptively multitask Win 16 applications when they are run in separate memory spaces.

Disadvantages include:

- More RAM and system resources are used when Win 16 applications are run in separate memory spaces.
- Some Win 16 applications that use shared memory instead of Object Linking and Embedding (OLE) or Dynamic Data Exchange (DDE) to communicate with other Win 16 applications may not work correctly when run in separate memory spaces.

 TEST TIP Win 16 applications that use shared memory to communicate with other Win 16 applications may not work correctly when run in separate memory spaces.

There are two methods you can use to run a Win16 application in a separate memory space: You can configure the properties of the shortcut to the application, or you can use a batch file that uses the Start/separate command.

Configuring the properties of the shortcut to the Win16 application is the easiest and most commonly used method of configuring a Win16 application to run in a separate memory space. A Shortcut tab is shown in Figure 11-1. Notice the Run in Separate Memory Space check box.

Figure 11-1 *Configuring a Win16 application to run in a separate memory space*

Win32 Environment

The Win32 environment is Windows NT's native application environment. It is the preferred and fastest environment for running applications on Windows NT 4.0, because no emulation or workarounds are required. Win32 environment applications consist of 32-bit Windows applications written specifically for Windows NT and/or Windows 95. Windows NT provides support for Win32 applications via the *Win32 subsystem*. Windows NT supports the Win32 subsystem on all hardware platforms supported by Windows NT.

Win32 applications are *source-compatible* across all supported hardware platforms. This means that Win32 applications must be recompiled for each hardware platform in order to be run on that platform.

Win32 Applications

Each Win32 application runs in its own separate memory space. Because of this, if a Win32 application crashes, other applications are *not* affected. Windows NT can pre-emptively multitask multiple Win32 applications.

POSIX Environment

Portable Operating System Interface for Computing Environments (POSIX) was developed as a set of accepted standards for writing applications for use on various UNIX computers. POSIX environment applications consist of applications developed to meet the POSIX standards. These applications are sometimes referred to as *POSIX-compliant* applications.

Windows NT provides support for POSIX-compliant applications via the *POSIX subsystem*. Windows NT supports the POSIX subsystem on all hardware platforms supported by Windows NT. To fully support POSIX-compliant applications, at least one NTFS partition is required on the Windows NT computer.

POSIX applications are source-compatible across all supported hardware platforms. This means that POSIX applications must be recompiled for each hardware platform in order to run on that platform.

Each POSIX application runs in its own separate memory space. Because of this, if a POSIX application crashes, other applications are *not* affected. Windows NT can preemptively multitask POSIX applications.

OS/2 Environment

OS/2 environment applications consist of 16-bit, character-based applications designed for OS/2 version 1.*x*. Applications designed for other versions of OS/2, including OS/2 2.*x*, 3.*x*, and Presentation Manager applications, are *not* supported by Windows NT. Windows NT provides support for OS/2 applications via the *OS/2 subsystem*. It supports the OS/2 subsystem only on Intel 486 and higher platforms. Windows NT does *not* support the OS/2 subsystem on any other hardware platforms.

However, some OS/2 applications, called *real-mode applications*, can be run in an MS-DOS environment. Because Windows NT supports MS-DOS NTVDMs on *all* hardware platforms that it supports, real-mode OS/2 applications can be run in an NTVDM on any of these platforms by using the Forcedos.exe command to start the application.

Each OS/2 application runs in its own separate memory space. This means that if an OS/2 application crashes, other applications are *not* affected. Windows NT can preemptively multitask OS/2 applications.

POP QUIZ **True or False?**

1. Windows NT Workstation can preemptively multitask MS-DOS applications.

2. Windows NT Workstation can run Win16 applications in separate NTVDMs.

3. Windows NT Workstation supports OS/2 2.*x* applications.

4. A *thread* is the largest unit of processing that can be scheduled by the Windows NT Schedule service.

5. Win32 application must be recompiled for each hardware platform.

Answers: *1.True 2. True 3. False 4. False 5. True*

Application Support on Diverse Hardware Platforms

Windows NT 4.0 supports several different types of applications on various hardware platforms. Not all application types are supported on every hardware platform. Some types of applications are source-compatible across hardware platforms. As mentioned previously, this means that the application must be recompiled for each hardware platform that you want to run it on.

Table 11.1 shows the support provided by Windows NT 4.0 for different application types on diverse hardware platforms. Each hardware platform is based on a different type of processor.

Application Priorities

The Windows NT Schedule service uses application priorities to determine which applications receive the most processor time. Applications that have a high priority receive more processor time than applications with a low priority.

An *application priority* is a number between 0 and 31 that is assigned to an application when it is started. By default, most user applications are assigned a priority of 8, the normal priority. A user application can be assigned a priority between 0 and 15. These applications can be written to a paging file.

A real-time or kernel mode application can be assigned a priority between 16 and 31. Real-time applications *can't* be written to a paging file. When running, these applications are always stored in RAM.

If you start an application with real-time priority, the application will not be swapped to the paging file, which is a disk-based allocation of space that is used as virtual RAM for a computer. It is common place to swap low-priority applications to the paging file to free up faster RAM space.

Table 11.1. Application Support on Windows NT 4.0 Computers with Various Processors

Application Type	How the Application Runs in Windows NT (Broken Down by Processor Type)				
	Intel 486 or Higher	DEC Alpha	PowerPC	MIPS R4000
MS-DOS and Win16	Runs in a Virtual DOS Machine (NTVDM)	Runs in Intel 486 emulation mode	Runs in Intel 486 emulation mode	Runs in Intel 486 emulation mode
Win32	Runs in Win32 subsystem; source code must be recompiled for Intel processor	Runs in Win32 subsystem; source code must be recompiled for DEC Alpha processor	Runs in Win32 subsystem; source code must be recompiled for PowerPC processor	Runs in Win32 subsystem; source code must be recompiled for MIPS R4000 processor
POSIX	Runs in POSIX subsystem; source code must be recompiled for Intel processor	Runs in POSIX subsystem; source code must be recompiled for DEC Alpha processor	Runs in POSIX subsystem; source code must be recompiled for PowerPC processor	Runs in POSIX subsystem; source code must be recompiled for MIPS R4000 processor
OS/2 1.x character-based	Runs in OS/2 subsystem; only OS/2 1.x character-based applications are supported – additional software is required to support other OS/2 applications	No OS/2 application support; however, real-mode OS/2 applications can be run in an MS-DOS NTVDM by using the Forcedos.exe command to start the application	No OS/2 application support; however, real-mode OS/2 applications can be run in an MS-DOS NTVDM by using the Forcedos.exe command to start the application	No OS/2 application support; however, real-mode OS/2 applications can be run in an MS-DOS NTVDM by using the Forcedos.exe command to start the application

Windows NT can dynamically raise and lower application priorities based on changing conditions in the computer. Most application priority changes are beyond the user's control, and are managed by the operating system. However, the base priority assigned to an application can be set by the user, and the foreground application can be assigned a one- or two-point boost in priority by the user.

Starting Applications at Various Priorities

In Windows NT, the `Start` command is used to start applications at various priorities. The `Start` command can be used in batch files and from the command prompt. The `Start` command *can't* be used in shortcuts to applications.

Six switches are commonly used with the Windows NT `Start` command. These switches are listed and described in Table 11.2.

TABLE 11.2 Windows NT Start Command Switches

Switch	Description
/low	Starts the application with a base priority of **4**.
/normal	Starts the application with a base priority of **8**. This is the priority that is normally assigned to most user applications. Windows NT typically starts user applications with a base priority of 8 when no other priority is specified.
/high	Starts the application with a base priority of **13**.
/realtime	Starts the application with a base priority of **24**. An application with this priority *can't* be written to a paging file. Applications started at the real-time base priority can slow the performance of the operating system itself. The real-time base priority should be used with extreme caution and is not recommended for most applications.
/min	Does *not* affect the base priority of an application. It starts an application in a minimized window. This switch can be used in conjunction with a priority switch and/or the /separate switch.

Switch	Description
/separate	Does *not* affect the base priority of an application. It starts a Win16 application in a separate memory space.

For the exam, you should know each of the NT Start Command Switches for settings various application priorities for the application. You are very likely to see at least one question about the priority settings on the exam.

For example, to start User Manager at a high priority and in a minimized window, the following command is used at the command prompt:
Start /min /high Usrmgr.exe

Configuring Foreground Application Priority Boost

Normally it is desirable to give the application running in the foreground (the active application) a higher priority than applications running in the background. By default, Windows NT assigns a two-point priority boost to the foreground application.

You can boost the foreground application's priority by zero, one, or two points. The foreground application priority boost is *applied* to an application when it becomes the foreground application, and is *removed* from that application when the application is minimized or when another application becomes the foreground application. Once the foreground application priority boost is configured, that boost is applied to the foreground application from then on until the foreground application priority boost is changed.

The System application in Control Panel is used to configure the amount of boost a foreground application is assigned by Windows NT, as the next section explains. The Performance tab for the System icon in Control Panel is shown in Figure 11-2. Notice that the Boost slider is set at Maximum, by default.

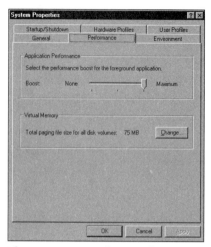

Figure 11-2 *Configuring foreground application performance boost*

You can configure the application performance for your Windows NT Workstation computer using these settings:

- **None** — No foreground application priority boost is applied.
- **Middle Setting** — A one-point application priority boost is applied to the foreground application.
- **Maximum** — A two-point application priority boost is applied to the foreground application. This is the default setting.

Windows NT Task Manager

Windows NT Task Manager is a Windows NT administrative utility that can be used to start and stop applications; to view performance statistics, such as memory and CPU usage; and to change a process's base priority.

There are four different ways to access Task Manager:

- By pressing Ctrl + Shift + Esc

- By pressing Ctrl + Alt + Delete, and then clicking the Task Manager command button in the Windows NT Security dialog box

- By right-clicking a blank space on the taskbar (on the Windows NT desktop), and then selecting Task Manager from the menu that appears

- By selecting Start ➪ Run, and then typing **taskmgr** in the Run dialog box

Stopping an Application

Task Manager is often used to stop or end an application that has crashed and has stopped responding to user input.

The Windows NT Task Manager dialog box is shown in Figure 11-3. Notice that the Applications tab is on top, by default. Highlight the application you want to stop. Click the End Task command button. Exit Task Manager.

Figure 11-3 *Using Task Manager to stop (end) an application*

Viewing Performance Statistics

You can also use Task Manager to view performance statistics for your Windows NT computer.

Start the Windows NT Task Manager and click the Performance tab. The Performance tab is shown in Figure 11-4. Notice the CPU Usage and Memory Usage graphs. The Processes tab, shown in Figure 11-5, shows the performance statistics for each application or service running on the computer.

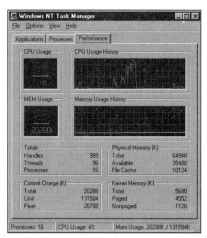

Figure 11-4 *Viewing performance statistics in Task Manager*

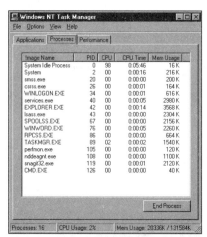

Figure 11-5 *Viewing application performance statistics in Task Manager*

True or False?

1. A Win32 application needs to be compiled separately for Intel platforms and RISC platforms.

2. A Win16 application needs to be compiled separately for Intel platforms and RISC platforms.

3. Starting an application with the /realtime priority will prevent it from being written to the page file.

4. You can automatically assign applications in the foreground a higher priority.

5. By default, applications run with a normal priority of 8.

Answers: *1. True 2. False 3. True 4. True 5. True*

Troubleshooting Common Problems

Occasionally you may experience problems when running an application on Windows NT. Some application problems have workarounds, and others can't be solved easily because they involve applications that simply aren't compatible with Windows NT.

Table 11.3 shows some common application problems and recommended solutions.

TABLE 11.3 Troubleshooting Application Problems in Windows NT

Problem	Recommended Solution
An application crashes and no longer responds to user input.	Use Task Manager to stop (end) the application. (This is sometimes called "killing" the application.)

Continued

TABLE 11.3 *Continued*

Problem	Recommended Solution
A 16-bit Windows (Win16) application often crashes, which results in all other Win16 applications locking up.	Use Task Manager to stop (end) all of the Win16 applications that are running. Configure the application that often crashes to run in its own separate memory space.
An application that makes a direct call to the hardware does not function properly on your Windows NT computer.	Windows NT does not support applications that make direct calls to hardware. Run this application on the operating system for which it was originally designed, or rewrite the application to function correctly in a Windows NT environment.
An OS/2 or POSIX application makes calls to APIs that aren't supported by Windows NT. The application doesn't function properly on your Windows NT computer.	Windows NT does not support calls to OS/2 Presentation Manager APIs (unless you have the special add-on product that supports Presentation Manager), and does not support many POSIX extensions. Run this application on the platform for which it was originally designed, or rewrite the application to function correctly in a Windows NT environment.
A standard Win32 application won't run on your PowerPC (or DEC Alpha, or MIPS R4000) computer.	Purchase a PowerPC (or DEC Alpha, or MIPS R4000) version of the application, or recompile the application for the PowerPC (or DEC Alpha, or MIPS R4000) platform. Win32 applications are source-compatible, and must be recompiled for each individual hardware platform.

Have You Mastered?

Now it's time to apply what you've learned in this chapter by testing your mastery of the material. These questions provide you with a means to determine if you are ready to move on to the next chapter or if you need to review the material again.

1. **You are running several 16-bit applications on your Windows NT Workstation computer. One of the applications occasionally fails and causes the other applications on the computer to stop responding. What can you do to prevent this application from affecting other 16-bit applications on the computer?**

   ☐ A. Give the application a priority setting of **low**.
   ☐ B. Give the application a priority setting of **realtime**.
   ☐ C. Run the application in a separate NTVDM.
   ☐ D. Run the application with the /min command-line switch.

   The correct answer is **C**. Windows NT Workstation allows you to run 16-bit applications in separate NTVDMs, which prevents applications from causing faults in other applications. The priority setting will have little difference in solving the problem unless the application was already running set at realtime and was hogging the processor. For more information, see the "Win16 Environment" section.

2. **You are running several MS-DOS applications on your Windows NT Workstation computer. You want to run several programs and TSRs when you start the Command Prompt to run the applications. Which files can you update so that these programs**

and TSRs are loaded when you start the Command Prompt? (Choose two.)

- [ ] A. `Autoexec.bat`
- [ ] B. `Autoexec.nt`
- [ ] C. `Config.sys`
- [ ] D. `Config.nt`

The correct answers are **B** and **D**. Windows NT Workstation uses `Autoexec.nt` and `Config.nt` each time a NTVDM is started, just as their `autoexec.bat` and `config.sys` counterparts would be used when MS-DOS started on a computer. If the commands were placed in the `autoexec.bat`, most of the entries, if not all, would be ignored by Windows NT Workstation as it loaded. For more information, see the "Application Environments" section.

3. **You are developing a 32-bit Windows application on your Intel-based Windows NT Workstation computer. When you are done writing the program, what will you need to do in order for it to run on a RISC computer running Windows NT Workstation?**

- [ ] A. Nothing, the platforms are Win32 compatible.
- [ ] B. Recompile the program for the RISC platform.
- [ ] C. Run the application with a priority setting of **high**.
- [ ] D. Run the application with a priority setting of **low**.

The correct answer is **B**. Win32 applications are source-compatible, which means that the source code is compatible across all Windows NT Workstation architectures, but still requires a compiled version for each platform. For more information, see the "Application Environments" section.

4. **You are installing a POSIX application on your Windows NT Workstation computer. What Windows NT Workstation configuration must you have to support this application?**

- [ ] A. At least 48MB RAM
- [ ] B. At least a Pentium/90 processor
- [ ] C. A FAT partition with at least 500MB Free
- [ ] D. A NTFS partition

The correct answer is **D**. Before you can run any POSIX-compliant applications, they must be installed on a NTFS partition. The amount of RAM or processor speed does not make a difference as it relates to running POSIX applications. For more information, see the "POSIX Environment" section.

5. **You are configuring some client-server applications on your Windows NT Workstation computer. You want to set a higher priority level for the client-server applications than the desktop applications that may be in use. What is the default priority level for normal applications running on Windows NT Workstation?**

    ☐ A. 4
    ☐ B. 8
    ☐ C. 16
    ☐ D. 24

The correct answer is **B**. When an application is run without any special priority assignments in the command line, the normal setting is level 8. The application may have instructions internally that change the priority, but as a general rule, applications run at level 8. For more information, see the "Application Priorities" section.

6. **You are running a complex random number generator program on your Windows NT Workstation computer. You notice that it is taking an extremely long time to generate the numbers you need. What can you do to increase the performance of the application without restarting it?**

    ☐ A. Run all of the other application in a separate memory space.
    ☐ B. Run all of the other applications in a minimized state.
    ☐ C. Use the Task Manager to boost the base priority of the application.
    ☐ D. Nothing can be done once the application has already started.

The correct answer is **C**. You can use the Windows NT Workstation Task Manager to change the base priority of any running application that you have permissions to. Running the other applications in separate NTVDMs or in a minimized state will very rarely improve the performance of other applications. However, there may be scenarios where running the application in a separate NTVDM will improve performance because the application can be preemptively multi-tasked. For more information, see the "Windows NT Task Manager" section.

7. **You are installing a 32-bit application on your Windows NT Workstation computer. What are some of the benefits you are likely to get from running a Win32 application instead of a Win16 application? (Choose two.)**

☐ A. Preemptive multitasking
☐ B. Shared memory space
☐ C. Single application thread
☐ D. Source compatibility across NT platforms

The correct answers are **A** and **D**. Applications running in the 32-bit world provide a number of advantages over their 16-bit counterparts. Win16 applications running in a common NTVDM must use a shared memory space and use a single process thread, which increases the likelihood of a application fault and decreases the system performance. For more information, see the "Application Environments" section.

8. **You are configuring application priority on your Windows NT Workstation computer. What priority level can cause system performance problems and possibly cause problems with other applications running on the computer?**

☐ A. Low
☐ B. High
☐ C. Real-time
☐ D. Performance

The correct answer is **C**. Using the Real-time priority for an application can dedicate so many system resources to the application that the system may have difficulty servicing other applications. As a result, extreme caution should be used when assigning the real-time priority to any application. For more information, see the "Application Priorities" section.

A

Practice Your Skills

Here is a chance to apply your practical, hands-on experience and material from this chapter. These exercises are designed for you to apply not only the material in the book, but to gain greater experience and exposure to the product. These exercises are a critical part of understanding the product and gaining valuable experience for using the product and passing the certification exam. For each of the following problems, consider the facts given and determine the possible causes of the problem and what course of action you might take to resolve the problem.

1. Choosing an application architecture

EXERCISE When you are choosing which application types to use on your Windows NT Workstation computer, what are some of the considerations that you should make?

ANALYSIS When choosing your application architecture for a Windows NT Workstation computer, it is important to understand what task you are trying to perform. Although Win32 applications function far better on a Windows NT Workstation computer, and they offer improved performance and reliability, there are still more Win16 applications. As a result, you are likely to run Win16 applications on a Windows NT Workstation in most environments. Thus, you will need to consider how these Win16 applications will be configured to run in your environment including separate NTVDMs and priorities.

2. Configuring application priorities

EXERCISE When you are configuring the priorities for various applications on your Windows NT Workstation computer, what are some important considerations?

ANALYSIS The most important consideration is to determine whether or not an application needs a priority setting other than the default. If it does, it is important to find out how that application's priority relates to other applications on the computer. Once each application has been assigned an importance relative to other applications, you can then assign the priority levels. The other consideration is if any of the assigned priorities will cause performance problems on the computer, as applications with higher priorities may demand too many system resources.

3. Using Task Manager to terminate applications

EXERCISE You are running a Win32 application on your Windows NT Workstation computer. The application has stopped responding to your input. You decide to terminate the application using the Task Manager. What is likely to happen as a result of terminating the application?

ANALYSIS When an application is terminated using the Task Manager, it's usually because the application has stopped responding. Some of the possible effects of termination include loss of user data, corrupt application files, DLL libraries left open, and possible ongoing problems with the computer until it is rebooted and all of the application files are closed. Additionally, many applications may lose user settings and changes that were made during the last sessions, as applications sometimes wait until they are exited before writing the settings to the disk.

4. Using Task Manager to boost application priority

EXERCISE You are running a Win32 application on your Windows NT Workstation computer. The application appears to be taking a long time to complete its task. You are considering boosting its base priority using the Task Manager. Why is it a good idea to view the performance statistics before boosting the priority?

ANALYSIS When an application appears to be taking a long time to complete a task, it is a good idea to check out its performance stats using the Task Manager. The performance tab will indicate whether the application is just slow, or may be locked up. If you assign a higher priority to a locked-up application, you could cause massive failures on your Windows NT Workstation computer. On the other hand, if the application is only getting a small percentage of the processor time, go ahead and increase the base priority.

Optimizing Performance

O NE OF THE MORE DIFFICULT AREAS to prepare for on the Workstation exam is monitoring and optimization. In this chapter I hope to provide you with a strong foundation to take into the exam and your environment. I first look at what Performance Monitor is and what its benefits are. I then examine some of the most common performance objects and what is required before they can be viewed in Performance Monitor. The chapter then moves on to the process of gathering and viewing statistics and each of the views available in Performance Monitor. The chapter wraps up with a quick look at troubleshooting bottlenecks and shows various tips on what to look for on the exam.

Exam Material in This Chapter

Based on Microsoft Objectives

Monitoring and Optimization

- Monitoring system performance by using various tools
- Identifying and resolving a given performance problem
- Optimizing system performance in various areas

Based on Author's Experience

- You need to understand what a Performance Monitor *object* is and what types of components have objects.

- You definitely need to know what Performance Monitors *counters* are and how you can use them to determine performance and locate bottlenecks.

- You need to know which objects and counters require services to be installed or configuration changes before they are accessible.

- You should be familiar with the various Performance Monitor views and their capabilities in different troubleshooting processes.

Are You Prepared?

Do you have what it takes? Try out these self-assessment questions to see if you have prepared for the material in this chapter or if you should review problem areas.

1. You are experiencing long wait times when trying to access files on your Windows NT Workstation computer. You suspect that an application may be writing to the hard disk excessively. What can you do to view the statistics of the hard disk using the Performance Monitor?

    ☐ A. Use the Disk Administrator to enable the PhysicalDisk objects.

    ☐ B. Use the `diskperf.exe` utility to enable the PhysicalDisk objects.

    ☐ C. Nothing, the objects are enabled by default.

    ☐ D. Log on to the Windows NT Workstation computer as member of the local Administrators group.

2. You are using the Performance Monitor to capture statistics that you will be archiving for future comparison and analysis. Which Performance Monitor view will allow you to capture statistics and store them for future retrieval?

    ☐ A. Chart view

    ☐ B. Alert view

    ☐ C. Log view

    ☐ D. Report view

3. You have been receiving messages from users that their network performance seems to have slowed down in the last

few days. You want to use Performance Monitor to alert you when the network segment performance for a select group of computers falls below a specified level. What two things do you need to do in order to accomplish this? (Choose two.)

☐ A. Install the SNMP service on the computers.
☐ B. Install the Network Monitor Agent on the computers.
☐ C. Use the Report view in Performance Monitor.
☐ D. Use the Alert view in Performance Monitor.

Answers:

1. B   *Before Performance Monitor can access the statistics for PhysicalDisks, the objects must first be enabled using the* diskperf.exe *utility. The objects are installed by default, but because of a small increase in system utilization, the objects are not enabled by default. See the "PhysicalDisk and LogicalDisk Objects" section.*

2. C   *The Log view of Performance Monitor allows you to collect current system statistics and store them in a log file for future analysis in Performance Monitor or within other third-party applications capable of reading CSV files. See the "Using Performance Monitor to Gather and View Statistics" section.*

3. B and D   *Before you can access the Network Segment performance object, the Network Monitor Agent must be installed to capture the values used by the counters. Then by using the Alert view, you can establish a threshold where the computer will alert you to the current activity. See the "Network Segment Object and its Counters" section.*

What Is Performance Monitor?

Performance Monitor is a Windows NT tool that ships with Windows NT Workstation. Performance Monitor automatically installs when you install Windows NT Workstation. Performance Monitor is often used when there's a problem to be resolved, but it can also be used for planning purposes. Performance Monitor can be used to

- Identify performance problems or bottlenecks.
- Determine current usage of system resources.
- Track performance trends over time.
- Predict future usage of system resources (capacity planning).
- Determine how system configuration changes affect system performance.

Performance Monitor Objects, Instances, and Counters

The system components that Performance Monitor can measure, such as processor, memory, and physical disk, are called *objects*. If a system has more than one of a particular object, such as multiple processors or multiple physical disks, there is said to be more than one *instance* of that object. Some objects, such as memory, do not have instances. This is because there can't be more than one of the particular object.

When you are taking the exam and are asked how to measure the performance of a system component, remember that physical components of a computer are called *objects*, including hard disks, processors, and memory.

295

Each instance of an object can be measured in different ways. Each possible measurement of an object is called a *counter*. Each counter is selected individually. An object can be selected multiple times with a different counter for each selection, as shown in Figure 12-1. Notice the Performance Monitor report shows multiple counters selected for the PhysicalDisk object.

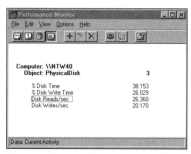

Figure 12-1 *Measuring multiple counters for a single object*

 Each object has at least one measurement counter that performs specific performance measurements. So if a Windows NT Workstation computer has multiple processors, there will be a unique counter value for each processor in the computer.

Not all Performance Monitor objects and counters are available when Windows NT is first installed. For example, the TCP (Transmission Control Protocol) object is not available until the *Simple Network Management Protocol* (SNMP) Service is installed. Additionally, some objects and counters must be enabled before they can be effectively used in Performance Monitor. The following sections explain how to add and enable certain Performance Monitor objects and counters.

TCP/IP Objects and Their Counters

By default, Performance Monitor does *not* make available TCP/IP object and their counters, even when TCP/IP is installed and configured on the Windows NT computer.

Be sure you know that the SNMP Service must be installed before you can monitor TCP/IP objects and counters in Performance Monitor. It is highly likely you will encounter questions where you are unable to see any TCP/IP counter values — the problem will likely be that SNMP is not installed on the computer.

Installing the SNMP Service adds four objects and their counters to Performance Monitor:

- IP (Internet Protocol)
- ICMP (Internet Control Message Protocol)
- TCP (Transmission Control Protocol)
- UDP (User Datagram Protocol)

These four objects and their counters are used by developers to optimize network usage of applications, and by administrators of large networks to troubleshoot and optimize TCP/IP network traffic.

Network Segment Object and its Counters

By default, the Network Segment object and its counters are *not* available in Performance Monitor. The Network Monitor Agent must be installed to make this object and its counters available.

The Network Monitor Agent must be installed to view the Network Segment objects and its counters. As before, watch for scenarios where you are unable to view Network Segment counter values because the Network Monitor Agent isn't installed.

The counters that are installed with the Network Segment object include: % Broadcast Frames, % Network Utilization, Total Bytes Received/second, and Total Frames Received/second.

The Network Segment object has an instance for each network adapter installed in the Windows NT computer. You can monitor counters for each instance of the Network Segment object. In other words, you can monitor network traffic on each network segment that your Windows NT computer is connected to.

The Network Segment object and its counters are used by network administrators to determine network utilization on individual network segments. In addition, this object and its counters are often used for network capacity planning.

PhysicalDisk and LogicalDisk Objects

By default, the PhysicalDisk and LogicalDisk objects and their counters are installed, but *not* enabled. Although you can select these objects and their counters in Performance Monitor, until they are enabled, the counters will always display a value of zero.

The reason these objects and their counters are not enabled by default is that monitoring these objects can cause up to a one-and-a-half-percent increase in processor utilization on an Intel 486 computer. On a Pentium computer, enabling these objects and their counters usually causes a negligible (less than one half of one percent) increase in processor utilization.

KNOW THIS — Disk Performance Counters

The Windows NT Diskperf.exe command-line utility is used to enable the PhysicalDisk and LogicalDisk objects and their counters. You must reboot the computer after running Diskperf.exe before these objects and their counters will be usable in Performance Monitor.

The Diskperf.exe command-line utility can be used to enable and disable the PhysicalDisk and LogicalDisk objects and their counters:

- `diskperf -y`   Enables the PhysicalDisk and LogicalDisk objects and their counters.
- `diskperf -ye` Enables the PhysicalDisk and LogicalDisk objects and their counters for stripe sets and stripe sets with parity.
- `diskperf -n`   Disables the PhysicalDisk and LogicalDisk objects and their counters.

POP QUIZ True or False?

1. Each physical component is called a performance counter.

2. The PhysicalDisk counters are not enabled by default.

3. You must install SNMP before you can use the TCP/IP objects.

4. Performance objects must have more than one instance.

5. The Network Monitor Agent must be installed to view the Network Segment objects.

Answers: *1. False 2. True 3. True 4. False 5. True*

Using Performance Monitor to Gather and View Statistics

Now that we've reviewed Performance Monitor objects and their counters, you're ready to use the Performance Monitor tool.

In this section, we'll review how to start Performance Monitor and how to use the "views" within Performance Monitor to gather and view statistics on a Windows NT computer's performance.

Chart View

The Performance Monitor Chart view displays activity in a graphical format. It can be used to view current performance activity, or to view archived performance activity from a Performance Monitor log file. (Log files are discussed later in this chapter.)

 TEST TIP Chart view displays activity in a graphical format and can be used to view current performance activity, or to view archived performance activity from a Performance Monitor log file.

Before you can view performance statistics in a Performance Monitor chart, you must first select one or more objects and their counters to be measured and displayed in a Chart view.

To select objects and their counters to be displayed in a Performance Monitor chart, you need to access the Add to Chart dialog box. The Add to Chart dialog box is shown in Figure 12-2. Notice that you can select objects, counters, and instances in this dialog box.

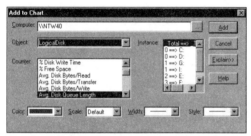

Figure 12-2 *Selecting objects, counters, and instances in the Add to Chart dialog box*

Figure 12-3 shows a Performance Monitor chart with several objects and counters selected. Notice the Last, Average, Min, Max, and Graph Time boxes toward the bottom of the chart.

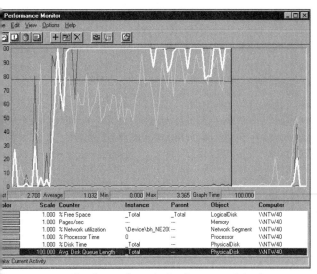

gure 12-3 *Viewing a chart in Performance Monitor*

When you highlight any counter in the section at the bottom of the ialog box, that counter's statistics are displayed in the Last, Average, Iin, Max, and Graph Time boxes directly below the chart:

- **Last:** This is the most recent measurement of the counter.

- **Average:** This is an average of the counter's measurement over the period of time represented by the chart.

- **Min:** This is the lowest (minimum) measurement of the counter during the period of time represented by the chart.

- **Max:** This is the highest (maximum) measurement of the counter during the period of time represented by the chart.

- **Graph Time:** This is the number of seconds represented by the entire chart. This is the total amount of time it takes Performance Monitor to graph from one side of the chart to the other.

Alert View

he Performance Monitor Alert view is used to display an alert when a ionitored counter's value exceeds or drops below a specified value.

Performance Monitor has no preset alerts. Alerts must be created in Alert view by selecting one or more counters to be monitored, and by entering a threshold value for each counter. When this threshold value is exceeded or falls below a minimum level (depending on how the alert is configured), an alert is triggered.

Alert view is used to display an alert when a object's counter value exceeds or drops below a specified level.

To add counters to be monitored in Alert view, you need to access the Add to Alert dialog box. The Add to Alert dialog box is shown in Figure 12-4. Notice that you can select objects, counters, and instances in this dialog box.

Figure 12-4 *Selecting objects, counters, and instances in the Add to Alert dialog box*

By default, Performance Monitor measures each specified counter in five second intervals, and compares each measurement with the threshold value. If the threshold value is exceeded or falls below a minimum level (depending on how the alert is configured), Performance Monitor generates an alert. If the threshold value is consistently exceeded or consistently falls below a minimum level, an alert will be generated every five seconds.

Report View

The Performance Monitor Report view displays activity in a report format. It can be used to view current performance activity, or to view archived performance activity from a Performance Monitor log file. (Log files are discussed later in this chapter.)

Report view displays activity in a textual report format and can be used to view current and historical performance activity.

Before you can view Performance Monitor statistics in Report view, you must select one or more objects and their counters to be measured and displayed in the report.

To select objects and their counters to be displayed in a Performance Monitor report, you need to access the Add to Report dialog box, shown in Figure 12-5. Notice that there are fewer options in this dialog box than are in the Add to Chart and Add to Alert dialog boxes.

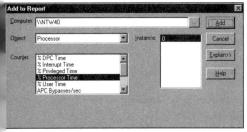

Figure 12-5 *Selecting objects and counters to be included in a Performance Monitor report*

The value displayed for each counter in the Report view represents an average of the last two Performance Monitor measurements for that counter. However, the value is not an average from the time Performance Monitor was started. Performance Monitor, by default, updates the report every five seconds.

Log View

The Performance Monitor Log view is used to save statistics gathered by Performance Monitor to a log file. The Performance Monitor log file can be viewed at a later time in Chart, Alert, or Report view.

Log view is used to save counter statistics to a file for use by other views or third-party software.

Before you can create a log file, you must select one or more objects to be monitored. To select objects, you need to access the Add To Log dialog box. The Add To Log dialog box is shown in Figure 12-6. Notice you can only select a computer and the objects to be monitored in this dialog box. The next section explains how to select objects for a Performance Monitor log in this dialog box.

Figure 12-6 *Selecting objects to be monitored for a Performance Monitor log*

 True or False?

1. The Report view can use archived Performance Monitor log files.

2. The Report view is a graphical display of performance counters.

3. The default refresh time for Performance monitor is every five seconds.

4. You do not need to add counters to a Log view because it logs everything.

5. Alert view displays an alert only when a counter exceeds a specified value.

Answers: *1. True   2. False   3. True   4. False   5. False*

What Is Performance Optimization?

Now that we have taken a look at monitoring performance, let's examine what we can do with that information. *Performance optimization* is the process of modifying computer and/or network hardware and software configurations with the intent of speeding up computer and/or network response. Performance optimization is performed for the following reasons:

- To get the most performance out of existing hardware
- In response to user or administrator observations of slow system performance

Performance optimization should be performed with a specific goal in mind. For most network administrators, performance optimization usually means resolving user reports of slow system performance. Determining the cause of the slow performance is referred to as *identifying a bottleneck.*

Identifying Bottlenecks

A *bottleneck* is the component in the system that is slowing system performance. In a networking environment, the bottleneck is the part of the system that is performing at peak capacity while other components in the system are not. In other words, if it weren't for the limiting component, the rest of the system could go faster.

When you are attempting to identify the bottleneck in your system, use Performance Monitor to measure performance of the computer's memory, processor, and disk. You can also use Performance Monitor to gather statistics about your network that may help you identify network bottlenecks.

TEST TIP It is very important that you review each of these highlighted performance objects and counters. These counters are the most commonly used items, and they are extremely likely to show up on your exam.

305

The following tables contain Performance Monitor counters that may help you in identifying bottlenecks. Table 12.1 shows the counters you can use to monitor a Windows NT computer's memory.

TABLE 12.1 Performance Monitor Memory Counters		
Object	**Counter**	**Description and How to Interpret**
Memory	Pages/sec	Measures the amount of 4KB memory pages that are read from or written to the paging file during a one-second time period. This counter is used to obtain an overall view of how memory is utilized by Windows NT. If the computer does not have enough memory, then excessive paging will occur. A consistently high number for this counter (greater than 2–3) indicates that the current amount of RAM may be insufficient for the computer.
Paging File	% Usage	This counter measures the percentage of paging file utilization. A consistently high percentage for this counter (approaching 100%) may indicate that you should add RAM to the system or enlarge the paging file. Enlarging the paging file won't speed up the system — only adding RAM will do that.

These two counters are likely to be used in scenarios where a Windows NT Workstation computer is experiencing slow performance and excessive disk access. Watch for exam questions that mention these traits and ask which performance objects/counters you should monitor.

Table 12.2 shows the counters you can use to monitor a Windows NT computer's processor.

TABLE 12.2 Performance Monitor Processor Counters

Object	Counter	Description and How to Interpret
Processor	% Processor Time	Measures the percentage of time that the processor is actively being used by processes other than the Idle process. This counter only measures one processor — if your system has multiple processors, use the System % Total Processor Time counter instead. A consistently high number for this counter (approaching 100%) may indicate that a faster processor (or an additional processor) may be required for adequate system performance. Check the memory counters *before* upgrading your processor — if the memory counters are consistently high, you might just need more RAM.
System	% Total Processor Time	This counter measures the percentage of time that *all* processors in the computer are actively being used by processes other than the Idle process. A consistently high number for this counter (approaching 100%) may indicate that faster processors (or an additional processor) may be required for adequate system performance. Check the memory counters *before* upgrading your processor(s) — if the memory counters are consistently high, you might just need more RAM.

TEST TIP These two counters are likely to be used in scenarios where a Windows NT Workstation computer is experiencing slow performance and long wait times for system services. Watch for exam questions that mention these traits and ask which performance objects/counters you should monitor.

Table 12.3 shows the counters you can use to monitor a Windows NT computer's disk.

TABLE 12.3 Performance Monitor Disk Counters

Object	Counter	Description and How to Interpret
PhysicalDisk	Avg. Disk Queue Length	This counter measures the average number of disk reads and writes waiting to be performed. A consistently high number for this counter (greater than 2–3) may indicate that a faster hard disk and/or disk controller, or a different disk configuration (such as a stripe set) may be required for adequate system performance. Check the memory counters *before* upgrading your disk(s) — if the memory counters are consistently high, you might just need more RAM.
PhysicalDisk	% Disk Time	This counter measures the percentage of time that the disk is actually busy performing reads and writes. A consistently high number for this counter (approaching 100%) may indicate that a faster hard disk and/or disk controller, or a different disk configuration (such as a stripe set) may be required for adequate system performance. Check the memory counters *before* upgrading your disk(s) — if the memory counters are consistently high, you might just need more RAM.
LogicalDisk	% Free Space	This counter measures the percentage of unused disk space. A consistently high or gradually increasing number for this counter (approaching 100%) indicates that the computer does *not* have sufficient disk space available. An additional disk or a replacement disk that has more capacity may be required.

These three counters are likely to be used in scenarios where a Windows NT Workstation computer is experiencing slow hard disk performance and excessively long periods waiting for files to load. Watch for exam questions that mention these traits and ask which performance objects/counters you should monitor.

Table 12.4 shows a Performance Monitor counter you can use to monitor the network.

TABLE 12.4 Performance Monitor Network Counter

Object	Counter	Description and How to Interpret
Network Segment	% Network utilization	This counter measures the total network utilization on a given network segment as a percentage of the maximum amount of network traffic possible on that segment. A consistently high number for this counter (approaching 100%) may indicate that there are too many computers or too much network traffic on that network segment. An additional network adapter may need to be installed in the computer, or a router may need to be installed on the network to further segment the network.

Once you've interpreted the Performance Monitor statistics and have identified the bottleneck in your system, you're ready to take steps to resolve that bottleneck. In the next section I review ways to optimize performance and to resolve bottlenecks.

Optimizing Performance and Resolving Bottlenecks

You don't have to make a large number of configuration or Registry setting changes to optimize the performance of Windows NT. Windows NT is designed to automatically tune itself to provide the best performance it can with the hardware resources available in the computer.

RAM

Perhaps the single most inexpensive and effective upgrade you can make to your Windows NT computer is to add additional RAM. I've never heard an administrator whine that "I just have too much RAM in my computers." You can *never* have too much RAM.

Adding RAM can reduce how often the computer reads or writes virtual memory pages to or from the paging file on the hard disk. This is called *reducing paging*. Because paging uses both processor time and disk time, when paging is reduced, the performance of the processor and the disk can also be improved.

 Remember the almost cardinal rule — adding RAM often reduces or eliminates excessive paging.

When RAM is added to the computer, Windows NT automatically increases the allocation of RAM made available to the disk cache. The disk cache temporarily stores requested files from the hard disk. Because the disk doesn't need to be accessed when a file is retrieved from the cache, files in the cache are more quickly available to users than files on the disk. Thus, increasing the size of the cache can improve disk performance because the number of disk accesses is reduced.

Paging Files

The best method for optimizing a paging file is adding more RAM. The more RAM in the computer, the less paging activity will occur.

 Optimizing paging files is likely to be on the exam, so check out the ways to improve access to the paging file.

That said, there are a few additional things you can do to optimize paging file performance. If the Performance Monitor Paging File % Usage and Paging File % Usage Peak counters indicate that the paging file is being used a consistently high percentage of the time, you might consider trying one or more of the following:

- Configure the paging file so that its initial size and maximum size are equal. This prevents fragmentation of the paging file.

- Place the paging file on the physical disk in your system that has the least amount of activity.

- Place the paging file on a stripe set.

- Place multiple, smaller paging files on multiple physical disks in your system.

- Place the paging file on any other partition than the boot partition.

Memory Dumps

If you have configured Windows NT to create a memory dump file (`memory.dmp`) when a stop error occurs, you *must* have a paging file on the boot partition that is at least as large as the amount of RAM in the computer. If the paging file isn't large enough or has been moved from the boot partition, a memory dump file won't be created.

Hard Disks

Optimizing disks is the process of speeding up hard disk response or adding to or replacing the existing disk(s).

Consider optimizing disks when planning for a new Windows NT computer that will perform a specific task, such as CAD or graphics.

Consider optimizing and/or upgrading disks when you determine, through performance monitoring, that the Windows NT computer's disk is a bottleneck to system performance. Before you upgrade a disk(s), ensure that memory (RAM) is *not* the bottleneck in your system.

You can increase disk performance by doing the following:

- Defragment the hard disk(s) in your computer.

- Upgrade to a faster disk controller and/or a faster hard disk(s).

- Configure a stripe set across two or more disks.

CPUs

When you determine, through performance monitoring, that the Windows NT computer's processor is a bottleneck to system performance, you should consider upgrading or adding a processor to the computer.

Before you upgrade or add a processor, ensure that memory (RAM) is *not* the bottleneck in your system.

Following are ways to improve processor performance, all of which involve replacing or adding hardware

- Replace the existing processor with a faster processor.
- Replace the existing motherboard and processor with a faster motherboard and processor.
- Upgrade from a single processor system to a multiprocessor system.

Have You Mastered?

Now it's time to apply what you've learned in this chapter by testing your mastery of the material. These questions provide you with a means to determine if you are ready to move on to the next chapter or if you need to review the material again.

1. **What does Performance Monitor call the physical components of a computer?**

   ☐ A. Objects
   ☐ B. Counters
   ☐ C. Instances
   ☐ D. Items

   The correct answer is A. Performance Monitor refers to physical components, such as processors and hard disks, as *objects*. Performance Monitor assigns each object at least one counter, which measures specific performance activity for an object. An instance is each occurrence of an object, so if a computer had two processors, it would have two instances of the processor object. For more information, see the "Performance Monitor Objects, Instances, and Counters" section.

2. **You want to measure the percentage of time that processes on a Windows NT computer actively use the processor. Which Performance Monitor object and counter should you use?**

   ☐ A. Object: Processor; Counter: %Processor Time
   ☐ B. Object: %Processor Time; Counter: Processor
   ☐ C. Object: Processor; Counter: %Privileged Time
   ☐ D. Object: %Privileged Time; Counter: Processor

The correct answer is **A**. Performance Monitor refers to the processor as an object, and the individual reporting items as counters. This Object/Counter pair will show what percentage of the time is spent on processes running on the Windows NT Workstation computer. For more information, see the "Identifying Bottlenecks" section.

3. **You are experiencing what appears to be slow network performance and long wait times on your Windows NT Workstation computer. You want to monitor the local network segment performance to determine if that is where the problem lies. What two things should you do? (Choose two.)**

    ☐ A. Install the SNMP Service.
    ☐ B. Install the Network Monitor Agent.
    ☐ C. Use Performance Monitor to view the Network Segment object.
    ☐ D. Use Performance Monitor to view the Network Segment counter.

The correct answers are **B** and **C**. Before you can view network traffic performance activity, you must first install the Network Monitor Agent. Then you can use Performance Monitor to view the Network Segment object, which has several counters associated with it. For more information, see the "Network Segment Object and its Counters" section.

4. **You are having difficulty maintaining a TCP/IP connection with a host over the Internet. You suspect that your connection is being timed out, and you want to verify the problem. What two things should you do? (Choose two.)**

    ☐ A. Install the SNMP Service.
    ☐ B. Install the Network Monitor Agent.
    ☐ C. Use Performance Monitor to view the TCP and IP objects.
    ☐ D. Use Performance Monitor to view the Network Segment object.

The correct answers are A and C. Before the IP, TCP, ICMP, and UDP objects can be viewed with Performance Monitor, you must first install the SNMP service, which is responsible for creating the counter values. Once the SNMP service is installed, you can then use Performance Monitor to view the various TCP and IP object counters. For more information, see the "TCP/IP Objects and Their Counters" section.

5. **You are experiencing slow disk performance on your Windows NT Workstation computer. You suspect that either your computer is writing to the page file too often, or there is a disk performance problem. When you start Performance Monitor, you notice all of the PhysicalDisk Counters show a value of zero. What do you need to do to view the PhysicalDisk objects?**

   ☐ A. Log on to the Windows NT Workstation computer as an administrator.
   ☐ B. Use diskperf.exe to enable the Performance Monitor objects.
   ☐ C. Use the Disk Administrator to enable the Performance Monitor objects.
   ☐ D. Install the PhysicalDisk Performance Monitor objects.

The correct answer is B. The PhysicalDisk related objects are installed by default, but are not enabled until the diskperf.exe utility is used. The objects are not enabled by default because they cause a slight decrease in system performance. The Disk Administrator cannot be used to enable the PhysicalDisk objects. For more information, see the "PhysicalDisk and LogicalDisk Objects" section.

6. **You are using Performance Monitor on your Windows NT Workstation computer. What three sources of performance data**

can you use in Performance Monitor when using the Report view? (Choose all that apply.)

- ☐ A. Current activity on local Windows NT Workstation computer
- ☐ B. Current activity on remote Windows NT Workstation computer
- ☐ C. Windows NT Event Logs
- ☐ D. Windows NT modem logs
- ☐ E. Archived Performance Monitor data from a log file
- ☐ F. Archived Performance Monitor data that has been exported to a CSV file

The correct answers are A, B, and E. The view that you are using in Performance Monitor actually makes no difference; all of the views are capable of inputting from any of these sources, except Log view, which can only use current activity. Performance Monitor has no way of importing information from the Event log, modem logs, or from a CSV file. For more information, see the "Using Performance Monitor to Gather and View Statistics" section.

7. **You are preparing a monthly utilization report of your Windows NT computers on the network. You would like to use the Performance Monitor data in an Excel spreadsheet to graphically map the historical performance and merge the graphs with a monthly Word report template. Which Performance Monitor view should you use?**

- ☐ A. Report
- ☐ B. Log
- ☐ C. Chart
- ☐ D. Alert

The correct answer is B. The Log view stores only the performance counter values, and no extra text that may confuse the import process into applications such as Excel. The log file can be exported to a CSV file and then imported to Excel or any other application capable of reading CSV files. For more information, see the "Using Performance Monitor to Gather and View Statistics" section.

8. **You are noticing an excessive amount of writing to the system page file. You suspect that you have insufficient RAM in your Windows NT Workstation computer. You want to obtain an overall view of how memory is being used on a particular Windows NT computer. Which Performance Monitor object and counter should you use?**

   ☐ A. Object: Memory; Counter: Pages/sec
   ☐ B. Object: Pages/sec; Counter: Memory
   ☐ C. Object: Processor; Counter: Pages/sec
   ☐ D. Object: Pages/sec; Counter: Processor

The correct answer is **A**. The Performance Monitor object is memory that has a counter called pages/sec, which shows the overall activity with the system RAM. It is important to remember which elements are objects and which are counters. The processor object does not track RAM activity, such as pages/sec. For more information, see the "Identifying Bottlenecks" section.

Practice Your Skills

Here is a chance to apply your practical, hands-on experience and material from this chapter. These exercises are designed for you to apply not only the material in the book, but to gain greater experience and exposure to the product. These exercises are a critical part of understanding the product and gaining valuable experience for using the product and passing the certification exam. For each of the following problems, consider the facts given and determine the possible causes of the problem and what course of action you might take to resolve the problem.

1. Performance Monitor Objects

EXERCISE Considering the dependencies of some Performance Monitor objects on services such as SNMP and Network Monitor Agent, why do you think these services are required to be installed before viewing these objects?

ANALYSIS The three major objects that require special configuration work are the TCP/IP, Network Segment, and disk performance objects. All three of these objects measure performance of the key communications channels for most Windows NT Workstation computers. Because the use of Performance Monitoring in any environment always leads to increased system utilization, the need to add a component to make these measurements ensures that the system administrator has purposely installed those Performance Monitoring components. Additionally, on computers that do not need those objects, eliminating the tracking of the performance counters maximizes the performance of the computer.

2. Viewing Remote Computer Statistics

EXERCISE You received a call from a user of a Windows NT Workstation computer on a remote network subnet. The user states that it is taking an extremely long time to connect to the corporate servers. You want to use Performance Monitor to view the statistics on the remote Windows NT Workstation computer. What must you do?

ANALYSIS Before Performance Monitor can remotely view the Network Segment object, the Network Monitor Agent must be installed. This is the same procedure that is required if you were going to monitor the object locally. Other than administrative permission to the computer, there are no other configuration requirements.

3. Using Performance Monitor views

EXERCISE You are using Performance Monitor to view the performance of a remote Windows NT Workstation computer. You will be monitoring the utilization of the system processor as the user of the computer performs various tasks. What should you consider when choosing the Performance Monitor view you should use?

ANALYSIS Performance Monitor offers four different views of the activity. Since the scenario stated that you are basically watching the information interactively, you should probably use the Chart view because it provides quick graphically analysis of the system activity, whereas the Report and Alert views are geared towards post-event monitoring and the Log view is good for evaluating the performance at a later time or in a third-party application.

4. Settings Performance Alerts

EXERCISE You want to be alerted whenever a hard disk on one of your Windows NT Server computers has less than 250MB of free disk space left. What should you do in Performance Monitor to do this?

ANALYSIS By setting up an Alert view in Performance Monitor and specifying the 250MB threshold limit, Performance Monitor can notify you when this event occurs. You can specify a command-line program to run to notify you as well, which could dial your beeper number and leave a text message about the problem.

5. Creating Network Baselines

EXERCISE What are some of the main benefits of using a Log view in Performance Monitor when viewing your network servers or network performance?

ANALYSIS By using the Log view within Performance Monitor, you can archive the performance data to be used as a baseline measurement on the performance of your network. Whenever you make a change, you can create new log files and compare the performance before and after to determine how your network and servers are responding to recent changes. This information can be used to show a general trend in the health of your network.

13

Advanced Troubleshooting

YOU'VE MADE IT TO THE LAST CHAPTER in the book. Before you run off and take your Windows NT Workstation exam, there are just a few last things to cover. One of the more common chores of a Windows NT administrator is troubleshooting problems caused either by the hardware, software, or the user. This chapter starts with a look at troubleshooting common boot sequence problems. Next, you look at using the Event Viewer to resolve service problems. The chapter wraps up with a look at the Windows NT Workstation registry, common registry hives, back up procedures, and searching the registry. So, get through this last chapter and then you can test yourself using the full-length Windows NT Workstation sample exam at the back of the book. Good luck!

Exam Material in this Chapter

Based on Microsoft Objectives

Troubleshooting

- Choose the appropriate course of action to take when the boot process fails

- Modify the registry using the appropriate tool in a given situation

- Implement advanced techniques to resolve various problems

Based on Author's Experience

- You need to be familiar with the boot sequence and its most common problems.

- You should know how the Last Known Good control set is created and the benefits of using it.

- You can expect to see some questions about using the Event Viewer to view the computer logs. In addition, you may be required to determine the cause of a problem based on a system log.

- You should understand the ways to modify the registry and the capabilities of each of the provided utilities.

- You should be familiar with the general layout of the registry and where common component information is stored.

Are You Prepared?

Do you have what it takes? Try out these self-assessment questions to see if you have prepared for the material in this chapter or if you should review problem areas.

1. **You have installed a new Win32 application on your Windows NT Workstation computer. After rebooting the computer, you receive a Missing Operating System error. What should you do to repair this problem?**

   ☐ A. Start an Emergency Repair process and choose the Verify Windows NT system files option.
   ☐ B. Copy the `boot.ini` file from another Windows NT computer to the C drive.
   ☐ C. You must reinstall Windows NT Workstation.
   ☐ D. Boot the computer using the Last Known Good control set.

2. **You have installed a new hard disk controller in your Windows NT Workstation computer. You have also installed the device driver for the hard disk controller. After rebooting the computer you receive an error that the hard disk driver failed to start. After checking with the manufacturer, you determine that there is a registry problem with the driver. Which Windows NT Registry hive contains the device driver entry?**

   ☐ A. HKEY_LOCAL_MACHINE
   ☐ B. HKEY_CURRENT_USER
   ☐ C. HKEY_CURRENT_CONFIG
   ☐ D. HKEY_CLASSES_ROOT
   ☐ E. HKEY_USER

3. Your Windows NT Workstation computer has a device driver that is failing to start when Windows NT loads. Whenever you try to start the driver manually, you receive a dialog box that indicates that a dependent service is not started. What can you do to determine what the dependent services are for this device driver?

☐ A. Use the Registry Editor to search for the device driver and determine the dependent services.

☐ B. Use the Last Known Good control set to determine the dependent services.

☐ C. Use the Event Viewer to determine the dependent services.

☐ D. You cannot determine dependent services on a Windows NT Workstation computer.

Answers:

1. A   *If some of the core Windows NT boot files are missing, the best way to correct the problem is to start an Emergency Repair process using the original Windows NT setup disks and the Emergency Repair Disk that was created for the computer. You can then check the Windows NT system files, and missing or corrupt files can be updated. See the "Troubleshooting the Boot Sequence" section of this chapter.*

2. A   *The standard location for hardware device driver settings and configurations is in the HKEY_LOCAL_MACHINE. If you are trying to locate Registry settings related to services or hardware devices, check this Registry hive first. See the section in this chapter, entitled "Using the Registry Editors."*

3. A   *Device drivers and services can be configured to require other supporting services or devices to be started before they can function, this is called a dependency. Only the Registry Editor and the Windows NT Diagnostics application can be used to view these dependencies. See the "Searching the Registry" section of this chapter.*

Troubleshooting the Boot Sequence

The *boot sequence* refers to the process of starting Windows NT, including initializing all of its services and completing the logon process. There are several common problems that can occur during the boot sequence; in order to successfully troubleshoot them, you must understand the steps that occur during the boot sequence.

Overview of the Boot Sequence

The Windows NT boot sequence consists of a series of sequential steps, beginning with powering on the computer and ending with completion of the logon process. Understanding the individual steps that make up the boot sequence will help you to troubleshoot problems that may occur during this process. Of course, the boot sequence steps vary according to the hardware platform you are using; this section discusses steps that apply to the Intel platform only.

The Windows NT boot sequence (Intel platform) is as follows:

1. **Power On Self Test:** The *Power On Self Test* (POST) is performed by the computer's BIOS every time the computer is powered on to test for the existence of specific components, such as processor, RAM, and video adapter. If any errors are detected during this phase, an error message or onscreen diagnostics display is shown.

2. **Initial Startup:** In this step, the computer's BIOS attempts to locate a startup disk, such as a floppy disk, or the first hard disk in the computer.

   If the startup disk is the first hard disk, the BIOS reads the *Master Boot Record* from the startup disk, and the code in the Master Boot Record is run. The Master Boot Record then determines which partition is the active partition, and loads sector 0 (also called the *partition boot sector*) from the active partition into memory. Then the code contained in sector 0 is run. This causes the `ntldr` file to be loaded into memory from the root folder of the active partition. `Ntldr` is then run.

If the startup disk is a floppy disk, the code from sector 0 on the floppy disk is loaded into memory. Then the code contained in sector 0 is run. This causes `ntldr` to be loaded into memory from the root folder of the floppy disk. `Ntldr` is then run.

3. **Selecting an operating system:** `Ntldr` switches the processor into a 32-bit flat memory mode. `Ntldr` then initializes the appropriate minifile system (either FAT or NTFS) to enable `ntldr` to locate and load the `boot.ini` file.

4. **Detecting hardware:** `Ntdetect.com` searches for computer ID, bus type (ISA, EISA, PCI, or MCA), video adapter, keyboard, serial and parallel ports, floppy disk(s), and pointing device (mouse).

   `Ntdetect.com` creates a list of the components it finds and passes this information to `ntldr`.

5. Selecting hardware profile and loading the kernel: `Ntldr` displays the following message:

```
OS Loader V4.0
Press spacebar now to invoke Hardware Profile/Last Known
Good menu.
```

`Ntldr` gives you approximately three to five seconds to press the spacebar. If you press the spacebar at this time, the Hardware Profile/Last Known Good menu is displayed as shown:

```
Hardware Profile/Configuration Recovery Menu
This menu enables you to select a hardware profile
to be used when Windows NT is started.
If your system is not starting correctly, then you may
switch to a
previous system configuration, which may overcome startup
problems.
IMPORTANT: System configuration changes made since the
last
successful startup will be discarded.
          Original Configuration
          Some other hardware profile
```

```
Use the up and down arrow keys to move the highlight
to the selection you want. Then press Enter.
To switch to the Last Known Good Configuration, press
'L'.
To Exit this menu and restart your computer, press F3.
Seconds until highlighted choice will be started
automatically: 5
```

If you press **L** while this screen is displayed, the Last Known Good control set will be used, and any configuration changes made during the last logon session will be discarded.

If you don't press the spacebar and have only one hardware profile, the default hardware profile is loaded.

If you don't press the spacebar and have more than one hardware profile, the Hardware Profile/Configuration Recovery Menu is displayed.

Once you've selected a hardware profile, ntldr loads Ntoskrnl.exe and executes the Windows NT kernel.

 The Last Known Good control set uses the registry set that was used during the last successful boot process. This enables you to revert back to a working set of system configuration files after making a change that could prevent a successful boot. On the exam, this will likely be the point of a question in which you recently made a hardware configuration change and are unable to boot the computer.

6. **Kernel initialization:** When the kernel starts, you'll see a screen indicating that the kernel has successfully started.

7. **Initializing device drivers:** At this point, the kernel loads either the default control set or, if you selected the Last Known Good Configuration, it loads the Last Known Good control set. The kernel then initializes all of the device drivers listed in the control set.

8. **Initializing services:** The kernel loads and starts the services listed in the control set being used.

9. **Logon process:** The Begin Logon dialog box is displayed, prompting the user to press Ctrl + Alt + Delete to log on. Then the user logs on, supplying an appropriate user name and password.

Once a user has successfully logged on, the boot sequence is complete, and the control set currently in use is copied to the Last Known Good Configuration.

Troubleshooting Common Boot Sequence Problems

There are many common problems that can occur during the Windows NT boot sequence. Table 13.1 lists these problems, along with their possible causes and recommended solutions.

TABLE 13.1 Troubleshooting the Windows NT Boot Sequence

Problem	Possible Cause	Recommended Solution
An error message is displayed during the POST.	This message most likely indicates a hardware failure.	Use the error message (or onscreen diagnostics) to determine the offending hardware device. Repair, replace, or reconfigure the hardware device as necessary.
An error message, such as "Invalid partition table" or "Missing operating system" is displayed after the POST.	This type of error message often indicates that either sector 0 of the active partition is damaged, or that important operating system files (such as ntldr) are missing.	Perform the Emergency Repair process and select the Inspect boot sector option during this process. If you suspect that there are missing files, also select the Verify Windows NT system files option during the Emergency Repair process.

Problem	Possible Cause	Recommended Solution
After you select MS-DOS from the boot loader menu, the following error is displayed: I/O error accessing boot sector	This message indicates that `ntldr` can't find the `Bootsect.dos` file.	Restore this file from tape; or, perform the Emergency Repair process, selecting the Inspect boot sector option during the process.
During the boot sequence, NT displays a message indicating that it cannot find a specific file, such as `Ntoskrnl.exe` or `ntldr`.	There are two possible causes for this problem: the specified file is missing or corrupt, or the `boot.ini` file does not specify the correct path to system files.	To restore a missing or corrupt file (except for the `boot.ini` file), perform the Emergency Repair process, selecting the Verify Windows NT system files and Inspect start up environments options during the process. To repair a `boot.ini` file, do the following: Boot to MS-DOS and edit the `boot.ini` file (assuming that the `boot.ini` file is on a FAT partition)
Your Windows NT computer crashes during a power outage. When you reboot the computer, a blue screen is displayed during the boot sequence.	The most likely cause of this problem is a corrupt file. Power outages can easily corrupt files on the hard disk.	Perform the Emergency Repair process, selecting the Inspect boot sector and Verify Windows NT system files options during the process.

continued

TABLE 13.1 *Continued*

Problem	Possible Cause	Recommended Solution
You make several configuration changes and then reboot your Windows NT computer. A blue screen is displayed during the boot sequence.	The most likely cause of this problem is the configuration changes made during the last logon session.	Reboot the computer, and select the Last Known Good Configuration during the boot sequence. If this does *not* repair the problem, perform the Emergency Repair process, selecting the Inspect Registry files option during the process.
A STOP error (blue screen) is displayed during the device driver or service initialization steps of the boot sequence.	The most probable causes of this error are a corrupt Registry entry, a corrupt device driver, or a corrupt service file.	Perform the Emergency Repair process, selecting the Inspect Registry files and Verify Windows NT system files options during the process.

Table 13.1 presents some very common boot sequence problems. Study each of these problems carefully, as one of these scenarios may be similar to a question on your Windows NT Workstation exam.

Using Event Viewer

Event Viewer is a Windows NT administrative tool that is used to view the System, Security, and Application Logs. The most common troubleshooting application of Event Viewer is determining why a service or device driver failed during system startup. After booting the computer, Windows NT notifies the user of such a failure by displaying a Service Control Manager warning dialog box.

When a Service Control Manager warning is displayed, you can use the Event Viewer System Log to determine which service or driver failed, and to view a detailed description of the failure. This information will often help you determine the cause of the failure and an appropriate solution. The Event Viewer System Log dialog box is shown in Figure 13-1. Notice the stop errors listed in the dialog box.

A *stop error* in the System Log is identified by a red stop sign preceding the event on the left-hand side of the dialog box. A stop error indicates that the service or driver listed in the Source column was incapable of initializing correctly during system startup.

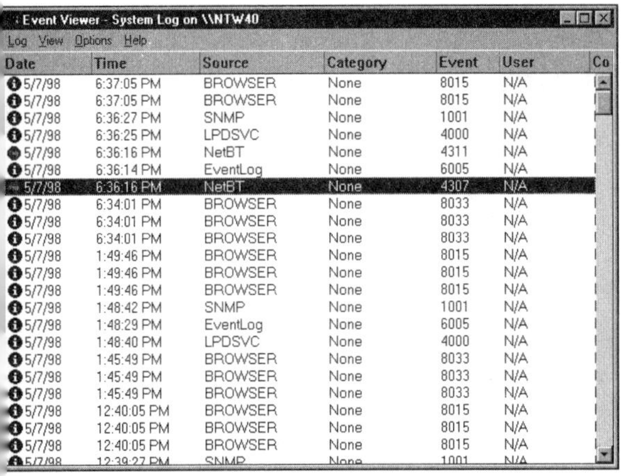

Date	Time	Source	Category	Event	User	Co
5/7/98	6:37:05 PM	BROWSER	None	8015	N/A	
5/7/98	6:37:05 PM	BROWSER	None	8015	N/A	
5/7/98	6:36:27 PM	SNMP	None	1001	N/A	
5/7/98	6:36:25 PM	LPDSVC	None	4000	N/A	
5/7/98	6:36:16 PM	NetBT	None	4311	N/A	
5/7/98	6:36:14 PM	EventLog	None	6005	N/A	
5/7/98	6:36:16 PM	NetBT	None	4307	N/A	
5/7/98	6:34:01 PM	BROWSER	None	8033	N/A	
5/7/98	6:34:01 PM	BROWSER	None	8033	N/A	
5/7/98	6:34:01 PM	BROWSER	None	8033	N/A	
5/7/98	1:49:46 PM	BROWSER	None	8015	N/A	
5/7/98	1:49:46 PM	BROWSER	None	8015	N/A	
5/7/98	1:49:46 PM	BROWSER	None	8015	N/A	
5/7/98	1:48:42 PM	SNMP	None	1001	N/A	
5/7/98	1:48:29 PM	EventLog	None	6005	N/A	
5/7/98	1:48:40 PM	LPDSVC	None	4000	N/A	
5/7/98	1:45:49 PM	BROWSER	None	8033	N/A	
5/7/98	1:45:49 PM	BROWSER	None	8033	N/A	
5/7/98	1:45:49 PM	BROWSER	None	8033	N/A	
5/7/98	12:40:05 PM	BROWSER	None	8015	N/A	
5/7/98	12:40:05 PM	BROWSER	None	8015	N/A	
5/7/98	12:40:05 PM	BROWSER	None	8015	N/A	
5/7/98	12:39:27 PM	SNMP	None	1001	N/A	

Figure 13-1 *Viewing the System Log in Event Viewer*

KNOW THIS

Viewing the Event Log

Some portions of the Windows NT Workstation event log are viewable only by members of the computer's local administrators group. The Security log is not viewable except by local administrators, but the system log is generally open for all viewers to see.

Examining stop error event details is the key to troubleshooting failed services or drivers. When multiple stop errors are listed, it's usually best to start your troubleshooting by first examining the *oldest* stop error in the list. The oldest stop error is the *first* stop error that occurred during the boot process — it is also the last stop error on the System Log list. This stop error is probably the cause of all the later stop errors listed.

To view stop error event detail, double-click the stop error in the System Log in Event Viewer. When you double-click the stop error, the Event Detail dialog box is displayed, as shown in Figure 13-2. Notice the description of the stop error in the Description text box. This stop error indicates that initialization of the NetBT service failed because the driver device could not be created.

Figure 13-2 *Viewing stop error in Event Detail*

True or False?

1. The POST is performed by the computer's BIOS every time the computer is powered on.

2. A Stop error in Event viewer indicates that the service or driver paused during its initialization.

3. During the boot process, once the device drivers are loaded, the current control set is copied to Last Known Good.

4. The Windows NT Boot process varies based on your hardware architecture.

Answers: *1. True 2. False 3. False 4. True*

Using the Registry Editors

Registry editors are tools that enable you to search and modify the Windows NT Registry. Following are the two primary tools for editing the Windows NT Registry:

- Windows NT Registry Editor (`regedt32.exe`)
- Windows 95 Registry Editor (`regedit.exe`)

Additionally, you can use the Windows NT System Policy Editor (`poledit.exe`) to modify the Registry. The use of the Policy Editor is limited to fields that you have manually configured because you can't search the Registry.

The Registry editors are primarily used for the following four types of tasks:

- To change Registry settings that can't be changed with any other user interface (such as Control Panel)
- To modify the Registry as directed by *Microsoft TechNet* or by Microsoft Technical Support to resolve a particular problem or to provide a particular feature
- To troubleshoot various startup problems
- To define a functional group of settings that you wish to configure in a central location for a single user/computer or for a group.

Registry Structure Overview

The Windows NT Registry is a database that contains all of the information required to configure an individual Windows NT computer correctly, its user accounts, and its applications. Registries are unique to each computer — you shouldn't use the Registry from one computer on another computer. The Registry is organized in a tree structure consisting of five subtrees and their keys and value entries. Within the subtrees, keys are similar to folders in a file system, and value entries are similar to files. Each subtree in the Registry contains different information, as follows:

- **HKEY_LOCAL_MACHINE:** This subtree contains various configuration information specific to the local computer, including hardware, software, device driver, and services startup configurations. Windows NT accesses this information during system startup and uses it to configure the computer correctly.

For the exam, look for a question about which subtree to check first when troubleshooting Windows NT. **Always** check the HKEY_LOCAL_MACHINE subtree first, because this subtree contains most of the service and driver configuration information for the operating system.

- **HKEY_CURRENT_USER:** This subtree contains the entire user profile for the user currently logged on. This includes the user's individual desktop settings, network drive and printer connections, and so on. HKEY_CURRENT_USER is a replica of the keys and values stored in HKEY_USERS\ *security identifier (SID) of currently logged on user.*

- **HKEY_CURRENT_CONFIG:** The subtree contains the hardware configuration currently being used by Windows NT. This subtree consists of a replica of the keys and values stored in HKEY_LOCAL_MACHINE\System\ CurrentControlSet\HardwareProfiles\Current.

- **HKEY_CLASSES_ROOT:** This subtree contains all of the associations between applications and their specific file name extensions. This subtree also contains all of the *object linking and embedding* (OLE) information used by various Windows applications, and consists of a replica of the keys and values stored in HKEY_LOCAL_MACHINE\Software\ Classes.

- **HKEY_USERS:** This subtree contains the user profile for the user currently logged on (the current user profile), as well as the default user profile.

Registry Keys

You should be familiar with the Registry tree layout before you take your Windows NT Workstation exam. You will likely be asked where common configurations are stored and how to troubleshoot registry errors. The best way to remember the purpose of each key is to remember an example of the information stored in each.

In the Windows NT Registry, various keys and their values are grouped together and stored in a single file. This file is called a *hive*. All of the Windows NT Registry hives are stored in the `winntroot>\System32\Config` folder. Table 13.2 shows the six hives and their respective Windows NT Registry locations.

TABLE 13.2 Windows NT Registry Hives

Hive File Name	Location in the Registry
SAM	HKEY_LOCAL_MACHINE\SAM
Security	HKEY_LOCAL_MACHINE\Security
Software	HKEY_LOCAL_MACHINE\Software
System	HKEY_LOCAL_MACHINE\System and HKEY_CURRENT_CONFIG
Ntuser.dat	HKEY_CURRENT_USER
Default	HKEY_USERS\.DEFAULT

Backing Up the Registry

Before you can use a Registry editor, you should back up the Registry — if you don't, you could end up with a system that won't boot.

The two primary tools you can use to back up the Windows NT Registry:

- The Windows NT Backup program
- The `Rdisk.exe` utility

When you back up the Registry using the Windows NT Backup program, you must choose to back up at least one file on the boot partition, and you must select the check box next to the Backup Local Registry option.

When you back up the Registry using the `Rdisk.exe` utility, two backup copies are made. First, `Rdisk` makes a backup copy of the Registry and stores it in the `<winntroot>\Repair` folder. Then `Rdisk` prompts you to insert a floppy disk (which will become the Emergency Repair Disk), and copies the `<winntroot>\Repair` folder contents to the floppy disk. This process is known as *updating the Emergency Repair Disk*. Be sure to update your computer's Emergency Repair Disk every time you make a successful configuration change to your Windows NT computer.

Remember this for the exam — you should always run `Rdisk` using the `/s` switch, because using this switch will cause the `SAM` and `Security` hives to be backed up. If you *don't* use the `/s` switch, these two hives won't be backed up. You may be asked how to backup the `SAM` and `Security` hives on a Windows NT Workstation in your exam.

Searching the Registry

Now that we've reviewed the structure of the Windows NT Registry and the importance of backing it up, you can begin using the Registry editor to search and modify the Registry. As mentioned previously, there are two primary tools you can use to edit the Windows NT Registry: the Windows NT Registry Editor (`regedt32.exe`) and the Windows 95 Registry Editor (`regedit.exe`).

The Windows 95 Registry Editor (`regedit.exe`) is the preferred tool because it can be used to search the Windows NT Registry by key, by value, or by the data contained in the value. This editor is more effective than the Windows NT Registry Editor, which can only search the

Registry by key. You can wade your way through the various Registry folders and subfolders manually by using the Windows NT Registry Editor, and you can use this editor to modify any Registry value — it's just more cumbersome to use as a search tool than the Windows 95 Registry Editor.

Watch out for this gotcha on the exam — While the Windows 95 Registry Editor is a better search tool, the Windows NT Registry Editor has a couple of features not included in the Windows 95 version. Some of those features include the capability to connect to and edit a remote Windows NT computer's Registry, and the capability to set security on various Registry keys.

A common type of search that is performed in Registry Editor is a search for a specific service or driver, with the intent of determining the service and group dependencies of that service or driver. Let's review this type of search, and how to determine the dependencies of the service or driver.

For troubleshooting purposes, once you have determined what the service and group dependencies for a particular service (or driver) are, you can verify that all of these services and drivers (that are required to be running *before* a particular service or driver can start) are, in fact, running. The easiest way to determine a particular service's or driver's service and group dependencies is by using the Services tab in Windows NT Diagnostics.

You can search the Windows NT Registry to locate a particular service or driver for the purpose of determining that service's or driver's service and group dependencies. Although you can use either Registry Editor to find dependencies, only the Windows NT Registry Editor (regedt32.exe) presents this information in a usable format. (The Windows 95 Registry Editor presents service and group dependencies in hexadecimal format.)

All service and driver Registry entries are stored in subkeys of KEY_LOCAL_MACHINE\System\CurrentControlSet\Services.

Suppose you want to use a Registry editor to determine service and group dependencies of the Messenger service. (You want to do this because Event Viewer indicates that the Messenger service failed to start because a dependency service of the Messenger service was not running.)

Highlight the service or driver for which you want to determine service and group dependencies. In the example, this is the Messenger service. Various Registry entries for the highlighted service or driver are displayed on the right-hand side of the window, as shown in Figure 13-3. Notice the DependOnGroup and DependOnService entries.

You can ignore the REG_MULTI_SZ: portion of the DependOnGroup and DependOnService entries — REG_MULTI_SZ just identifies the type of data that will be placed in the Registry — in this case, multiple string values.

In this example, notice that the Messenger service's DependOnGroup entry does not contain any data (other than the ignored REG_MULTI_SZ). This means this service has no group dependencies.

Figure 13-3 *Viewing the Messenger service's Registry entries*

Also notice that the Messenger's service DependOnService entry lists the LanmanWorkstation and NetBios services as its service dependencies. This means the Messenger service will not start if the LanmanWorkstation (Workstation) and the NetBios services are not running.

True or False?

1. The Registry is divided into five hives.

2. You cannot use the Policy Editor to search the Registry.

3. Windows NT services can have dependent services.

4. Only the Windows NT Registry Editor can be used to connect to a remote Registry.

Answers: *1. True 2. True 3. True 4. True*

Have You Mastered?

Now it's time to apply what you've learned in this chapter by testing your mastery of the material. These questions provide you with a means to determine if you are ready to move on to the next chapter or if you need to review the material again.

1. Your Windows NT computer crashes during a power outage. When you reboot the computer, a blue screen is displayed during the boot sequence. What should you do to resolve the boot problem?

☐ A. Perform the Emergency Repair process, selecting the Inspect boot sector and Verify Windows NT system files.

☐ B. Perform the Emergency Repair process to restore the Windows NT Registry.

☐ C. Run the Windows NT Diagnostics program.

☐ D. Reboot the computer, and select the Last Known Good Configuration during the boot sequence.

The correct answer is **A**. The most likely cause of this problem is a corrupt file. Power outages can easily corrupt files on the hard disk. Performing the Emergency Repair process, and selecting the Inspect boot sector and Verify Windows NT system files options will probably resolve the missing or corrupted files. For more information, see the "Overview of the Boot Sequence" section of this chapter.

2. **You make several configuration changes and then reboot your Windows NT computer. A blue screen is displayed during the boot sequence. What should you do to resolve the boot failure?**

    ☐ A. Perform the Emergency Repair process, selecting the Inspect boot sector and Verify Windows NT system files.

    ☐ B. Perform the Emergency Repair process to restore the Windows NT Registry.

    ☐ C. Run the Windows NT Diagnostics program.

    ☐ D. Reboot the computer, and select the Last Known Good Configuration during the boot sequence.

The correct answer is **D**. The most likely cause of this problem is the configuration changes made during the last logon session. The Last Known Good Configuration contains the system settings that reflect the configuration of the computer before any recent changes were made that could prevent the computer from booting. For more information, refer back to the "Troubleshooting Common Boot Sequence Problems" section.

3. **You receive a Service Control Manager warning message that indicates that a service or device driver failed during system startup. Which Windows NT administrative tool should you use to obtain more information about the failure?**

    ☐ A. Windows NT Diagnostics application

    ☐ B. Windows NT Registry Editor

    ☐ C. Windows NT Event Viewer

    ☐ D. Windows NT System Log Viewer

The correct answer is **C**. The Windows NT Event Viewer is used to view the Windows NT logs that will indicate which system services failed during the startup or boot process. Additionally, the logs may indicate other services that failed that may point to the cause of other failures. For more information, read back through the "Using Event Viewer" section.

4. **You receive a call from a user who is having problems with her Windows NT Workstation computer. Using your Windows NT Workstation computer and Event Viewer you determine that there is a Registry configuration change that needs to be made on the user's computer. What can you do so that you can remotely modify her Registry from your Windows NT Workstation computer?**

☐ A. Use the Windows 95 Registry Editor.
☐ B. Use the Windows NT Registry Editor.
☐ C. First connect a drive to the user's computer, and then use the Windows 95 Registry Editor.
☐ D. First make a connection to the user's IPC$ share, and the use the Windows 95 Registry Editor.

The correct answer is **B**. The Windows NT Registry Editor is the only application that can be used to open and modify a system Registry remotely. The Windows 95 Registry Editor does not have the capacity to open a Registry remotely, regardless of what you do ahead of time. For more information, see the "Using the Registry Editors" section of this chapter.

5. **You are preparing to install some new hardware devices on your Windows NT Workstation computer. Before you do, you want to ensure that your system registry is completely backed up. What switch must you use with the** Rdisk **utility if you want the** SAM **and** Security **hives backed up?**

☐ A. Use the /Complete switch.
☐ B. Use the /All switch.
☐ C. Use the /S switch.
☐ D. Use the /C switch.

The correct answer is **C**. The Rdisk application will not backup the SAM and Security hives unless the /S switch is used. If you create a Repair Disk without the switch, you will have an incomplete backup. If you do backup the SAM and Security hives, you need to secure the disk, as anyone with access to the disk could potentially crack the security information and gain access to your computer. For more information, refer to the "Backing Up the Registry" section.

6. **You have installed a hardware device in your Windows NT Workstation computer, and have configured the device as a manual startup component. When you use Device in Control Panel, the device states that a dependent service is not running. What can you do to determine what the dependent services are for this new device?**

☐ A.   Use the Windows NT Registry Editor to search for the dependencies tree.

☐ B.   Use the Windows 95 Registry Editor to search for the device driver and view the dependent services.

☐ C.   Use the Windows NT Event Viewer to view the Application logs.

☐ D.   Use the Windows NT Event Viewer to view the System logs.

The correct answer is **B**. The Windows 95 Registry Editor can be used to determine dependent services and groups. The Registry Editor enables you to search for the service or device and then view the dependent services in the device's data values. The Windows NT Event Viewer does not show group or service dependencies. For more information, read back through the "Searching the Registry" section.

7. **Your Windows NT Workstation computer is failing whenever you access the CD-ROM drive. You find out that you can change the access mode Windows NT uses when accessing the CD-ROM drive by changing a Registry value. Which Registry hive most likely contains the key for the CD-ROM device?**

☐ A.   HKEY_LOCAL_MACHINE

☐ B.   HKEY_CURRENT_USER

☐ C.   HKEY_CURRENT_CONFIG

☐ D.   HKEY_CLASSES_ROOT

The correct answer is **A**. The HKEY_LOCAL_MACHINE contains Registry keys for hardware and software configuration settings. The HKEY_CURRENT_USER hive contains Registry settings for the user currently logged in on the Windows NT Workstation computer For more information, see the "Using the Registry Editors" section.

8. Your Windows NT Workstation computer indicated that a service failed to load or start during the boot process. When you use the Windows NT Event Viewer to view the system log, what Stop event should you look for first to troubleshoot the problem?

  ☐ A. The latest Stop event in the log
  ☐ B. The oldest Stop event in the log
  ☐ C. The latest Informational event in the log
  ☐ D. The oldest Informational event in the log

The correct answer is **B**. When troubleshooting system failures, by looking at the oldest Stop event, you can work your way forward through the progressive system errors. This not only shows you the history of the problem, it will probably show the original circumstances that caused the error. For more information, see the "Using Event Viewer" section.

Practice Your Skills

Here is a chance to apply your practical, hands-on experience and material from this chapter. These exercises are designed for you to apply not only the material in the book, but to gain greater experience and exposure to the product. These exercises are a critical part of understanding the product and gaining valuable experience for using the product and passing the certification exam. For each of the following problems, consider the facts given and determine possible causes of the problem and what course of action you might take to resolve the problem.

1. Using the Last Known Good Control Set

EXERCISE Microsoft Windows NT Workstation provides a working configuration set called the Last Known Good configuration. This configuration set is created so that, after making system changes that prevent a computer from successfully booting, a user can boot the computer using a configuration that is known to work. At what point does Windows NT Workstation determine that the current control set is a good configuration and should be copied to the Last Known Good set?

ANALYSIS Once the computer successfully boots to the desktop logon screen and a user logs on, the configuration control set is assumed to be a valid configuration. Even if a device or service fails after the user logs on, the computer is at least capable of booting to the desktop thereby permitting diagnosis of system problems.

2. Using an Emergency Repair Disk

EXERCISE Using the Rdisk application, you can back up your system Registry and security database. When a system failure occurs that prevents you from booting your Windows NT Workstation computer, and the Last Known Good set does not resolve the problem, what are the advantages of performing an Emergency Repair process rather than reinstalling Windows NT Workstation?

ANALYSIS Performing an Emergency Repair usually resolves most system failures by verifying and updating corrupt or missing Windows NT Workstation files. As a result, existing user preference and application settings and installed data files are retained; whereas, if Windows NT Workstation was reinstalled, these settings would likely be lost during the reinstall.

3. Using the Windows NT Registry Editors

EXERCISE Microsoft Windows NT Workstation provides two Windows Registry Editors: Windows NT Registry Editor and Windows 95 Registry Editor. While the Windows 95 Registry Editor provides the capability to search the Registry to a great detail, what unique features are offered by the Windows NT Registry Editor?

ANALYSIS The Windows NT Registry Editor provides two unique features, the first is the capability to connect to other Windows NT computers and modify their system Registries. Second, the Windows NT Registry Editor can define security permissions to portions of the Registry hive. These two features are not available in the Windows 95 Registry Editor.

4. Storing Information in the Registry

EXERCISE Microsoft Windows products are used to store configuration and preference settings in the WIN.INI and SYSYTEM.INI files when they were installed. Windows NT uses the Registry to contain this same information. What are some of the benefits to be gained by using a Registry?

ANALYSIS By using a standard Registry with defined hives for specific purposes, there is no longer a need for configuration files for each application. In addition, by centrally locating all of the configuration settings, a user can easily update those settings, and applications adhering to the standard can automatically use existing preferences when configuring settings. A central Registry also enables remote administration capabilities by permitting administrative access to the Registry.

Practice Exam

1. You are installing Microsoft Peer Web Service on your Windows NT Workstation computer. The client computers will be using a variety of Web browsers that support different security standards. What level of security should you use on the Web site to ensure availability to all client types?

- [ ] A. Use Clear Text logon authentication.
- [ ] B. Use Certificates for logon authentication.
- [ ] C. Use Windows NT Challenge/Response logon authentication.
- [ ] D. Use Pass-through authentication.

2. You are adding 10 Windows NT Workstation computers to a new network. The Windows NT Workstation computers will be the only Windows NT computers on the network. You need to design a network configuration to manage user accounts and security privileges. What should you do?

- [ ] A. Place all of the computers in a workgroup.
- [ ] B. Place all of the computers in a workgroup and configure one of the Windows NT Workstation computers as a PDC.
- [ ] C. Configure one of the Windows NT Workstation computers as a PDC and place of the other computers in the domain.
- [ ] D. Configure one of the Windows NT Workstation computers as a PDC and the rest of the computers as BDCs in the domain.

MCSE NT WORKSTATION 4.0 ACE IT!

3. You want to install Windows 98 and Windows NT Workstation
on your new computer. You want to dual-boot between
Windows 98 and Windows NT Workstation. What should
you do?

- [ ] A. Install Windows NT Workstation, boot to the
Windows NT desktop, and run the Windows 98
setup program.
- [ ] B. Install Windows NT Workstation, boot the com-
puter with an MS-DOS disk, and start the
Windows 95 setup program.
- [ ] C. Format the partition as FAT32, install Windows
98, and then install Windows NT Workstation.
- [ ] D. Format the partition as FAT16, install Windows
98, and then install Windows NT Workstation.

4. You want to install Windows NT Workstation on 200 new
computers. You want to install Windows NT Workstation using
a minimal amount of interaction at the new computers. You
decide to install Windows NT Workstation over the network.
What should you do?

- [ ] A. Use the Windows NT Setup Manager to create a
boot disk.
- [ ] B. Use the Network Client Administrator on a
Windows NT Server computer to create a boot
disk.
- [ ] C. Use the Network Client Administrator on a
Windows NT Workstation computer to create a
boot disk.
- [ ] D. Use the contents of the `clients` folder to creat
a boot disk.

350

5. Your network contains three Windows NT Server computers in a Windows NT Server domain. There are also 45 Windows NT Workstation computers in the domain. Which computer(s) will be used as the domain master browser?

    ☐ A. The Primary Domain Controller

    ☐ B. All of the Backup Domain Controllers

    ☐ C. Any of the Windows NT Workstation computers

    ☐ D. All of the PDC and BDC computers

6. You are installing Windows NT Workstation using a shared folder and a sysdiff image. After the installation is completed and the computer is rebooted, you notice that the sysdiff image was not applied. What should you do?

    ☐ A. Add the command `Start $OEM$\cmd.bat` in to the `autoexec.bat` file on the computer.

    ☐ B. Create a `cmdlines.txt` file with the `sysdiff /apply` command in the Windows NT Workstation installation folder.

    ☐ C. Create a `cmdlines.txt` file with the `sysdiff /apply` command and place it in the `$OEM$` subfolder of the installation folder.

    ☐ D. Add the command `cmdlines.txt` to the UDF file used for each workstation.

7. You are planning to install Windows 98 and Windows NT Workstation on 250 new computers. What format should you use on drive C?

    ☐ A. NTFS

    ☐ B. FAT32

    ☐ C. FAT

    ☐ D. HPFS

8. Your computer has Windows 3.11 installed on the only hard
disk. You install Windows NT Workstation on the computer.
After completing the installation, you convert the partition to
NTFS so you can use file and folder compression. When you
reboot the computer you are unable to boot to Windows 3.11.
What should you do?

☐ A. Use the convert utility to convert the drive back
from NTFS to FAT, and reinstall Windows NT
Workstation and Windows 3.11.

☐ B. Use the Disk Administrator to convert the drive
from NTFS to FAT.

☐ C. Back up your computer, repartition the drive,
reformat the partition as FAT, install Windows
3.11 and Windows NT, and restore your backup.

☐ D. Uninstall Windows NT Workstation 4.0, and convert the partition back to FAT.

9. You have a portable computer that runs Windows NT
Workstation. You have installed a SCSI PC-Card adapter that
you use at the office to access a photo scanner. Because of the
power drain from the PC-Card adapter, you want to prevent the
SCSI drivers for the card from loading when away from the
office. What can you do?

☐ A. Configure the startup properties for the adapter
as disabled.

☐ B. Configure the startup properties for the adapter
as system.

☐ C. Create a hardware profile and enable the adapter
only in the profile for the office.

☐ D. Create a hardware profile called OFFICE and one
called MOBILE, NT will do the rest.

10. You have been experiencing problems connecting from your
    Windows NT Workstation computer to your corporate RAS
    server. You want to be able to view historical information on
    the modem connections. What can you do?

    ☐ A. Use the Windows NT Event Viewer.
    ☐ B. Use the Windows NT Performance Monitor.
    ☐ C. Configure the modem to record a log file.
    ☐ D. Use the server icon in the Control Panel.

11. Your Windows NT Workstation computer displays an error
    message that one or more services failed to start during the
    boot process. When you use the Event Viewer and look at the
    system log the device states that a dependent service was not
    started. What can you do to determine the dependent services
    for this failed service? (Choose two.)

    ☐ A. Use the Windows NT Diagnostics utility to view
          the dependencies on the Services tab.
    ☐ B. Use the Windows 95 Registry Editor to search for
          the device driver and view the dependent ser-
          vices.
    ☐ C. Use the Windows NT Event Viewer to view the
          Application logs.
    ☐ D. Use the Windows NT Event Viewer to view the
          Security logs.

12. Your Windows NT Workstation computer is configured to
    access NetWare servers and Windows NT Server computers.
    You access Windows NT Server computer more often than
    NetWare servers. What can you do to improve your
    performance when accessing Windows NT Server computer?

    ☐ A. Change the application performance setting to
          increase **Background** application speed.
    ☐ B. Configure the network bindings.
    ☐ C. Change the Network access order.
    ☐ D. Disable the Server service for the network
          adapter.

13. You are installing Windows NT Workstation on a new computer. After completing the installation you attempt to access the new computer over the network from your computer. You are able to see it when you browse the network, but you receive an access denied message when you attempt to connect. You are using the guest account on your computer. What is the most likely problem?

    ☐ A. The Guest account is disabled by default on the new computer.
    ☐ B. The Guest account has a user profile configured and it cannot be located.
    ☐ C. The computer belongs to a domain, and domain does not permit local Guest accounts.
    ☐ D. The Guest account has a home directory configured and it cannot be located.

14. Your network consists of Windows NT Workstation computers and Windows NT Server computers. You want to add an icon for a human resources benefits application to the desktop of all the computers. Where should you place the icon?

    ☐ A. In the `<winntroot>\Profiles\All Users\Desktop` folder on each computer.
    ☐ B. In the `<winntroot>\Profiles\Default User\Desktop` folder on each computer.
    ☐ C. In the `<users>\Profiles\All Users\Desktop` folder on each computer.
    ☐ D. In the `<users>\Profiles\Default Users\Desktop` folder on each computer.

15. You are installing Windows NT Workstation onto 75 new computers over the network using a Network Client Administrator boot disk. You want to install an in-house custom application at the same time you install Windows NT Workstation. What should you do?

    ☐ A. Add a `commands` section to the `unattended.txt` file and enter the application's setup application name in the section.

    ☐ B. Add a `commands` section to a `UDF` file and enter the application's setup program name in the section.

    ☐ C. Create a `$OEM$` subdirectory in the Windows NT Workstation installation shared folder, place the application files in the folder, and create the required `cmdlines.txt` file.

    ☐ D. Use the `sysdiff.exe` utility to add the application's setup application to your shared folder installation directory.

16. You are the network administrator for a network consisting of Windows NT Server computers and Windows NT Workstation computers. You want to update three DLL files on your servers located in a remote facility. What can you do?

    ☐ A. Connect to the server's Admin$ share.

    ☐ B. Connect to the server's C$ share.

    ☐ C. Connect to the server's IPC$ share.

    ☐ D. Do nothing, you cannot remotely access the hard drive of a Windows NT Server computer.

17. You are in the process of upgrading a Windows NT Workstation computer. You back up all of the existing user files by copying them to a shared folder on a Windows NT Server computer. What will happen to the NTFS file permissions when the files are moved to the server?

  ☐ A. The NTFS file permissions will be retained after the move.
  ☐ B. The NTFS file permissions will default to Read Only permissions for the Everyone group.
  ☐ C. The NTFS file permissions will default to Full Control permissions for the Everyone group.
  ☐ D. The NTFS permissions will inherit the permissions of the new parent folder.

18. Your Windows NT Workstation computer is running low on disk space on the boot partition. You are experiencing problems when you spool large print jobs on your computer. What should you do?

  ☐ A. Move the spool directory off of the boot partition.
  ☐ B. Assign separator pages to all of the printers.
  ☐ C. Change the spool format to EMF.
  ☐ D. Change the spool format to RAW.

19. You are planning on migrating your company's Windows 3.11 computers to Windows NT Workstation. You are in the process of testing several custom-developed internal applications to see how they will perform on a Windows NT Workstation computer. You discover that one of them is attempting to access the hardware directly. What can you do?

  ☐ A. Run the application in a Separate Memory space.
  ☐ B. Grant your user account the "Logon as Service" right.
  ☐ C. Configure the computer to dual-boot Windows 3.11 and run the application in Windows 3.11.
  ☐ D. Format a disk as FAT to run the application on.

20. **You want to optimize the performance of your Windows NT Workstation computer. How should you configure the page file on the computer?**

    ☐ A. Configure one large page file on the Windows NT boot partition.

    ☐ B. Configure one page file for each disk in the computer, including the Windows NT boot partition.

    ☐ C. Configure one page file for each disk in the computer, except the Windows NT boot partition.

    ☐ D. Configure one large page file on a partition other than the Windows NT boot partition.

21. **Your network consists of Windows NT Workstation computers and Windows NT Server computers. You want to prevent the Windows NT Workstation computers from maintaining the browse list. What should you do?**

    ☐ A. Configure the computers as Potential Browsers.

    ☐ B. Configure the computers as Non-Browsers.

    ☐ C. Configure the computers as Backup Browsers.

    ☐ D. Configure the computers as Master Browsers.

22. **You are using TCP/IP to access resources on a Windows NT network. Your network is subnetted and has several routes on the network. You want to provide a central location for connecting to computers using NetBIOS names. What should you use?**

    ☐ A. Use a Hosts.sam file.

    ☐ B. Use a WINS server.

    ☐ C. Use a DHCP server.

    ☐ D. Use a LMHosts.sam file.

23. You are configuring a Dial-Up Networking connection from your Windows NT Workstation computer to your corporate RAS server. When you connect using Dial-Up Networking, you can access Windows NT Server servers on the local segment, but you cannot access servers on remote segments. What should you do?

☐ A. Configure TCP/IP to use the default router on the remote network.
☐ B. Configure TCP/IP to disable PPP LCP extensions.
☐ C. Do not use a Multilink connection.
☐ D. Grant your user account Dial-in permission on the RAS server.

24. You are installing Client Service for NetWare and the NWLink IPX/SPX Compatible Transport on your Windows NT Workstation computer. You computer has two network adapter cards installed. Because of the multiple network adapters, what must you configure?

☐ A. An external network number
☐ B. An internal network number
☐ C. Frame type
☐ D. Default Context
☐ E. Default Tree
☐ F. Preferred Server

25. Your computer runs Windows NT Workstation. You want to be able to view network activity statistics for your computer. What should you do? (Choose two.)

☐ A. Install the SNMP Service.
☐ B. Install the Network Monitor Agent.
☐ C. Use Performance Monitor to view the Network Segment object.
☐ D. Use Performance Monitor to view the Network Segment counter.

26. You are installing a new Windows NT Workstation computer. You can access Windows NT Server computers on the local subnet using TCP/IP. When you attempt to access NT Server computers on remote subnets or print to remote printers, you are unable to access the resource. What configuration setting is the most likely problem?

- [ ] A. TCP/IP Address
- [ ] B. Subnet mask
- [ ] C. Default router
- [ ] D. Host name

27. You are in the process of configuring user access permission on a group of Windows NT Workstation computers. Which of the following can you do with a local group? (Choose two.)

- [ ] A. Add another local group from the same computer.
- [ ] B. Add another local group from a different computer.
- [ ] C. Add a local group from the workstation's Primary Domain Controller.
- [ ] D. Add a global group from the workstation's domain.

28. Your Windows NT Workstation computer is experiencing problems connecting to network resources using TCP/IP. Your computer is configured to use a DHCP server. What can you do to view your assigned TCP/IP configuration?

- [ ] A. Use Network in the Control Panel to view the TCP/IP protocol configuration.
- [ ] B. Use the `ipconfig /all` command.
- [ ] C. Use the Internet Service Manager to view your TCP/IP configuration.
- [ ] D. Use the `ping /all` command.

29. You are experiencing slow response times from a host when using TCP/IP. You want to determine if the network is causing a delay in routing your TCP/IP traffic or if the host is just slow. What should you do to verify if the network is slow?

   ☐ A. Use the `net use` command.
   ☐ B. Use the `net view` command.
   ☐ C. Use the `ipconfig` command.
   ☐ D. Use the `ping` command.

30. You are performing maintenance on one of your Windows NT Workstation computers. Several people on the network access shared folders on the computer. You want to prevent users from accessing the files while you work on the computer. What can you do?

   ☐ A. Change the network access order so Microsoft Networks is last.
   ☐ B. Place the computer in a workgroup rather than an NT Domain.
   ☐ C. Disable the server service on the network adapter.
   ☐ D. Disable the workstation service on the network adapter.

31. You are assigning the members of your corporate helpdesk Manage Documents permissions for all of your printers. What else must you do in order for them to print to the printers?

   ☐ A. Grant them Read Only permission to the `<winnt>\spool` directory.
   ☐ B. Grant them Print permission.
   ☐ C. Add them to the Power Users user group.
   ☐ D. Revoke the Manage Documents permission, and grant Print permission.

32. **When you start Performance Monitor and look at the TCP/IP objects, all of the counters are 0. You want to be able to see actual statistics for your TCP/IP protocol performance. What should you do? (Choose two.)**

    ☐ A. Install the SNMP Service.

    ☐ B. Install the Network Monitor Agent.

    ☐ C. Use Performance Monitor to view the TCP and IP objects.

    ☐ D. Use Performance Monitor to view the Network Segment object.

33. **You are upgrading your Windows 3.11 computer to Windows NT Workstation 4.0. You insert the Windows NT Workstation CD-ROM and run** `Winnt32.exe` **to start the installation. You receive an error stating that** `Winnt32.exe` **could not run. What should you do?**

    ☐ A. Replace the CD-ROM drive with a drive supported by Windows NT Workstation.

    ☐ B. Run `Winnt32.exe` with the /B switch.

    ☐ C. Start the upgrade with `Winnt.exe`.

    ☐ D. Remove all of the network components in Windows 3.11 before starting the upgrade.

34. **You are the network administrator for a network that contains a Windows NT Server domain. You are moving a common shared area on an NT Server to another server on the network with more storage capacity. When you attempt to move some of the files, you receive access denied messages. What should you do?**

    ☐ A. Use the Windows Explorer to take ownership of the files, and then move them.

    ☐ B. Change the user password for the owner of each restricted file, log in as the user, change the permissions, and then move the files.

    ☐ C. Use the User Manager for Domains to change the ownership of the files.

    ☐ D. Log in as a member of the Server Operators group and then move the files.

35. You are configuring a Dial-Up Networking connection on your Windows NT Workstation computer. You have configured your connection to use your two modems and to use Multilink to bind the modems together. When you dial your corporate RAS server, the Multilink connection fails. What should you do?

   ☐ A. You do not have permission to use Multilink.
   ☐ B. The RAS Server is configured to refuse Multilink connections.
   ☐ C. Your modems do not support Multilink.
   ☐ D. You are using a SLIP connection.

36. You are installing the Remote Access Service on your Windows NT Workstation computer. You will be using a variety of client types to dial into the computer. What level of security should you use?

   ☐ A. Accept only Microsoft-encrypted authentication.
   ☐ B. Accept any authentication including clear text.
   ☐ C. Accept only encrypted authentication.
   ☐ D. Require data encryption.

37. You use your Windows NT Workstation computer to access a mainframe host using the DLC protocol. You want to be able to use Dial-Up Networking to connect to your RAS server and access the mainframe host. How will the RAS server handle the DLC protocol?

   ☐ A. The client computer is only permitted to access the RAS server.
   ☐ B. The RAS server will refuse connections made using DLC.
   ☐ C. The RAS server provides a DLC gateway.
   ☐ D. Dial-Up Networking does not support the DLC protocol.

38. You are upgrading your company's Windows 3.1 computers to Windows NT Workstation. Before you upgrade everyone, you test all of the applications the users will need to run on the Windows NT Workstation computers. One of the Windows 3.1 applications has a tendency to fail under certain situations. You want to protect other Windows 3.1 applications from being affected if this one fails. What can you do on the Windows NT Workstation computers?

- [ ] A. Give the application a priority setting of low.
- [ ] B. Give the application a priority setting of real-time.
- [ ] C. Run the application in a separate NTVDM.
- [ ] D. Run the application with the /min command-line switch.

39. You are configuring the hard disks in your Windows NT Workstation. The computer has four 3GB hard disks. The first hard disk contains the boot and system partitions for Windows NT Workstation. You want to configure the remaining three so that if one of the disks fail, you can still access all of your data. What should you do?

- [ ] A. Configure the three disks as a stripe set.
- [ ] B. Configure the three disks as a volume set.
- [ ] C. Configure the three disks as a stripe set with parity.
- [ ] D. Configure the three disks as a mirror set.

40. You have started a security monitoring application using the /real-time command switch. All of the other applications on the computer are running extremely slowly and are failing due to the slow response times. What can you do to resolve this problem without stopping the security application?

- [ ] A. Run all of the other applications in a separate memory space.
- [ ] B. Run all of the other applications in a minimized state.

☐ C. Use the Task Manager to reduce the base priority of the application.

☐ D. Nothing can be done once the application is started.

---

41. **When you start performance monitor and look at the PhysicalDisk objects, all of the counters are 0. You want to be able to see actual statistics for your disk performance. What should you do? (Choose two.)**

☐ A. Log on to the Window NT Workstation computer as an administrator.

☐ B. Use `diskperf.exe` to enable the Performance Monitor objects.

☐ C. Use the Disk Administrator to enable the Performance Monitor objects.

☐ D. Install the PhysicalDisk Performance Monitor objects.

---

42. **You are optimizing your Windows NT Workstation computer. You want to increase the speed at which your computer spools and prints jobs to a print server. What can you do?**

☐ A. Configure your spool settings to use EMF.

☐ B. Configure your spool settings to use RAW.

☐ C. Print your documents using drag-and-drop.

☐ D. Configure your spool settings to print directly to the printer.

---

43. **You want to forward spooled print jobs from a Windows NT Workstation to a NetWare print queue. What must you install on the Windows NT Workstation computer? (Choose two.)**

☐ A. Install Client Service for NetWare.

☐ B. Install NWLink IPX/SPX Compatible Transport.

☐ C. Configure a separator page.

☐ D. Configure the spool format as RAW.

44. You want to remotely modify the registry on one of your Windows NT Server computers. You are using a Windows NT Workstation computer. What should you do?

　　□ A. Use the Windows 95 Registry Editor.
　　□ B. Use the Windows NT Registry Editor.
　　□ C. First connect a drive to the server's computer, and then use the Windows 95 Registry Editor.
　　□ D. First make a connection to the server's IPC$ share, and the use the Windows 95 Registry Editor.

45. You are adding a new software application to your Windows NT Workstation computer. When you reboot the computer the boot process fails and the computer displays a blue screen. When you reboot the computer the same problem occurs. What should you do?

　　□ A. Perform the Emergency Repair process, selecting the Inspect boot sector and Verify Windows NT system files.
　　□ B. Perform the Emergency Repair process to restore the Windows NT Registry.
　　□ C. Run the Windows NT Diagnostics program.
　　□ D. Reboot the computer, and select the Last Known Good Configuration during the boot sequence.

46. You are installing Remote Access Service on your Windows NT Workstation computer. The remote users will be calling long distance from various locations using their portable laptop modems. You want to incur the bulk of long distance charges at your corporate office where you have negotiated better phone rates. How should you configure RAS?

　　□ A. Configure the user accounts for Call Back security set as **Set By Caller**.
　　□ B. Configure the user accounts for Call Back security set as **Preset To**.
　　□ C. Assign the user accounts a mandatory profile.
　　□ D. Add the user accounts to the Users group.

47. You are installing 25 new Windows NT Workstation computers in the executive offices at your company. You need to make sure that the documents stored on the Windows NT Workstation computers are protected from prying eyes. You want to protect the files from unauthorized access even if the user is sitting at the computer. What should you do?

☐ A. Place the files in a shared folder with restricted access permissions.
☐ B. Place the files on a FAT32 partition with restricted access permissions.
☐ C. Place the files on an NTFS partition with restricted access permissions.
☐ D. Place the files on an HPFS partition with restricted access permissions.

48. You are optimizing the performance on your Windows NT Workstation computer using Performance Monitor. When you view the Paging File - % Usage counter, you notice it is averaging 99 percent. What should you do to your computer to resolve this problem?

☐ A. Add a faster CPU.
☐ B. Add a faster hard disk.
☐ C. Add more hard disk space.
☐ D. Add more RAM.

49. Which Windows NT Workstation group enables members to share folders and add devices, but cannot add members to the administrators group or change the administrator password?

☐ A. Administrators local group
☐ B. Power Users local group
☐ C. Server Operators local group
☐ D. Users local group

50. You are creating a batch file to update your recovery disk and back the SAM and Security registry hives. What command should you use?

     ☐ A. Rdisk /Complete.

     ☐ B. Rdisk /All.

     ☐ C. Rdisk /S.

     ☐ D. Rdisk /C.

Exam Key

1. A
2. A
3. D
4. B
5. A
6. C
7. C
8. C
9. C
10. C
11. A and B
12. C
13. A
14. A
15. C
16. B
17. D
18. A
19. C
20. C
21. B
22. B
23. A
24. B
25. B and C

26. C
27. A and D
28. B
29. D
30. C
31. B
32. A and C
33. C
34. A
35. B
36. B
37. D
38. C
39. C
40. C
41. B
42. A
43. A and B
44. B
45. D
46. A
47. C
48. D
49. B
50. C

Exam Analysis

1. The use of Windows NT Challenge/Response can limit the number of supported platforms. This security model often requires additional add-on software or nonstandard processes that current or future browsing platforms may not support. *For more information refer to Chapter 9.*

2. Because the Windows NT Workstation computers will be the only ones on the network, you can only place them in a workgroup. To place the computers in a domain, you would need at least one Windows NT Server computer acting as a PDC. *For more information refer to Chapter 1.*

3. Because only Windows NT can use NTFS partitions, and FAT32 is not usable by Windows NT, the only possible format for the C drive is FAT. In addition, if Windows 98 is installed after Windows NT, the boot loader program will be incorrectly over written. You are better off installing Windows NT after Windows 98. *For more information refer to Chapter 3.*

4. The Network Client Administrator (NCA) can create a bootable disk to start up a computer and begin the installation of Windows NT Workstation without installing drivers or software on the PC first. The NCA is available only on a Windows NT Server computer. The NT Setup Manager is used to create an unattended installation file. *For more information refer to Chapter 2.*

5. The PDC is always the domain master browser and there is only one domain master browser per domain. *For more information refer to Chapter 8*

6. The `cmdlines.txt` file when placed in the `$OEM$` directory will be run automatically if the `OEMPREINSTALL` command is entered in the `unattended.txt` file. If the `cmdlines.txt` will only be used if it is placed in the `$OEM$` directory, it will not be used if placed anywhere else. *For more information refer to Chapter 2.*

7. The only file system accessible to both Windows NT and Windows 98 is FAT16. If the C drive is formatted as NTFS, Windows 98 will not be capable of accessing the drive to be installed. Additionally, FAT32 is available only in Windows 98 and is not supported by Windows NT 4.0. *For more information refer to Chapter 3.*

8. The `convert` utility can only convert a drive from NTFS to FAT, no vice versa. As a result, once a drive is formatted as NTFS, you must repartition and format the drive. *For more information refer to Chapter 3.*

9. A hardware profile contains configuration settings for the hardware device drivers that will or will not be loaded during a session. If you have a SCSI adapter that you use only in the office the device driver does not need to be loaded when traveling around. The name of the hardware has no significance for Windows NT, so it will not do anything automatically as a result. *For more information refer to Chapter 4.*

10. The only way to view historical information on the status and performance of modem connections is with a log file. Neither the Event Viewer nor the Performance Monitor can view the performance information of a modem. *For more information refer to Chapter 4.*

1. The Windows NT Diagnostics utility and Windows 95 Registry Editor can be used to determine dependent services and groups. The Windows NT Diagnostics utility enables you to select a service and view its dependencies, the Registry Editor enables you to search for the service or device and then view the dependent services in the device's data values. *For more information refer to Chapter 13.*

2. By configuring the Network access order, you can establish which Network Operating System will be the first one used when connecting to other computers. Rather than waiting for the NetWare resources to timeout and then reverting to the Microsoft network, you can configure the Microsoft network to be accessed first. *For more information refer to Chapter 4.*

3. When Windows NT Workstation is installed, the Guest account is disabled by default. This is done to prevent unauthorized access to local and network resources without your consent. *For more information refer to Chapter 5.*

4. There is no way to define a company-wide roaming All Users profile, so you must make the change on each Windows NT computer. The All Users profile is loaded for each user on a Windows NT Workstation computer — even if they have a roaming profile defined. The Default User profile is only used when a user logs on to the computer and does not have a local or roaming profile already defined for him. *For more information refer to Chapter 5.*

5. The OEM directory and `cmdlines.txt` are used to install applications that have their own scripted install. The `commands` section does nothing to include your application with the roll out. If you have a scripted install, it is generally better to use the OEM directory, rather than using sysdiff. *For more information refer to Chapter 2.*

16. By default, Windows NT automatically creates an administrative share for every hard drive partition in your computer. The administrative shares are named for their logical drive letter assignment and the $ sign is appended to hide the share from network browsers. The IPC$ is used for interprocess communications and cannot be used to access logical volumes or Windows NT computers. *For more information refer to Chapter 6.*

17. When files are moved between NTFS partitions on different disks or computers, the NTFS permissions inherit the settings of the new parent folder. NTFS permissions are not maintained when moved off of a computer. *For more information refer to Chapter 6*

18. If your Windows NT Workstation boot partition is limited in disk space, the burden of printing large documents can reduce available disk space to 0 and cause extreme performance penalties. You should move the spool directory off of the boot partition and place it on another partition. *For more information refer to Chapter 7.*

19. Windows NT does not support any application that requires direct access to the computer hardware. Direct access may compromise the security features of Windows NT or interfere with its architecture. Of the available solutions, configuring a dual-boot computer is the best resolution to the problem. *For more information refer to Chapter 1.*

20. Spreading the page files over multiple disks, Windows NT can access the page files in parallel, rather than waiting for a file to be read, and then working with a page file. *For more information refer to Chapter 4.*

21. If a computer is configured as a nonbrowser, it will not participate in the browser-election process nor will it build a browse list. *For more information refer to Chapter 8.*

2. Using a WINS server enables you to browse a Microsoft network using TCP/IP and to connect to network devices using NetBIOS names. The WINS server is responsible for converting a NetBIOS name to a registered TCP/IP address for the client. *For more information refer to Chapter 8.*

3. When you are able to connect to a RAS server and access hosts local to the RAS server, but are unable to reach other hosts, the problem is usually a TCP/IP default router configuration error. By using the default router on the remote network, the PPP connection uses the default router assigned by the RAS server. *For more information refer to Chapter 10.*

4. Because the computer has two network adapters, you must configure an internal network address for the NWLink IPX/SPX Compatible Transport protocol. *For more information refer to Chapter 8.*

5. Before you can view network traffic performance activity, you must install the Network Monitor Agent. You can then use Performance Monitor to view the Network Segment object, which has several counters associated with it. *For more information refer to Chapter 12.*

6. If a computer is capable of accessing resources on a local subnet, but cannot communicate across subnets, the problem is likely an incorrect default router setting. Without a default router defined, the workstation has no means to pass traffic to computers that reside on remote subnets. *For more information refer to Chapter 9.*

7. Local groups are contained in the security database of a local computer; they are not accessible by other computers. As a result, a local group can contain only other local groups from the same computer or a global group from the workstation's domain. *For more information refer to Chapter 5.*

28. The command line `ipconfig` application can be used to display the current TCP/IP configuration for each network adapter in a computer. This application shows the TCP/IP address, subnet mask, and default gateway, among other things, for each adapter. Network in the Control Panel will not show the current TCP/IP assignments, it will only indicate that the computer is configured to use DHCP. *For more information refer to Chapter 9.*

29. The `ping` command can be used in conjunction with the remote host name or TCP/IP address to determine the network response time. If the response time is reasonably fast, but the client is experiencing slow response when accessing resources on the host, the host is most likely the problem. *For more information refer to Chapter 9.*

30. By disabling the server service, Windows NT does not accept connection requests for shared folders and shared printers. This can also be used for computers that should not ever accept client connections. *For more information refer to Chapter 4.*

31. In addition to granting the Manage Documents permission, you must also grant at least Print permission to enable them to use the printers. *For more information refer to Chapter 7.*

32. Before the IP, TCP, ICMP, and UDP objects can be viewed with Performance Monitor, you must install the SNMP service, which is responsible for creating the counter values. Once the SNMP service is installed, you can use Performance Monitor to view the various TCP and IP object counters. *For more information refer to Chapter 12.*

33. You can only use `Winnt32.exe` on Windows NT computers, as it is a threaded, 32-bit application that does not support MS-DOS, Windows 3.1, or Windows 95/98. On these computers you must you `Winnt.exe`, which performs the same functions but in a 16-bit memory space. *For more information refer to Chapter 1.*

4. The only way you can change the permissions for a file, if you are not the owner/creator and do not have change permission, is to take ownership of the files. You must be logged in as a member of the administrators local group, and then you can change the file permissions. *For more information refer to Chapter 6.*

5. Windows NT RAS does not enable Multilink connections by default; the server administrator must enable it. If the server you are calling does not permit Multilink connections, you will only be able to connect using a single modem line. *For more information refer to Chapter 10.*

6. Because you will be using a variety of client platforms to connect to your Windows NT Workstation computer, you should use the lowest common security authentication — clear text. Otherwise, you are likely to encounter problems connecting from platforms that do not support Challenge/Response authentication. *For more information refer to Chapter 10.*

7. The Remote Access Service does not support the DLC protocol. As a result, you will be unable to create a Dial-Up Networking connection using this protocol alone. *For more information refer to Chapter 10.*

8. Windows NT Workstation enables you to run 16-bit applications in separate NTVDMs, which prevent the application from causing faults in other applications. The priority setting will make little difference in solving the problem unless the application was already running at real-time and was hogging the processor. *For more information refer to Chapter 11.*

9. A stripe set with parity provides fault tolerance so that when a single disk fails, all of the user data is still accessible through the other remaining disks. *For more information refer to Chapter 3.*

40. You can use the Window NT Workstation Task Manager to change the base priority of any running application to which you have permissions. Running the other applications in separate NTVDMs or in a minimized state will rarely improve the performance of other applications. *For more information refer to Chapter 11.*

41. The PhysicalDisk related objects are installed by default, but are not enabled until the `diskperf.exe` utility is used. The objects are not enabled by default as they cause a slight decrease in system performance. The Disk Administrator cannot be used to enable the PhysicalDisk objects. *For more information refer to Chapter 12.*

42. The EMF spool setting configures your computer to perform only half of the print-rendering process and then sends the print job to the print server, which finishes the processing and prints out the document, completing the print processing. The methods by which you submit your print job, such as drag-and-drop, have little to do with print performance. *For more information refer to Chapter 7.*

43. Before a Windows NT computer can forward print jobs to a NetWare print queue, the computer must have Client Service for NetWare and NWLink IPX/SPX Compatible Transport installed. You do not need to have a separator page defined, nor does the spool format need to be changed in order to forward to a NetWare queue. *For more information refer to Chapter 7.*

44. The Windows NT Registry Editor is the only application that can be used to open and modify a system Registry remotely. The Windows 95 Registry Editor does not have the capacity to open a Registry remotely. *For more information refer to Chapter 12.*

45. The most likely cause of this problem involves the configuration changes made during the last logon session. The Last Known Good Configuration contains the system settings that reflect the configuration of the computer before any recent changes were made that prevented the computer from booting. *For more information refer to Chapter 13.*

6. To centrally bill the bulk of long distance charges, you can use Call Back security set to **Set By Caller.** This enables authorized callers to input a dial back number and have the RAS server call them back at their present location. This way, the RAS server phone line will incur the bulk of the charges, rather than the user. *For more information refer to Chapter 5.*

7. NTFS is the only file system that can set access permissions on the local hard disks. FAT32 and FAT do not have any means of applying access rights at the file-system level. *For more information refer to Chapter 3.*

8. When the Paging File - %Usage counter shows a number approaching 100%, this indicates the computer is short on RAM. You should add more RAM and the counter should begin to show a lower trend. *For more information refer to Chapter 12.*

9. Only the Power Users group can share folders and add devices, but it cannot make changes to the administrators group or the administrator account. This is beneficial in allowing knowledgeable users to modify their workstations to individual preferences, but they cannot lock out administrator access. *For more information refer to Chapter 6.*

10. The Rdisk application will not back up the SAM and Security hives unless the /s switch is used. If you create a Repair Disk without the switch, you will have an incomplete backup. *For more information refer to Chapter 13.*

Exam Revealed

You want to install Windows NT Workstation over the network on a computer that has not had its hard disk formatted. What should you do?

- [ ] A. Use the Windows NT Setup Manager to create a boot disk.
- [ ] B. **Use the Network Client Administrator on a Windows NT Server computer to create a boot disk.**
- [ ] C. Use the Network Client Administrator on a Windows NT Workstation computer to create a boot disk.
- [ ] D. Use the contents of the `clients` folder to create a boot disk.

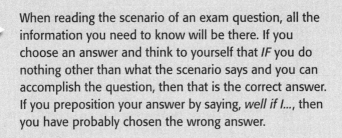

When reading the scenario of an exam question, all the information you need to know will be there. If you choose an answer and think to yourself that *IF* you do nothing other than what the scenario says and you can accomplish the question, then that is the correct answer. If you preposition your answer by saying, *well if I...*, then you have probably chosen the wrong answer.

2. You are using an `unattended.txt` file to install Windows NT
   Workstation on 250 new computers. You also want to apply the
   Windows NT Service Pack 3 at the same time you install NT
   Workstation. You already have a scripted installation of the
   Service Pack. What should you do?

   - [ ] A. Add a `commands` section to the unattended.txt file
     and enter the Service Pack installation script pro-
     gram name in the section.
   - [ ] B. Add a `commands` section to a UDF file and enter
     the Service Pack installation script program name
     in the section.
   - [ ] C. **Create a OEM subdirectory in your shared
     folder for Windows NT Workstation, place the
     installation script and required files in the fold-
     er, and create the required cmdlines.txt file.**
   - [ ] D. Use the sysdiff.exe utility to add the installation
     script to your shared folder installation directory.

   If you are unable to determine the correct answer, use the
   Mark option at the top of the exam window. You can
   review the remaining questions in the exam because
   many times another question may give you the details or
   information to help answer questions you skipped. Wait
   for the end of the exam and then review your marked
   items. Use the scratch paper to write down notes on
   questions you need more information on to answer.

3. You use your Windows NT Workstation to print large
   presentation documents. You want to increase the speed at
   which your computer spools and sends off your print jobs to the
   print server. What can you do?

   - [ ] A. **Configure your spool settings to use EMF.**
   - [ ] B. Configure your spool settings to use RAW.
   - [ ] C. Print your documents using drag-and-drop.
   - [ ] D. Print your document using an application and no
     drag-and-drop.

When an exam question uses the word *can*, the scenario can usually be resolved or answered in a number of ways, but generally the question provides only one correct answer. If you can think of another correct way of solving the problem, then you need to continue that train of thought and see if any of the provided answers will provide the same effect.

4. You are installing Client Service for NetWare and the NWLink IPX/SPX Compatible Transport on your Windows NT Workstation computer. Your computer has one network adapter and you want to use resources on a NetWare 3.x server. What information must you have to configure these two components? (Choose three.)

☐ A. **An external network number**
☐ B. An internal network number
☐ C. **Frame type**
☐ D. Default Context
☐ E. Default Tree
☐ F. **Preferred Server**

If the exam question indicates to choose a specific number of items, all of the selected answers must be correct; no credit is given for partially correct answers. Questions that indicate a specific number are far easier than those that say *Choose all that apply*.

5. Your Window NT Workstation computer seems to respond very slowly to your requests. You want to measure the percentage of time that processes on your computer are actively using the processor. Which Performance Monitor objects and counters should you monitor?

☐ A. **Object: Processor**
Counter: %Processor Time

☐ B. Object: %Processor Time
Counter: Processor

☐ C. Object: Processor
Counter: %Privileged Time

☐ D. Object: %Privileged Time
Counter: Processor

▷ Don't get to anxious when it comes to questions in which all of the answers appear the same, and often make you wish they would just go away. First write down the four answer choices, and then scratch out the ones that are obviously wrong. This will usually leave two answers remaining, look back at the scenario and see if you missed any information. This will usually lead you to the correct answer. Never just guess at the correct answers because it looks complicated, it usually isn't.

6. You receive a call from a user who is having problems with his Windows NT Workstation computer. Using your Windows NT Workstation computer and Event Viewer you determine that a Registry configuration change needs to be made on his computer. You want to remotely modify the user's Registry from your Windows NT Workstation computer. What should you do?

☐ A. Use the Windows 95 Registry Editor.
☐ B. **Use the Windows NT Registry Editor.**

☐ C. First connect a drive to the user's computer, and
then use the Windows 95 Registry Editor.

☐ D. First make a connection to the user's IPC$ share,
and the use the Windows 95 Registry Editor.

Be on the lookout for wording that would otherwise
make the distracters look like correct answers. The purpose of the scenario and distracters is to give options for
people who don't know the product or who didn't read
the scenario closely enough. In this case, without this
wording, both answers A and B would be correct, but
think to yourself, what's the purpose of the rest of the
scenario? This may be a give away that you are missing
something.

**You are configuring your Windows NT Workstation computer
and want to increase the performance of your computer. You
notice that your hard drive is very busy, and you suspect that
the page file is being used heavily. What can you do?**

☐ A. Configure 1 large page file on the partition that
contains the Windows NT boot files.

☐ B. Configure 1 page file for each disk in the computer, including the Windows NT boot partition.

☐ C. **Configure 1 page file for each disk in the computer, except the Windows NT boot partition.**

☐ D. Configure 1 large page file on a partition other
than the Windows NT boot partition.

If the distracters prevent you from easily determining the
correct answer, take the time to draw out the scenario
and eliminate all of the distracters. In this case, make a
diagram of the disks, and draw out the locations of the
page file and see how it may affect performance on the
computer. You should either see the correct answer glar-
ing out at you, or at least one or two distracters you can
eliminate.

8. You are installing Remote Access Server on your Windows NT Workstation computer. You want to increase the security on the Remote Access Server to ensure that only authorized users are allowed to connect using Dial-Up Networking. What should you do?

☐ A. **Configure the user accounts for Call Back security set as Set By Caller.**

☐ B. Configure the user accounts for Call Back security set as Preset To.

☐ C. Assign the user accounts a mandatory profile.

☐ D. Add the user accounts to the Users group.

If you can see why one answer is more correct than the other, try to imagine a real life scenario and think throug the process and see what happens. In this case, when a user calls in and Call Back is set as Set By Caller, the use can enter the number to call them back at. How does th help to increase security? Whereas, if the user calls in an Call Back already has a preset number, it will only call th user back at that number. If the user account had been hacked, the RAS server will call the user back at their defined number, maybe an office number or home num ber. The hacker won't be there and therefore won't be able to connect to the server – that *is* increased security.

9. You are the network administrator for a network that contair a Windows NT Server domain. An employee has left the company to go to work for a competitor. You deleted the user': accountto ensure that the employee will not be able to access the network. The employee's manager has requested that all o the employee's files be moved to the manager's personal folde for review. When you attempt to change the permissions for th files to permit the manager to work with the files, you are unable to set the permissions. What should you do?

☐ A. **Use the Windows Explorer and Take Ownership of the files and then change the permissions**.

☐ B. Recreate the user account and change the permissions to permit the manager to work with the files.

☐ C. Move the files off of the NTFS partition and onto another one so that the permissions are inherited from the volume.

☐ D. Logon as a member of the Power Users group and change the permissions for the files.

▶ When the exam question scenario indicates that you are the network administrator, that generally means you have all of the administrator privileges required to complete the task. That's not to say that a correct answer may be to grant yourself administrator privileges, but if none of the answer choices mention user permissions, it a safe bet that you have the required permissions. Rarely will the correct answer be contingent on knowing if you are the administrator for a specific domain.

). You are experiencing difficulty connecting to a TCP/IP host computer on a remote subnet on your network. Previously you have had no problems working with this remote host, but recently you are unable to reach the host. You want to determine if there is a communications problem between your Windows NT Workstation computer and the remote host. What can you do?

☐ A. Change your computer's subnet mask to match that of the remote host.

☐ B. Change your computer's default gateway to match that of the remote host.

☐ C. Use the ipconfig command.

☐ D. Use the ping command.

When evaluating the scenario, you need to pay attention to exactly what is being asked. In this case, the scenario says that you are experiencing difficulty with a connection that has worked okay until now. It is unlikely that a configuration change was performed on the computer, so the and B deal with configuration issues, so you can probably rule them out in the scenario. That leaves just two answers to decide between.

Glossary

A

access control list (ACL) The ACL is a list that contains user and group security identifiers (SIDs), with the associated privileges of each user and group. Each object, such as a file or folder, has an access control list associated with it. *See also* security identifier (SID).

account policy The account policy is the set of rules indicating how passwords and account lockout are managed in Windows NT. Account policy is managed by using the Account Policy dialog box in User Manager.

active partition The active partition is a primary partition on the first hard disk in a computer that has been marked active by a partitioning program, such as Fdisk or Disk Manager. A computer loads its operating system from the active partition.

answer files (Unattend.txt) Answer files are text files that contain localized responses to the queries posed by the Windows NT setup program during installation. You can use an answer file in conjunction with a network installation startup disk to fully automate the installation of Windows NT on a single computer (in other words, perform an unattended installation). The default name for an answer file is Unattend.txt, but you can use any file name you want for your answer files.

AppleTalk AppleTalk is a routable network protocol developed by Apple Computer, Inc. This protocol is associated with Macintosh computers.

application programming interface (API) An API is a set of operating system functions that can be called by an application running on the computer. Windows NT supports the Win32, Win16, POSIX, MS-DOS, and OS/2 1.*x* APIs.

authentication Authentication is the verification of a user account name and password by Windows NT. Authentication can be performed by the local Windows NT computer or by a Windows NT Server domain controller.

B

backup browser A backup browser is a computer that maintains a backup copy of the browse list. The backup browser receives the browse list from the master browser, and then makes the browse list available to any computer that requests it. All computers on the network, when they request a copy of the browse list, do so from a backup browser. A backup browser updates its browse list by requesting an update from the master browser every 12 minutes. There can be more than one backup browser on each subnet. Any Windows NT Server, Windows NT Workstation, Windows 95, or Windows for Workgroups computer can perform the role of the backup browser. *See also* Computer Browser service and master browser.

backup domain controller (BDC) A BDC is a Windows NT Server computer that is configured to maintain a backup copy of the domain Directory Services database (SAM). The BDC receives updates to the Directory Services database from the Primary Domain Controller (PDC) via a process called synchronization. *See also* primary domain controller and synchronization.

binary tree A binary tree is the type of search used by the NTFS file system to locate files and folders quickly on an NTFS partition. A binary tree search is much faster than a sequential read or search. *See also* sequential read.

bindings Bindings are associations between a network service and a protocol, or between a protocol and a network adapter.

BIOS BIOS stands for *Basic Input/Output System*. The BIOS is a program that is stored in ROM (read-only memory) on a computer's motherboard. The BIOS contains instructions for performing the Power On Self Test (POST).

blue screen A blue screen is displayed by Windows NT when it encounters a STOP error that it cannot recover from. A blue screen contains information about the type of error that occurred, a list of loaded drivers, and a processor stack dump.

boot loader A boot loader is a program that is used to load a computer's operating system. In Windows NT, the boot loader is a program called `ntldr`, and it creates a menu (the boot loader menu) by parsing the contents of the `Boot.ini` file. Once the user selects an operating system from this menu (or the default time period expires), `ntldr` begins the process of starting the selected (or default) operating system.

boot partition The boot partition is the partition that contains the Windows NT system files. The boot partition contains the folder that Windows NT is installed in.

boot sequence The Windows NT boot sequence consists of a series of steps, beginning with powering on the computer and ending with completion of the logon process. The boot sequence steps vary according to the hardware platform you are using.

bottleneck A bottleneck is the component in the system that is slowing system performance. In a networking environment, the bottleneck is the part of the system that is performing at peak capacity while other components in the system are not working at peak capacity. In other words, if it weren't for the limiting component, the rest of the system would go faster.

browsing Browsing is the process of viewing a list of computers and their available shared resources, or viewing a list of files and folders on a local or network-connected drive.

built-in groups Built-in groups are the default groups created by the operating system during a Windows NT installation. Different groups are created on Windows NT domain controllers than are created on non-domain controllers.

C

C2 secure environment C2 is a designation in a range of security le els identified in the computer security specifications developed by the National Computer Security Center. If installed and configured correctly, Windows NT meets the C2 level of security.

cache Cache is a section of memory used to temporarily store files from the hard disk.

CDFS CDFS stands for *Compact Disc Filing System*. CDFS supports access to compact discs, and is only used on CD-ROM devices.

client A client is a computer that is capable of accessing resources on other computers (servers) across a network. Some computers are configured with both client and server software. *See also* server.

Client Service for NetWare (CSNW) CSNW is a Windows NT Workstation service that enables a Windows NT Workstation compu to access files and print queues on NetWare 3.*x* and 4.*x* servers.

complete trust domain model This is a decentralized domain mod that consists of two or more domains that contain both user accounts and shared resources. In the complete trust domain model, a two-way trust relationship must be established between each and every domai Because of the excessive number of trusts required for this model, the complete trust domain model is not often implemented. *See also* trus relationship and two-way trust.

Computer Browser service This Windows NT service is responsible for the process of building a list of available network servers, called a browse list. The Computer Browser service is also responsible for determining the role a computer plays in the browser hierarchy: domain master browser, master browser, backup browser, or potential browser. *See also* backup browser, domain master browser, master browser, and potential browser.

Computer name A computer name is a unique name, up to 15 characters in length, that is used to identify a particular computer on the network. No two computers on the same internetwork should have the same computer name.

Computer policy A computer policy is a collection of Registry settings created in System Policy Editor that specify a local computer's configuration. A computer policy enforces the specified configuration on all users of a particular Windows NT (or Windows 95) computer.

Control Panel Control Panel is a group of mini applications that are used to configure a Windows NT computer.

D

Default Computer policy The Default Computer policy is a computer policy that applies to all computers that don't have an individual computer policy. *See also* computer policy.

Default gateway A default gateway is a TCP/IP configuration setting that specifies the IP address of the router on the local network segment.

Default User policy The Default User policy is a user policy that applies to all users who don't have an individual user policy. *See also* user policy.

Default User profile The Default User profile is a user profile folder created during the Windows NT installation process. The settings in the Default User profile are applied, by default, to new user profiles as they are created. The Default User profile can be modified by using the Registry Editors or by using Windows NT Explorer. *See also* user profile.

demand paging Demand paging is a process used by the Windows NT Virtual Memory Manager that involves reading pages of memory from the paging file into RAM, and writing pages of memory from RAM into the paging file as required by the operating system. *See also* paging file.

desktop The desktop is the screen that is displayed after Windows NT 4.0 boots and you log on. The desktop replaces the Program Manager interface from earlier versions of Windows and Windows NT.

desktop operating system A desktop operating system is an operating system that is designed to be used by an individual user on his or her desktop. A desktop operating system is not designed to be used on network server.

DHCP DHCP stands for *Dynamic Host Configuration Protocol*. This protocol is used to dynamically assign IP addresses to client computer on a network.

Dial-Up Networking Dial-Up Networking is a Windows NT service that enables a computer to use its modem to make a network connection over a telephone line to another computer. Dial-Up Networking i installed during the installation of the Remote Access Service (RAS) o a Windows NT computer. *See also* Remote Access Service (RAS).

directory A directory is a folder. In Windows NT terminology, the terms *directory* and *folder* are synonymous. The two terms are used interchangeably throughout Windows NT documentation and the Windows NT user interface.

directory replication Directory replication was designed to copy logon scripts from a central location, usually the PDC, to all domain controllers, thus enabling all users to execute their own logon scripts matter which domain controller validates their logon. Replication involves copying subfolders and their files from the source folder on t source server to the destination folder on all Windows NT computers on the network that are configured as replication destinations. *See als* Directory Replicator service.

Directory Replicator service The Directory Replicator service is a Windows NT service that copies (replicates) files from a source Windows NT computer to a destination Windows NT computer. *See also* directory replication.

Directory Services *See* Windows NT Directory Services.

Directory Services database *See* Security Accounts Manager (SAM) database.

DNS *See* Microsoft DNS Server.

domain A domain is a logical grouping of networked computers in which one or more of the computers has shared resources, such as a shared folder or a shared printer, and in which all of the computers share a common central domain Directory Services database that contains user account and security information.

domain controller A domain controller is a Windows NT Server computer that maintains a copy of the domain Directory Services database (also called the SAM). *See also* backup domain controller, primary domain controller, and Security Accounts Manager (SAM) database.

domain master browser The domain master browser is a computer that maintains a list of available network servers located on all subnets in the domain. Additionally, the domain master browser maintains a list of available workgroups and domains on the internetwork. The domain master browser is the primary domain controller. *See also* Computer Browser service.

domain name A domain name is a unique name, up to 15 characters in length, assigned to identify the domain on the network. A domain name must be different than all other domain names, workgroup names, and computer names on the network.

Dr. Watson for Windows NT Dr. Watson is a Windows NT tool that is used to debug application errors.

dual boot Dual boot refers to a computer's capability to permit a user to select from more than one operating system during the boot process. (Only one operating system can be selected and run at a time.)

Emergency Repair Disk The Emergency Repair Disk is a floppy disk created during (or after) the Windows NT installation process that is used to repair Windows NT when its configuration files have been damaged or corrupted.

enhanced metafile (EMF) An enhanced metafile is an intermediate print job format that can be created very quickly by the graphic device driver interface. Using an EMF enables Windows NT to process the print job in the background while the foreground process continues.

Event Log service The Event Log service is a Windows NT service that writes operating system, application, and security events to log files. These log files can be viewed by an administrator using Event Viewer. *See also* Event Viewer.

Event Viewer Event Viewer is a Windows NT administrative tool that enables an administrator to view and/or archive the System, Application, and Security Logs.

exabyte An exabyte is a billion gigabytes (1,152,921,504,606,846,976 bytes).

Executive Services (Windows NT Executive) Executive Services is the entire set of services that make up the kernel mode of the Windows NT operating system.

extended partition An extended partition is a disk partition that can be subdivided into one or more logical drives. An extended partition can't be the active partition. *See also* active partition.

ault tolerance Fault tolerance refers to the capability of a computer r operating system to continue operations when a severe error or failre occurs, such as the loss of a hard disk or a power outage.

le allocation table (FAT) file system FAT is a type of file system at is used by several operating systems, including Windows NT. 'indows NT does not support security or auditing on FAT partitions. he maximum size of a FAT partition is 4GB.

le attributes File attributes are markers assigned to files that scribe properties of the file and limit access to the file. File attributes clude: Archive, Compress, Hidden, Read-only, and System.

le system A file system is an overall architecture for naming, storing, d retrieving files on a disk.

lder A folder is a directory. In Windows NT terminology, the terms *rectory* and *folder* are synonymous. The two terms are used interangeably throughout Windows NT documentation and the Windows Γ user interface.

ame type A frame type (also called a *frame format*) is an accepted, ndardized structure for transmitting data packets over a network.

lly qualified domain name (FQDN) An FQDN is a fancy term ' the way computers are named and referenced on the Internet. The mat for an FQDN is: `server_name.domain_name.root_domain` ame. For example, a server named `wolf` in the `alancarter` domain the `com` root domain has a fully qualified domain name of `lf.alancarter.com`. Fully qualified domain names always use lowase characters.

G

gateway A gateway is a computer that performs protocol or data format translation between two computers that use different protocols or data formats.

gigabyte (GB) A gigabyte is 1,024 megabytes (MB), or 1,073,741,824 bytes.

global group A global group is a Windows NT Server group that can only be created in the domain Directory Services database. Global groups are primarily used to organize users that perform similar tasks or have similar network access requirements. In a typical Windows NT configuration, user accounts are placed in a global group, then the global group is made a member of one or more local groups, and each local group is assigned permissions to a network resource. The advantage of using global groups is ease of administration — the network administrator can manage large numbers of users by placing them in global groups. Global groups are only available in Windows NT Server domains — they are not available in workgroups or on a stand-alone server. *See also* local group.

Graphics Device Interface (GDI) The GDI is a specific Windows NT device driver that manages low-level display and print data. The GDI used to be part of user mode in Windows NT 3.51, but is now part of the kernel mode (Executive Services) in Windows NT 4.0.

group dependencies Group dependencies are groups of services or drivers that must be running before a given service (or driver) can start

group policy A group policy is a policy that applies to a group of users. Group policies apply to all users that are members of a group (that has a group policy), and that do not have individual user policies

Hardware Compatibility List (HCL) The HCL is a list of hardware that is supported by Windows NT. The HCL is shipped with Windows NT. You can access the latest version of the HCL at **www.microsoft.com/ntworkstation**.

Hertz (Hz) Hz is a unit of frequency measurement equivalent to one cycle per second.

Hive A hive is a group of Windows NT Registry keys and values that are stored in a single file. *See also* key, Registry, and value.

Host A host is a computer that is connected to a TCP/IP network, such as the Internet.

HPFS HPFS stands for *high performance file system*. This is the file system used by OS/2. Windows NT used to support HPFS, but HPFS support was dropped for NT version 4.0.

Internetwork An internetwork consists of multiple network segments connected by routers and/or WAN links.

Interrupt (IRQ) An interrupt (or interrupt request) is a unique number between two and fifteen that is assigned to a hardware peripheral in a computer. No two devices in the computer should have the same interrupt, unless the devices are capable of sharing an interrupt, and are correctly configured to do so.

Intranetwork An intranetwork is a TCP/IP internetwork that is not connected to the Internet. For example, a company's multicity internetwork can be called an intranetwork as long as it is not connected to the Internet. *See also* internetwork.

kernel A kernel is the core component of an operating system.

kernel mode Kernel mode refers to a highly privileged mode of operation in Windows NT. "Highly privileged" means that all code that runs in kernel mode can access the hardware directly, and can access any memory address. A program that runs in kernel mode is always resident in memory — it can't be written to a paging file. *See also* user mode.

key A key is a component of the Registry that is similar to a folder in a file system. A key can contain other keys and value entries. *See also* Registry and value.

kilobyte (K) A kilobyte is 1,024 bytes.

L

line printer daemon (LPD) LPD is the print server software used in TCP/IP printing. LPD is supported by many operating systems, including Windows NT and UNIX.

local group A local group is a Windows NT group that can be created in the domain Directory Services database on a domain controller or the SAM on any non-domain controller. Local groups are primarily used to control access to resources. In a typical Windows NT configuration, a local group is assigned permissions to a specific resource, such as a shared folder or a shared printer. Individual user accounts and global groups are then made members of this local group. The result is that members of the local group then have permissions to the resource. Using local groups simplifies the administration of network resources because permissions can be assigned once, to a local group, instead of separately to each user account. *See also* global group.

local print provider A local print provider is a Windows NT kernel mode driver that manages printing for all print devices managed by the local computer.

LocalTalk LocalTalk is a specification for the type of network cabling, connectors, and adapters developed by Apple Computer, Inc. for use with Macintosh computers.

logging on Logging on is the process of supplying a user name and password, and having that user name and password authenticated by a Windows NT computer. A user is said to "log on" to a Windows NT computer.

logical drive A logical drive is a disk partition (or multiple partitions) that has been formatted with a file system and assigned a drive letter.

logon hours Logon hours are the assigned hours that a user can log on to a Windows NT Server domain controller. The logon hours configuration only affects the user's ability to access the domain controller — it does not affect a user's ability to log on to a Windows NT Workstation computer or to a non-domain controller.

logon script A logon script is a batch file that is run when a user logs on. All MS-DOS 5.0 (and earlier versions) batch commands can be used in logon scripts.

M

mandatory user profile A mandatory user profile is a user profile that, when assigned to a user, can't be modified by the user. A user can make changes to desktop and work environment settings during a single logon session, but these changes are not saved to the mandatory profile when the user logs off. Each time the user logs on, the user's desktop and work environment settings revert to those contained in the mandatory user profile. A mandatory user profile is created by renaming the user's `ntuser.dat` file to `ntuser.man`. *See also* user profile.

master browser A master browser is the computer on the subnet that builds and maintains the browse list for that subnet. The master browser distributes this browse list to backup browsers on the subnet and to the domain master browser. *See also* backup browser, Computer Browser service, and domain master browser.

Maximum Password Age The Maximum Password Age is the maximum number of days a user may use the same password.

megabyte (MB) A megabyte is 1,024 kilobytes, or 1,048,576 bytes.

member server A member server is a Windows NT Server computer that is not installed as a domain controller, and that has joined a Windows NT Server domain.

memory dump The term memory dump refers to the process of Windows NT copying the contents of RAM into a file (the `memory.dmp` file) when a STOP error or blue screen occurs.

Microsoft DNS Server Microsoft DNS Server is a Windows NT Server service. This service is a TCP/IP-based name resolution service. It is used to resolve a host name or an FQDN to its associated IP address.

million bits per second (Mbps) Mbps is a measurement of data transmission speed that is used to describe WAN links and other network connections.

Minimum Password Age The Minimum Password Age is the minimum number of days a user must keep the same password.

Minimum Password Length Minimum Password Length specifies the minimum number of characters required in a user's password.

MS-DOS MS-DOS is a computer operating system developed by Microsoft. MS-DOS stands for *Microsoft Disk Operating System*.

multihomed A computer is said to be multihomed when it has more than one network adapter installed in it.

multiple master domain model This domain model consists of two or more master domains that contain user accounts, and any number of resource domains that contain shared resources. In this model, a two-way trust is used between each of the master domains, and a one-way trust is used from each resource domain to each and every master domain. *See also* trust relationship, one-way trust, and two-way trust.

multiprocessing Multiprocessing refers to the capability of an operating system to use more than one processor in a single computer simultaneously.

N

NetBEUI NetBEUI is a nonroutable protocol designed for use on small networks. NetBEUI is included in Windows NT 4.0 primarily for backward compatibility with older Microsoft networking products.

network access order The network access order specifies which protocol or service Windows NT will use first when it attempts to access another computer on the network.

network adapter A network adapter is an adapter card in a computer that enables the computer to connect to a network.

network Client Administrator Network Client Administrator is a Windows NT Server tool you can use to create an installation disk set install network clients or services on client computers. You can also use Network Client Administrator to create a network installation startup disk. A network installation startup disk, when run on a computer that needs to be set up (the target computer), causes the target computer to automatically connect to the server and to start an interactive installation/setup routine.

network device driver A network device driver is a Windows NT kernel mode driver that is designed to enable Windows NT to use a network adapter to communicate on the network.

Network Monitor Network Monitor is a Windows NT Server administrative tool that allows you to capture, view, and analyze network traffic (packets).

network number Network numbers are 32-bit binary numbers that uniquely identify an NWLink IPX/SPX Compatible Transport network segment for routing purposes. Because network numbers uniquely identify a network segment, they are used by IPX routers to correctly forward data packets from one network segment to another.

non-browser A non-browser is a computer that is not capable of maintaining a browse list either because it was configured not to do so, or because the operating system on this computer is incapable of main taining a browse list. *See also* Computer Browser service.

NT Hardware Qualifier (NTHQ) The NT Hardware Qualifier (NTHQ) is a utility that ships with Windows NT. NTHQ examines and identifies a computer's hardware configuration, including the hardware settings used by each adapter.

NTFS *See* Windows NT file system.

NTFS permissions NTFS permissions are permissions assigned to individual files and folders on an NTFS partition that are used to control access to these files and folders. NTFS permissions apply to local users as well as to users who connect to a shared folder over the network. If the NTFS permissions are more restrictive than share permissions, the NTFS permissions will be applied. *See also* share permissions.

NWLink IPX/SPX Compatible Transport NWLink IPX/SPX Compatible Transport is a routable transport protocol typically used in a combined Windows NT and NetWare environment. NWLink IPX/SPX Compatible Transport is Microsoft's version of Novell's IPX/SPX protocol. (IPX/SPX is the protocol used on most Novell NetWare networks.) NWLink provides protocol compatibility between Windows NT and NetWare computers. In addition to its functionality in a NetWare environment, NWLink also fully supports Microsoft networking.

O

ODBC ODBC stands for *Open Database Connectivity*. ODBC is a software specification that enables ODBC-enabled applications (such as Microsoft Excel) to connect to databases (such as Microsoft SQL Server and Microsoft Access). The ODBC application in Control Panel is used to install and remove ODBC drivers for various types of databases. Additionally, this application is used to configure ODBC data sources.

OEM subfolder The OEM subfolder is used to store source files that are used to install applications, components, or files that do not ship with Windows NT. This subfolder is used during an automated setup of Windows NT.

one-way trust When a single trust relationship exists between two domains, it is called a one-way trust. Both domains must be configured by an administrator in order to establish a trust relationship. Trusts are configured in Windows NT by using User Manager for Domains. The trusted domain should be configured first, and then the trusting domain. *See also* trust relationship, trusted domain, and trusting domain.

P

packet A packet is a group of bytes sent over the network as a block of data.

paging file A paging file (sometimes called a page file or a swap file) is a file used as a computer's virtual memory. Pages of memory that are not currently in use can be written to a paging file to make room for data currently needed by the processor. *See also* virtual memory.

partition A partition is a portion of a hard disk that can be formatted with a file system, or combined with other partitions to form a larger logical drive. *See also* logical drive.

pass-through authentication Pass-through authentication is a process by which one Windows NT computer passes a user name and password on to another Windows NT computer for validation. Pass-through authentication makes it possible for a user to log on to a Windows NT Workstation computer by using a user account from a Windows NT Server domain.

Password Uniqueness Password Uniqueness specifies how many different passwords a user must use before a previous password can be reused.

Peer Web Services Peer Web Services is a Windows NT Workstation Internet publishing service that supports World Wide Web (WWW), File Transfer Protocol (FTP), and Gopher services. Peer Web Services is optimized to serve a small number of clients, such as might be found on a small company intranet.

Performance Monitor Performance Monitor is a Windows NT tool that is used to gather statistics on current performance of a Windows NT computer. Performance Monitor statistics can be displayed in a Chart, Alert, or Report view; or can be saved to a log file for later viewing.

permissions Permissions control access to resources, such as shares, files, folders, and printers on a Windows NT computer.

Plug and Play Plug and Play is a specification that makes it possible for hardware devices to be automatically recognized and configured by the operating system without user intervention.

Point-to-Point Multilink Protocol Point-to-Point Multilink Protocol is an extension of the Point-to-Point Protocol. Point-to-Point Multilink Protocol combines the bandwidth from multiple physical connections into a single logical connection. This means that multiple modem, ISDN, or X.25 connections can be bundled together to form single logical connection with a much higher bandwidth than a single connection can support. *See also* Point-to-Point Protocol.

Point-to-Point Protocol (PPP) Point-to-Point Protocol (PPP) is a newer connection protocol that was designed to overcome the limitations of the Serial Line Internet Protocol (SLIP). PPP is currently the industry standard remote connection protocol, and is recommended for use by Microsoft. PPP connections support multiple transport protocols, including: TCP/IP, NWLink IPX/SPX Compatible Transport, and NetBEUI. Additionally, PPP supports dynamic server-based IP addressing (such as DHCP). PPP supports password encryption, and the PPP connection process does not usually require a script file. *See also* Serial Line Internet Protocol (SLIP).

Point-to-Point Tunneling Protocol (PPTP) Point-to-Point Tunneling Protocol (PPTP) permits a virtual private encrypted connection between two computers over an existing TCP/IP network connection. The existing TCP/IP network connection can be over a local area network or over a Dial-Up Networking TCP/IP connection (including the Internet). All standard transport protocols are supported within the Point-to-Point Tunneling Protocol connection, including NWLink IPX/SPX Compatible Transport, NetBEUI, and TCP/IP. A primary reason for choosing to use PPTP is that it supports the RAS encryption feature over standard, unencrypted TCP/IP networks, such as the Internet.

POSIX *Portable Operating System Interface for Computing Environments* (POSIX) was developed as a set of accepted standards for writing applications for use on various UNIX computers. POSIX environment applications consist of applications developed to meet the POSIX standards. These applications are sometimes referred to as POSIX-compliant applications. Windows NT provides support for POSIX-compliant applications via the POSIX subsystem. Windows NT supports the POSIX subsystem on all hardware platforms supported by Windows NT. To fully support POSIX-compliant applications, at least one NTFS partition is required on the Windows NT computer. POSIX applications are source compatible across all supported hardware platforms. This means that POSIX applications must be recompiled for each hardware platform in order to be run on that platform.

potential browser A potential browser is a computer that does not currently maintain or distribute a browse list, but is capable of doing so. A potential browser can become a backup browser at the direction of the master browser. *See also* backup browser, Computer Browser service, and master browser.

preemptive multitasking In preemptive multitasking, the operating system allocates processor time between applications. Because Windows NT, not the application, allocates processor time between multiple applications, one application can be preempted by the operating system, and another application enabled to run. When multiple applications are alternately paused and then allocated processor time, they appear to run simultaneously to the user.

primary domain controller (PDC) A PDC is a Windows NT Server computer that is configured to maintain the primary copy of the domain Directory Services database (also called the SAM). The PDC sends Directory Services database updates to Backup Domain Controllers (BDCs) via a process called synchronization. *See also* backup domain controller, Security Accounts Manager (SAM) database, and synchronization.

primary partition A primary partition is a disk partition that can be configured as the active partition. A primary partition can only be formatted as a single logical drive. *See also* active partition.

print device In Windows NT, the term print device refers to the physical device that produces printed output — this is what most people refer to as a printer.

print device driver A print device driver is a Windows NT kernel mode driver that formats print jobs into a RAW format. (The RAW format is ready to print, and no further processing is required.) A print device driver can also convert EMF formatted print jobs into a RAW format. *See also* enhanced metafile (EMF).

print job A print job is all of the data and commands needed to print a document.

print monitor A print monitor is a software component that runs in kernel mode. A print monitor sends ready-to-print print jobs to a print device, either locally or across the network. Print monitors are also called port monitors.

print processor A print processor is a kernel mode driver that manages printer device drivers and the process of converting print jobs from one format into another.

print queue In Windows NT terminology, a print queue is a list of print jobs for a specific printer that are waiting to be sent to a print device. The print queue is maintained by the Windows NT Spooler service. *See also* Spooler service.

print server A print server is a software program on a computer that manages print jobs and print devices. The Windows NT Spooler service functions as a print server. The term print server is also used to refer to a computer used primarily to manage multiple print devices and their print jobs. *See also* Spooler service.

printer In Windows NT, the term printer does not represent a physical device that produces printed output. Rather, a printer is the software interface between the Windows NT operating system and the device that produces the printed output. In other operating systems, what Windows NT calls a printer is often referred to as a print queue.

printer pool When a printer has multiple ports (and multiple print devices) assigned to it, this is called a printer pool. Users print to a single printer, and the printer load-balances its print jobs between the print devices assigned to it.

RAM *Random access memory*, or RAM, is the physical memory installed in a computer.

Rdisk.exe Rdisk.exe is a Windows NT utility that is used to update the Emergency Repair Disk. Using Rdisk /s causes this utility to back up the SAM and Security hives in the Registry. (If the /s switch is not used, the SAM and Security hives in the Registry are not backed up.) *See also* Emergency Repair Disk.

refresh The term refresh means to update the display with current information.

Registry The Windows NT Registry is a database that contains all of the information required to correctly configure an individual Windows NT computer, its user accounts, and applications. Registries are unique to each computer — you shouldn't use the Registry from one computer on another computer. The Registry is organized in a tree structure consisting of five subtrees, and their keys and value entries. *See also* key and value.

Registry editors Registry editors are tools that enable you to search and modify the Windows NT Registry. There are two primary tools for editing the Windows NT Registry: the Windows NT Registry Editor (regedt32.exe), and the Windows 95 Registry Editor (regedit.exe) Additionally, you can use the Windows NT System Policy Editor (poledit.exe) to modify a limited number of settings in the Registry. However, you can't use System Policy Editor to search the Registry.

Remote Access Admin Remote Access Admin is a Windows NT administrative tool that is primarily used to start and stop the Remote Access Service (RAS), to assign the dialin permission to users, and to configure a call back security level for each user. Remote Access Admin can also be used to view COM port status and statistics, to disconnect users from individual ports, and to remotely manage RAS on other Windows NT computers.

Remote Access Service (RAS) Remote Access Service (RAS) is a Windows NT service that enables dial-up network connections between a RAS server and a Dial-Up Networking client computer. RAS includes software components for both the RAS server and the Dial-Up Networking client in a single Windows NT service. RAS enables users of remote computers to use the network as though they were directly connected to it. Once the dial-up connection is established, there is no difference in network functionality, except that the speed of the link is often much slower than a direct connection to the LAN.

roaming user profiles Roaming user profiles are user profiles that a stored on a server. Because these profiles are stored on a server instead of a local computer, they are available to users regardless of which Windows NT computer on the network they log on to. The benefit of using roaming user profiles is that users retain their own customized desktop and work environment settings even though they may use several different Windows NT computers.

router A router is a network device that uses protocol-specific addressing information to forward packets from a source computer on one network segment across one or more routers to a destination computer on another network segment.

routing Routing is the process of forwarding packets from a source computer on one network segment across one or more routers to a destination computer on another network segment by using protocol-specific addressing information. Devices that perform routing are called routers.

S

SAP Agent The *Service Advertising Protocol* (SAP) Agent is a Windows NT service that advertises a Windows NT computer's services (such as SQL Server and SNA Server) to NetWare client computers. The SAP Agent requires the use of NWLink IPX/SPX Compatible Transport. The SAP Agent should be installed when NetWare client computers will access services on a Windows NT computer.

SCSI SCSI stands for *Small Computer System Interface*. SCSI is a hardware specification for cables, adapter cards, and the devices that they manage, such as hard disks, CD-ROMs, and scanners.

Security Accounts Manager (SAM) database The SAM is a Windows NT Registry hive that is used to store all user account, group account, and security policy information for a Windows NT computer or a Windows NT domain. On a domain controller, the SAM is also referred to as the domain Directory Services database.

security identifier (SID) A security identifier (SID) is a unique number assigned to a user account, group account, or computer account in the Security Accounts Manager (SAM) database. *See also* Security Accounts Manager (SAM) database.

Security Log The Security Log is a file that is managed by the Windows NT Event Log service. All auditing of security events is written to the Security Log. An Administrator can view the Security Log by using Event Viewer.

segment In network terminology, a segment refers to a network subnet that is not subdivided by a bridge or a router. The term segment can also be used as a verb, describing the process of dividing the network into multiple subnets by using a bridge or a router.

sequential read A sequential read is a read performed (normally by the operating system) from the beginning of a file straight through to the end of the file. No random access to different parts of the file can occur during a sequential read.

Serial Line Internet Protocol (SLIP) The Serial Line Internet Protocol (SLIP) is an older connection protocol, commonly associated with UNIX computers, that only supports one transport protocol — TCP/IP. SLIP connections don't support NWLink IPX/SPX Compatible Transport or NetBEUI. The version of SLIP supported by Windows NT 4.0 requires a static IP address configuration at the client computer — dynamic IP addressing is not supported. Additionally, password encryption is not supported by this version of SLIP. A script file is usually required to automate the connection process when SLIP is used.

server A server is a computer on a network that is capable of sharing resources with other computers on the network. Many computers are configured as both clients and servers, meaning that they can both access resources located on other computers across-the-network, and they can share their resources with other computers on the network. *See also* client.

Server Manager Server Manager is a Windows NT Server administrative tool that allows remote management of shared folders, remote starting and stopping of services, remote management of Directory

Replication, remote viewing to determine which users are currently accessing shared resources, and remote disconnection of users from shared resources on a Windows NT Server computer.

Server service The Server service is a Windows NT service that enables Windows NT computers to share their resources with other computers on the network.

service dependencies Service dependencies are services and drivers that must be running before a particular service (or driver) can start.

Setup Manager Setup Manager is a Windows NT tool that is used to create an answer file (`Unattend.txt`) for use in automating the installation of Windows NT. *See also* answer files.

share name A share name is a name that uniquely identifies a shared resource on a Windows NT computer, such as a shared folder or printer.

share permissions Share permissions control access to shared resources, such as shared folders and shared printers on a Windows NT computer. Share permissions only apply to users who access a shared resource over the network.

shared folder A shared folder is a folder on a Windows NT computer that can be accessed by other computers on the network because the folder has been configured to be shared and has been assigned a share name.

single domain model The single domain model consists of one domain, and does not use trust relationships. All user accounts and shared resources are contained within one domain.

single master domain model The single master domain model consists of one master domain that contains all user accounts, and one or more resource domains that contain shared resources. This domain model uses one-way trusts from each resource domain to the master domain. *See also* trust relationship and one-way trust.

SNMP SNMP stands for *Simple Network Management Protocol*. The Windows NT SNMP service, once installed on a Windows NT computer, gathers TCP/IP statistics on the local computer and transmits those statistics to any SNMP management station on the network that is correctly configured to receive them. Additionally, installing the SNMP service enables various TCP/IP counters within Windows NT Performance Monitor.

special groups Special groups are groups created by Windows NT during installation that are used for specific purposes by the operating system. These groups don't appear in User Manager. Special groups are only visible in Windows NT utilities that assign permissions to network resources, such as a printer's Properties dialog box, and Windows NT Explorer. You can assign permissions to and remove permissions from special groups. You can't assign users to special groups, and you can't rename or delete these groups. Special groups are sometimes called system groups. There are five special groups: Everyone, Interactive, Network, System, and Creator Owner.

Spooler service The Windows NT Spooler service manages the entire printing process on a Windows NT computer. The Spooler service performs many of the tasks that are associated with a print server.

stand-alone server A stand-alone server is a Windows NT Server computer that is not installed as a domain controller, and that has not joined a Windows NT Server domain.

static routing Static routing is basic, no-frills IP routing. No additional software is necessary to implement static routing in multihomed Windows NT computers. Static routers are not capable of automatically building a routing table. In a static routing environment, administrators must manually configure the routing table on each individual router. If the network layout changes, the network administrator must manually update the routing tables to reflect the changes.

stripe set A stripe set is a disk configuration consisting of 2 to 32 hard disks. In a stripe set, data is stored, a block at a time, evenly and sequentially among all of the disks in the set. Stripe sets are sometimes referred to as disk striping. Disk striping alludes to the process wherein a file is written, or striped, one block at a time, first to one disk, then to the next disk, and then to the next disk, and so on, until all of the data has been evenly distributed among all of the disks.

subfolder A subfolder is a folder that is located within another folder. Subfolders can contain other subfolders, as well as files.

subnet mask A subnet mask specifies which portion of an IP address represents the network ID and which portion represents the host ID. A subnet mask enables TCP/IP to correctly determine whether network traffic destined for a given IP address should be transmitted on the local subnet, or whether it should be routed to a remote subnet. A subnet mask should be the same for all computers and other network devices on a given network segment. A subnet mask is a 32-bit binary number, broken into four 8-bit sections (octets), that is normally represented in a dotted decimal format. Each 8-bit section is represented by a whole number between 0 and 255. A common subnet mask is 255.255.255.0. This particular subnet mask specifies that TCP/IP will use the first three octets of an IP address as the network ID, and use the last octet as the host ID.

synchronization Synchronization is a process performed by the NetLogon Service. In this process, domain Directory Services database update information is periodically copied from the primary domain controller (PDC) to each backup domain controller (BDC) in the domain.

Sysdiff.exe Sydiff.exe is a Windows NT utility that is used to automate the installation of applications that don't support scripted installation and that would otherwise require user interaction during the installation process.

system partition The system partition is the active primary partition on the first hard disk in the computer. (This is usually the C: drive.) The system partition contains several files that are required to boot Windows NT, including: ntldr, Ntdetect.com, Boot.ini, and sometimes Bootsect.dos, and Ntbootdd.sys, depending on the installation type and hardware configuration. *See also* boot partition.

system policy The Windows NT system policy file is a collection of user, group, and computer policies. System policy restricts the user's ability to perform certain tasks on any Windows NT computer on the network that the user logs on to. System policy can also be used to enforce certain mandatory display settings, such as wallpaper and color scheme. You can also create a system policy file that applies to users of Windows 95 computers. System policy gives the administrator far more configurable options than a mandatory profile. Administrators can use system policy to provide a consistent environment for a large number of users, or to enforce a specified work environment for "problem users" who demand a significant amount of administrator time.

System Policy Editor System Policy Editor is a Windows NT Server tool that is used to edit Windows NT and Windows 95 system policy files. *See also* system policy.

T

Task Manager Windows NT Task Manager is a Windows NT administrative utility that can be used to start and stop applications; to view performance statistics, such as memory and CPU usage; and to change a process's base priority.

TCP/IP The *Transmission Control Protocol/Internet Protocol* (TCP/IP) is a widely used transport protocol that provides robust capabilities for Windows NT networking. TCP/IP is a fast, routable enterprise protocol. TCP/IP is the protocol used on the Internet. TCP/IP is supported by many other operating systems, including: Windows 95, Macintosh, UNIX, MS-DOS, and IBM mainframes. TCP/IP is typically the recommended protocol for large, heterogeneous networks.

terabyte A terabyte is 1,024 gigabytes, or 1,099,511,627,776 bytes.

terminate-and-stay-resident (TSR) program A terminate-and-stay-resident program is an MS-DOS program that stays loaded in memory, even when it is not running.

thread A thread is the smallest unit of processing that can be scheduled by the Windows NT Schedule service. All applications require at least one thread.

trust relationship A trust relationship, or *trust*, is an agreement between two Windows NT Server domains that enables authenticated users in one domain to access resources in another domain. A trust relationship enables users from the trusted domain to access resources in the trusting domain. *See also* one-way trust, trusted domain, trusting domain, and two-way trust.

trusted domain The trusted domain is the domain that contains the user accounts of users who want to access resources in the trusting domain. The trusted domain is said to be trusted by the trusting domain. When graphically displaying a trust relationship, an arrow is used to point from the trusting domain to the trusted domain. *See also* trust relationship and trusting domain.

trusting domain The trusting domain is the domain that has resources to share with users from the trusted domain. The trusting domain is said to trust the trusted domain. When graphically displaying a trust relationship, an arrow is used to point from the trusting domain to the trusted domain. *See also* trust relationship and trusted domain.

two-way trust A two-way trust consists of two one-way trusts between two domains. *See also* one-way trust and trust relationship.

Unattend.txt *See* answer files.

UNC (universal naming convention) UNC is an accepted method of identifying individual computers and their resources on the network. A UNC name consists of a server name and a shared resource name in the following format: `\\Server_name\Share_name`. `Server_name` represents the name of the server that the shared folder is located on. `Share_name` represents the name of the shared folder. A UNC name in this format can be used to connect to a network share. For example, a shared folder named `Public` located on a server named `Server1` would have the following UNC name: `\\Server1\Public`.

Uniqueness Database Files (*.UDF) Uniqueness Database Files (UDFs) are text files, similar to answer files, that make it possible for one answer file to be used for the installation of many computers that have different identifying characteristics. For example, each computer has a different computer name and user name. A UDF, used in conjunction with a network installation startup disk and an answer file, enables you to fully automate the installation of Windows NT on multiple computers on a network. The UDF is structured like an answer file, and uses the same types of entries that an answer file uses. The UDF has an additional section, named UniqueIds. When the appropriate command-line switch is used, selected entries in the UDF replace entries with the same name in the answer file. *See also* answer files.

UPS UPS stands for *uninterruptible power supply*. A UPS is a fault-tolerance device that enables a computer to continue operations for a short period of time after a power outage.

user account A user account is a record in the Security Accounts Manager (SAM) database that contains unique user information, such as user name, password, and logon restrictions.

user account database *See* Security Accounts Manager (SAM) database.

User Manager User Manager is a Windows NT Workstation administrative tool that is used to administer user accounts, group accounts, and security policy on a Windows NT Workstation computer.

user mode Within the Windows NT architecture, user mode is referred to as a less privileged processor mode because it does not have direct access to hardware. Applications and their subsystems run in user mode. User mode applications are limited to assigned memory address spaces and can't directly access other memory address spaces. User mode uses specific application programming interfaces (API's) to request system services from a kernel mode component. *See also* application programming interface (API) and kernel mode.

user name A user name is the name assigned to a user account in the Security Accounts Manager (SAM) database.

user policy A user policy is a collection of Registry settings that restricts a user's program and network options, and/or enforces a specified configuration of the user's work environment.

user profile A user profile is a series of Registry settings and folders in the user's profile folder that define a user's work environment. The contents of a user profile include user-specific settings for: Windows NT Explorer, Notepad, Paint, HyperTerminal, Clock, Calculator, and other built-in Windows NT applications; screen saver, background color, background pattern, wallpaper, and other display settings; applications written to run on Windows NT; network drive and printer connections; and the Start menu, including program groups, applications, and recently accessed documents.

user rights User rights authorize users and/or groups to perform specific tasks on a Windows NT computer. User rights are not the same as permissions — user rights enable users to perform tasks, whereas permissions enable users to access objects, such as files, folders, and printers. *See also* permissions.

V

value A value is an individual entry in the Windows NT Registry. A value cannot contain keys or other values. *See also* key and Registry.

verbose mode Verbose mode refers to running an application in such way that the application returns the maximum amount of information and detail to the user. The verbose mode is initiated on many applications by using the /v switch.

virtual device driver A virtual device driver is a 32-bit protected mode device driver that is used in Windows 95 and Windows for Workgroups. Virtual device drivers are not supported by Windows NT.

virtual memory Virtual memory is the physical space on a hard disk that Windows NT treats as though it were RAM. *See also* paging file.

Virtual Memory Manager Virtual Memory Manager is a Windows NT kernel mode component that manages memory in a Windows NT environment by using demand paging. *See also* demand paging and virtual memory.

volume A volume is a logical drive. *See also* logical drive.

volume set A volume set is a combination of 2 to 32 partitions that are formatted as a single logical drive. A volume set does not use disk striping to store data on its partitions. *See also* logical drive and stripe set.

Windows NT Diagnostics Windows NT Diagnostics is a Windows NT administrative tool that allows you to view detailed system configuration information and statistics. This tool can help you troubleshoot system configuration problems. Windows NT Diagnostics can also be very useful in determining service and device driver dependencies.

Windows NT Directory Services Windows NT Directory Services is a Microsoft catchall phrase that refers to the architecture, features, functionality, and benefits of Windows NT domains and trust relationships. Windows NT Directory Services (often referred to as Directory Services), as implemented in Windows NT 4.0, is not X.500 compliant. However, Microsoft plans on releasing a new version of Windows NT Directory Services, called the Active Directory, that will be X.500 compliant in a future release of Windows NT.

Windows NT file system (NTFS) NTFS is the most powerful file system supported by Windows NT. Only Windows NT (both Windows NT Workstation and Windows NT Server) supports NTFS — no other operating systems currently support this file system. Windows NT auditing and security are only supported on partitions that are formatted with NTFS.

Windows NT Workstation Windows NT Workstation is a 32-bit operating system that is optimized to run as a desktop operating system. It can also be used on personal computers that are networked in a peer-to-peer workgroup configuration, or on a workstation computer that is part of a Windows NT Server domain configuration. Windows NT Workstation supports most MS-DOS-based applications, most 16-bit and 32-bit Windows-based applications, POSIX 1.*x* applications, and most OS/2 1.*x* applications. It does not support any application that requires direct hardware access because this could compromise Windows NT Workstation's security. It also does not support software applications that require a terminate-and-stay-resident program or a virtual device driver. Windows NT Workstation is a high-end, powerful operating system that supports multiple processors for true multiprocessing.

WINS *Windows Internet Name Service* (WINS) is a Windows NT Server service that provides NetBIOS name resolution services to client computers. A Windows NT Server computer that has WINS installed on it is called a WINS server.

workgroup A workgroup is a logical grouping of networked computers in which one or more of the computers has shared resources, such as a shared folder or a shared printer. In a workgroup environment, the security and user accounts are maintained individually on each separate computer.

Workstation service The Workstation service is a Windows NT service that enables a Windows NT computer to access shared resources on other computers across the network.

Index

H

L

AN Manager for MS-DOS, 32
AN Manager for OS/2, 32
ANs (Local Area Networks), 32, 235, 238
ptop computers
  Dial-Up Networking connections with,
    113
  docking stations and, 93
  hardware profiles and, 92–94
  ast Known Good configuration,
    326–327, 330
ft-arrow (<), 56, 58
st (RX) permission, 146
cal groups
  basic description of, 115–116
  shared folders and, 139
calmon print monitor, 166
g files, 81–82, 300–301, 303–304
g view, 303–304
gicalDisk object, 298–299, 308
gon Script Name text box, 112
gon process, 328
gon scripts, 112, 196
ng.nam, 194
tus Notes, 239
w switch, 276
D (line printer daemon) print servers,
    168, 177
R (line printer remote), 168
T1 parallel port, 166

M

AC (hardware) addresses, 192, 209
cintosh, 86, 209
  printing and, 167–168
  TCP/IP and, 87
nage Documents permission, 174
x box, 300, 301
ximum option, 278
Rs (Master Boot Records), 325
A bus, 326

memory. *See also* kernel; RAM (random-
    access memory)
  boot sequence and, 325
  bottlenecks and, 305, 306
  counters, 306, 307, 308
  dump file (memory.dmp), 92, 311
  as objects, 295
  requirements, 9
  spaces, running OS/2 applications in,
    273
  spaces, running Win16 applications in
    separate, 270–271
Memory object, 306
Memory Usage graph, 280
memory.dmp, 92, 311
Messenger service, 337–338
microprocessor(s)
  bottlenecks and, 305, 307
  computers with various, application
    support for, 275–276
  counters, 307
  DEC Alpha processors, 268, 275, 282
  Intel 486 processors, 268, 270, 275
  MIPS R4000 processors, 268, 275, 282
  multiprocessors systems, 312
  ntldr and, 326
  as objects, 295, 307
  paging and, 310
  performance optimization and, 295,
    298–299, 305, 307, 310, 312
  PowerPC processors, 268, 275, 282
  requirements, 9
  troubleshooting, 282
  upgrading, 312
Microsoft Peer Web Services
  basic description of, 215–220
  configuring, 216–218
  installing, 216–218
Microsoft Peer Web Services Setup dialog
    box, 216–218
Microsoft TCP/IP Printing service, 168
Microsoft TechNet, 333
Microsoft Technical Support, 333
Microsoft Windows 3.*x*
  applications designed for, 269–271
  configuring disks and, 55
  RAS and, 235
  upgrading from, 15
Microsoft Windows 95
  configuring disks and, 55, 56
  installation disk sets, 33

(continued)

P

my2cents.idgbooks.com